Mobile Device Security

A Comprehensive Guide to Securing
Your Information in a Moving World

Mobile Device Security

Security

A Comprehensive Guide to Securing
Your Information in a Moving World

STEPHEN FRIED

CRC Press
Taylor & Francis Group
Boca Raton   London   New York

CRC Press is an imprint of the
Taylor & Francis Group, an **informa** business
AN AUERBACH BOOK

Auerbach Publications
Taylor & Francis Group
6000 Broken Sound Parkway NW, Suite 300
Boca Raton, FL 33487-2742

© 2010 by Taylor and Francis Group, LLC
Auerbach Publications is an imprint of Taylor & Francis Group, an Informa business

No claim to original U.S. Government works

Printed in the United States of America on acid-free paper
10 9 8 7 6 5 4 3 2 1

International Standard Book Number: 978-1-4398-2016-2 (Hardback)

Library of Congress Cataloging-in-Publication Data

Fried, Stephen, 1962-
    Mobile device security : a comprehensive guide to securing your information in a moving world / Stephen Fried.
        p. cm.
    Includes bibliographical references and index.
    ISBN 978-1-4398-2016-2 (alk. paper)
    1. Data protection. 2. Mobile communication systems--Security measures. 3. Computer security. I. Title.

HF5548.37.F75 2010
005.8--dc22   2009052612

Visit the Taylor & Francis Web site at
http://www.taylorandfrancis.com

and the Auerbach Web site at
http://www.auerbach-publications.com

For Angela, who makes everything possible

Contents

Acknowledgments

No book is ever a solo effort. Although the author gets the credit and visibility, it is only through the efforts of a team of people contributing their time and expertise that the work can be accomplished. Therefore, I'd like to acknowledge the superb efforts of the people who helped make this book possible.

First, Rich O'Hanley and the team at Taylor & Francis have been extremely helpful and supportive of my work. Rich's initial topic ideas became the catalyst for this book, and his support throughout the process has been both encouraging and reassuring.

This book began as an Internet survey of the current approaches and attitudes about mobile devices. Though most of the respondents were anonymous, they have all helped form the basis and approach for many of the topics in this book. Thank you to everyone who responded and gave countless suggestions, ideas, and opinions on the topic. In particular, many thanks also go to Mace Moneta, whose original thoughts helped convince me that it's impossible to separate mobile data from mobile devices in any meaningful discussion about mobile security.

Throughout the editing process, there were numerous people who reviewed the text and provided countless suggestions for improvements and clarifications. I appreciate that they were not shy about giving me their opinions and aided in steering me out of trouble spots in the narrative. In particular, I'd like to thank George McBride, David Curry, and Jeff Davis for the commitment of their time and expertise in thoroughly reviewing the draft of the text. Their efforts made this book a better, and more enjoyable, work.

Finally, I'd like to thank my wife, Angela, for enduring the writing process right alongside me, reading and editing drafts, and providing endless support and encouragement throughout the process. Without her love and patience, I never would have been able to complete the book.

Stephen Fried

About the Author

Stephen Fried is a seasoned information security professional with more than 25 years experience in information technology. For the past 14 years, Stephen has concentrated his efforts on providing effective information security leadership to large organizations. He has led the creation of security programs for Fortune 500 companies and has extensive background in such diverse security issues as risk assessment and management, security policy development, security architecture, infrastructure and perimeter security design, outsource relationship security, off-shore development, intellectual property protection, security technology development, business continuity, secure e-business design, and information technology auditing. A frequent invited speaker at conferences, Stephen is also active in many security industry organizations. He is a contributing author to the *Information Security Management Handbook* and has also been quoted in *Secure Enterprise* and *CIO Decisions*.

Trademarks

Adobe Acrobat® is a registered trademark of Adobe Systems Incorporated.

AIM® is a registered trademark of AOL Inc.

Amazon® is a registered trademark of Amazon.com, Inc.

Apple®, iPhone®, iPod®, Mac OS®, iTunes®, and FileVault® are registered trademarks of Apple Inc.

Facebook® is a registered trademark of Facebook, Inc.

Fedex® is a registered trademark of Federal Express Corporation.

Gartner® is a registered trademark of Gartner, Inc.

Good™ and Good Mobile Messaging™ are trademarks of Good Technology, Inc.

Google™ and Gmail™ are trademarks of Google Inc.

Ironkey® is a trademark of Ironkey, Inc.

Kingston® is a registered trademark of Kingston Technology Corporation.

LinkedIn™ is a trademark of Linkedin Corp.

Lotus Notes® is a registered trademark of IBM Corporation.

Merriam-Webster® and Collegiate® are registered trademarks of Merriam-Webster, Incorporated.

Microsoft®, PowerPoint®, Windows Mobile®, Excel®, Outlook®, Active Directory®, BitLocker®, Windows Vista®, and Windows 7® are registered trademarks of Microsoft Corporation.

PGP® is a registered trademark of PGP Corporation.

Reuters™ is a trademark of Thomson Reuters.

RIM® and BlackBerry® are registered trademarks of Research In Motion Limited.

Starbucks® is a registered trademark of Starbucks Corporation.

Symbian™ is a trademark of the Symbian Foundation.

TrueCrypt® is a registered trademark of the TrueCrypt Foundation.

Twitter™ is a trademark of Twitter, Inc.

UPS™ is a trademark of United Parcel Service of America, Inc.

Victorinox™ and "Swiss Army"™ are trademarks of Victorinox AG.

Walmart™ is a trademark of Wal-Mart Stores, Inc.

Webshots® is a registered trademark of CNET Networks, Inc.

Yahoo!® and Flickr® are registered trademarks and Yahoo! Messenger is a trademark of Yahoo! Inc.

Introduction

What are you doing to secure your mobile data?

That question is being asked more often today, especially among business managers and information security professionals trying to secure their organizations against the latest threats coming at them from every angle. Mobile data and the mobile devices carrying that data are the current hot topics as organizations struggle to deal with the increased scrutiny of data security protection in all forms. Every passing week brings more news stories about lost laptops, missing backup tapes, and data breaches exposing millions of personal data records. These are certainly not new problems, and organizations have been trying to deal with these (and similar information-protection) issues for a very long time. However, the public's consciousness is now elevated as a result of increasingly frequent incidents of identity theft and online fraud bolstered by a constant barrage of media coverage concerning data loss incidents.

Ironically, many of these cases do not involve the use of mobile media. They are caused by more "traditional" forms of information theft such as network eavesdropping, social engineering, and old-fashioned computer hacking. However, the stories that seem to draw the most attention are the ones that involve the loss of information from mobile devices: the lost laptop, the missing portable hard disk, and the stolen flash drive. For some reason, these seem to generate the greatest response from the public and cause the most worry among corporate information managers. Perhaps it's because people can relate more easily to a missing laptop than something more esoteric, like a UNIX server compromised by a buffer overflow attack. They understand how easily a flash drive is lost because they've probably lost one or two themselves, much more than they understand how a man-in-the-middle attack works. They can imagine a malicious employee copying their private financial records to a CD because they use the same process for copying their family photos to a CD for storage or mailing.

This rise in security consciousness by both the general public and within businesses, as well as the increased media coverage of mobile device incidents, has had a ripple effect on the way organizations approach their information security programs and how they respond to mobile data protection. Some have banned all such devices from their enterprise, citing the need for high security and the inability to properly secure such devices as the driving forces behind the decision. Others have taken a more moderate approach, incrementally adding device and data protections to address the specific mobile security issues that threaten them. Still others have yet to address the issue at all, waiting for the "perfect solution" or the "silver bullet" that will solve their mobile security problems. None of these approaches is a perfect fit, and all these organizations are struggling with their decisions.

Even politicians are struggling to address the mobile data security issue. As the number of mobile data loss incidents rises, the public's intolerance for such apparently inadequate security practices has caused them to complain loudly to their elected officials. Already working to address privacy, fraud, and breach notification through increasingly comprehensive legislation, state and national representatives are now including mobile data issues specifically in such legislation, often citing mobile devices as requiring security commensurate with—and sometimes in addition to—traditional information management technologies like computers, networks, and databases. Although mobile devices share many of the same characteristics and security risks with their more stationary counterparts, it appears that even our legislators are caught up in mobile security fever. The result is that many organizations, already struggling to comply with the multitude of current security and privacy regulations, must now add mobile security to the list of compliance initiatives. Because it is a relatively new technology with little in the way of definitive security solutions to implement, organizations must seek out technology experts, external consultants, and industry partners and ask them the same question: "What are you doing to secure your mobile data?"

The fact that they're asking this question at all gives you a hint about the state of mobile security technology and the inability to easily integrate mobile data security into an organization's information security program. Unlike firewalls, antivirus services, and authentication technologies (with their mature history and robust data protection solutions), the security of mobile data and devices is still a relatively new field. There are many "solutions" on the market offering to protect a wide variety of mobile data and devices, but the field is fragmented, the technology still maturing, and organizations are still trying to determine how they want to approach the issue. Thus, there are too many variables to consider either the field or the solutions to be mature. In short, there are many more questions than answers, and organizations are struggling to create a mobile data strategy that protects their (and their customers') information while still allowing the business to function efficiently.

Finding some of those answers and creating that strategy is what this book is all about.

How Did We Get Here?

Computing has always been about information movement and management. Computers were initially created because we had more information than we (as humans) were able to manage and process ourselves, and we needed more "brain horsepower" than we were able to amass individually or collectively. Once the earliest rudimentary computers were invented, it quickly became apparent that the real power in computing rested in the ability to store information—a great deal of information—and recall that information for use and analysis. As a result, the processing and storage capacity for subsequent computers continually increased, creating an explosion in both the amount of information we could process and the need to efficiently store that information for later use. New technologies were created to manage that data storage, starting with punch cards and paper tape, then quickly moving to magnetic tape and the invention of the disk drive. Suddenly, the amount of data an organization could store seemed endless, limited only by the organization's physical storage capacity and its ability to afford additional storage media.

Once that early development was under way, advances in storage devices continued swiftly. Increased disk capacity and miniaturization allowed drives to store larger amounts of data in smaller-sized containers. However, one obstacle still remained: the ability to easily move information from one system to another so that different computers (and the users of those computers) could share the same information, work on the same problems, and jointly harness the computing resources that were rapidly increasing in power and capacity. Two significant achievements helped achieve that goal: the invention of the data network and the invention of portable storage devices.

The creation of data networks allowed, for the first time, multiple computers to work together to share programs and information. A great deal of historical and technical literature has been dedicated to discussing the history of data networking and its contribution to modern information management, so this book will not dwell on the topic. However, it is not an exaggeration to say that without the creation and continued advancement of data networks, modern computing and information management would not be the advanced engine of business, government, and personal communications that it is today.

The other great contribution to computing—portable storage devices—deserves just as much discussion and praise, as it has enabled the easy movement of data in ways unimagined in the early days of computing and still difficult to fathom today. The invention of small, cheap, portable storage allowed information, for the first time, to exist and move beyond the system where it was created. Data created on a mainframe system in London could be processed by a minicomputer in Hong Kong, then transferred to a PC in San Francisco, all aided by its storage and transport on a tape cartridge, DVD, or flash drive. The London-based user of that data was no longer tied to a particular machine and could follow the data through all those locations or store it on a portable storage device and pass it off to his colleagues in those other cities. Although we now take this capability for granted, it was a major breakthrough for its time and paved the way for the unrestricted flow of information that many in the modern business and social world enjoy today.

Subsequently, the creation of inexpensive, easily available portable storage allowed the separation of data storage as an entity distinct from the system used to process the data and established each of these components as independent, yet related, technologies. It changed the way each of these two components was viewed, and the development of each became a separate (yet intertwined) branch of technology. Entire technology ecosystems were built around each, and both areas—computing and storage—became industries in their own right. Portable storage evolved from simple magnetic tape reels and large drums of spinning magnetic platters to ever-shrinking sizes and ever-increasing capacity of miniaturized circuitry. Over time, we witnessed the evolution of portable storage to include floppy disks, tape cartridges, disk cartridges, mini drives, and eventually solid-state (or "flash") memory. Every iteration brought increased capacity, smaller physical size, and greater opportunities for quicker mobilization of data.

That's where our security troubles began.

The Beginning of the End

As each generation of storage media has become smaller, faster, higher in capacity, and easier to transport, it has seen a corresponding increase in the security problems surrounding the protection of data on that media. There was a time when security was not a big concern for computing services in general and storage devices in particular. Data storage devices were all contained in the data center, or at least within a single facility. "Portable" meant moving a disk pack across the floor from one machine to another, but that was the extent of its "portability." However, once storage devices started becoming smaller and more portable, their use as a method for information transport correspondingly increased. Data storage was no longer tied to a particular computer or computing facility. It was now independent, able to move to any number of locations and systems, and became increasingly difficult to control. In addition, as successive generations of portable storage became available, they became more system-independent, capable of interfacing with a wide variety of systems and networks and relying less and less on any proprietary infrastructure to operate. This was a huge benefit to consumers of this technology, who were growing weary of proprietary standards and the inability to use various storage technologies on different systems.

From a security perspective, however, the loss of this technology specialization also increased the risk of random data movement, and interchangeable storage devices increased the opportunity for data loss. With new, cross-platform storage technology, an information thief was no longer required to possess the same hardware as the system she was stealing data from; she just needed to have hardware that was compatible with the portable storage technology she was using to move the data—compatibility that was becoming increasingly standardized on a wide variety of mobile devices.

It all came to a head with the explosion of flash memory storage technology in the mid-1990s. This breakthrough in technology allowed the creation of small, inexpensive, and (most important) high-capacity storage devices. As a result, data storage became incorporated into a wide variety of mobile devices, including stand-alone solid-state data drives, entertainment devices (like music and video players), digital cameras, and mobile phones. By the early 2000s, flash memory became so commonplace and useful for both personal and business applications that devices of all kinds incorporated data storage as part of their basic functionality. It seemed as if every new device had the ability to store data in some form, and "dual-use" devices—possessing both functional and storage capabilities—became widely adopted as personal and business productivity tools. That's where the security of these devices, and the data they contained, began to get worrisome for those seeking to protect that data.

As these devices have continued to proliferate, the security problems with this convergence of utility and storage on the same device have become more apparent, and security experts are struggling to properly protect both the devices and the data. In addition, as storage capacity gets built into numerous devices, the balance of power for controlling and protecting data has shifted away from the owners of the data and toward the consumer of the data and the owners of these new devices. A user no longer needs specialized equipment to store data generated and used by the device. The device is both the data generator *and* the storage medium.

Where We Are Now

All these security and technology issues have finally converged, and that leads us to the central problem of mobile device protection; how do you allow productive use of the device while restricting and protecting access to the data on that device? As the benefit of these devices for legitimate business and personal use grows, so does their usefulness for nefarious purposes. Because data storage is often incorporated as part of some other useful function (such as a phone, camera, voice recorder, or music player), information thieves and malicious insiders can use these devices to store large quantities of stolen data and remove them surreptitiously from an organization. As a result, organizations are struggling to find ways to protect this newly mobile data while, at the same time, enabling productive use of the devices within their work force. While it would seem easy to simply banish all such devices from an organization (as some have tried), the devices have become so ingrained in our daily work and personal lives that such decrees often fail.

It would seem that we now have something of a culture clash on our hands. On the one side, we have the consumers of mobile devices and portable storage systems who see real benefit and business value from their use and wish to bring that value to their organizations. On the other side are the security, privacy, and information protection groups who have the responsibility to protect the organization (and its customers) against data loss and information breaches. They see these devices as yet another avenue for a security failure and are working feverishly to develop methods for better securing the technology. These two constituencies—end users and security groups—seem to be at odds constantly over this issue. Add to that the recent awareness and calls for increased diligence from lawmakers and the public, and the mix creates a volatile combination of unbridled technology, uncontrolled data, and a panicked public.

It's in the middle of that mix where you may now find yourself. That's why you're reading this book. So, what are you doing to secure *your* mobile data?

The Real Problems

In the final analysis, the current security issues surrounding mobile data and the use of mobile devices to store and process that data are related to three fundamental truths:

- *The information we need to survive (professionally and personally) can now be moved easily and inexpensively.* The technology available to us (via flash drives, smartphones, and rewritable media) permits—indeed, encourages—the mobility of data. It is no longer confined to a fixed point; it can move quickly and easily from system to system.
- *Information can easily move from medium to medium in an instant.* Because mobile devices have the ability to move data in and out quickly, and the content and format of that data is independent of the device, that data can move quickly through multiple devices in rapid succession. Consequently, the security of that information depends on a combination of the security mechanisms provided to the data as well as the security mechanisms available on the various devices where it resides.
- *As that vital information moves further away from its source (i.e., the data owner) it becomes more difficult to control and protect.* The originator of a piece of information may have requirements and assumptions for how that information is to be protected. As it moves further and further from that originator, his ability to enforce those protections diminishes. By the time that information reaches its final destination, the original protections in place to secure it may no longer be effective.

Apply these three statements to the way mobile devices are commonly used today by the average consumer. Whether it be a flash drive, PDA, smartphone, or laptop computer, these devices exist *specifically* to move and manage data. Most of these devices, however, don't have many (if any) built-in security provisions for information protection. When organizations do try to implement security to better protect the organization's information, they find that the security technology fails completely; it is insufficient to cover the full spectrum of risks and threats targeting mobile data and devices, or end users resist its implementation in the name of expedience and efficiency. It's a difficult situation for all involved. End users generally want to protect their information (some of it, after all, is their personal data) but don't want to work too hard for it. Security practitioners want to make security of the devices easier for end users, but the available technology and cultural environment do not allow that to happen. Finally, device manufacturers continuously introduce new devices with new features, often failing to consider their security or information-protection implications.

What You'll Learn in This Book

This is a book about securing mobile data and mobile devices. One of the first things you should know, however, is that there is no such thing as absolute security. This is true for all aspects of security, not just for mobile data and devices. Therefore, you will need to make some very difficult but critical decisions about what aspects of security are most important to you. You will need to understand the benefits, risks, and costs of each of the many choices you will face, and then determine the extent to which you are willing to limit your users' ability to take advantage of the benefits of mobile devices in the name of protecting your organization's confidential and sensitive information. This book is here to help.

To provide you with the information you will need, the book guides you through all aspects of the security issues for mobile data and devices—from basic risk identification through building a business case to create an effective mobile security program. The book takes a step-by-step approach, ensuring that you thoroughly understand the concepts and issues of each area before moving on to the next. Most important, the book will highlight the benefits of mobile device use, describe the security issues various devices and activities bring with them, and discuss alternative courses of action an organization can take to achieve that all-important risk/benefit balance. As a result, the chapters in this book use the following logical progression:

- **Chapter 1: What Are You Trying to Protect?** The first step in the process is to truly understand the problem you are facing and clearly define your objectives. This chapter introduces you to the essential definitions required to understand security issues for mobile data and devices and helps you begin to determine your most pressing mobile security concerns and needs.
- **Chapter 2: It's All about the Risk.** Understanding the various risks you will encounter when dealing with mobile data, and how those risks can change, is essential to developing an effective mobile security program. This chapter discusses the general risks found when mobilizing data and provides a methodology for identifying, analyzing, and evaluating that risk.

- **Chapter 3: The Many Faces of Mobility.** There is a plethora of mobile devices available today and just as many ways to store and move data among them. This chapter discusses the diversity of mobile devices and the many ways data can interact with them.
- **Chapter 4: Data at Rest, Data in Motion.** Both the biggest strengths and the biggest security concerns of mobile data come from the ever-changing interaction between mobile devices and mobile data. This chapter looks at the different places that mobile data can be located and the ways its security can change as it moves from place to place.
- **Chapter 5: Mobile Data Security Models.** Establishing an effective framework for your organization's mobile security program can start you on the way toward successfully protecting your company's mobile data. This chapter provides methods for modeling the interaction between mobile data and mobile devices, and discusses the advantages and disadvantages of each of these approaches.
- **Chapter 6: Encryption.** Using encryption technology is one of the best ways to protect mobile data. This chapter discusses basic encryption concepts and shows how they can be used effectively to protect data in a mobile environment.
- **Chapter 7: Defense-in-Depth: Mobile Security Controls.** There are a variety of methods and technologies you can implement to protect mobile data in your enterprise. This chapter discusses some of those technologies and shows how they can be layered and combined to create a more resilient and effective mobile data protection program.
- **Chapter 8: Defense-in-Depth: Specific Technology Controls.** Some mobile technologies are best secured through the application of specific types of controls. This chapter reviews the most common mobile device controls and discusses the options for implementing them in your mobile environment.
- **Chapter 9: Creating a Mobile Security Policy.** Your security policy is the place where you set expectations for appropriate mobile use and data protection in your organization. This chapter takes you through the process of creating a mobile security policy and discusses the various approaches you might consider.
- **Chapter 10: Building the Business Case for Mobile Security.** Even the best security program will not help the organization if the company's leadership won't approve its implementation. This chapter discusses the essential elements of a mobile security business case and provides examples of the information such a proposal might contain.

A Note on Technology and Terminology

Every effort has been made to make this book as comprehensive as possible and to present all the options available to you to help you establish your own mobile security program. It is directed primarily at high-level technical and program management personnel within an organization. While the book does go into some technical details about different types of currently available mobile technologies, it does so judiciously. There will be few references to specific mobile security products, because the security product market is constantly changing, particularly when it comes to protecting mobile data and the security capabilities of new mobile devices. Any discussion of a particular product's features or capabilities will most certainly be outdated by the time the book goes to print. As a result, different types of available protections are described at length, but discussions of particular products that have those protections, or available features within those products, are avoided.

There are also a number of actors involved in any discussion of security. There are those on the "good" side of the security equation, such as employees, security professionals, organizational management, and law enforcement. These are the people who are trying to help the organization achieve its business goals and who are in a position to strengthen the organization's security efforts by enforcing security policy and following good security practices.

There are also those on the "bad" side of the equation. These are the people who will attempt to subvert your information security controls to gain unauthorized access to your systems and data. These bad actors go by various names, depending on the situation. They are known as "attackers," "hackers," "information thieves," "fraudsters," "malicious actors," "threat agents," or (if they are your own employees) "malicious insiders." In some situations, there may be more than one of these bad actors trying to get your information or subvert your security controls. To cover all such descriptions and keep the narrative flowing, all such actors will be referred to uniformly as "attackers." Attackers come from all different nationalities, races, religious affiliations, political persuasions, and genders. Despite their inherent diversity, however, the attackers in the various scenarios presented here all have one thing in common; they are all trying to steal your information, and taking that information while it resides on mobile devices is the latest attack in their repertoire.

Final Thoughts

The journey to securing mobile data can be long and arduous, and it will require you to find the proper balance between security, user acceptance, technology capabilities, and resource commitment to create the best possible mobile security program for your organization. Each person who reads this book will apply its message differently, because security in every organization is a bit different: different risks, different circumstances, and different goals. As you read through this material, be sure to inject your own experiences and circumstances into the text and use the examples given as the basis for developing your own approach to mobile security.

By viewing the chapters as a progression of knowledge, experiences, and strategies, you will be better prepared to address the specific mobile security issues prevalent in your own organization. In addition, you will become well versed in all the various aspects of mobile data, mobile technology, and the benefits and challenges of applying different security and protection controls to different mobile data scenarios. Most of all, when you are done, you will be able to definitively answer that most popular of questions: What are you doing to secure your mobile data?

Chapter 1

What Are You Trying to Protect?

One can scarcely pick up a business or technical journal without reading about the promise and future of "mobility." It seems as if everything today is, or wants to be, mobile. There are mobile phones, mobile computers, mobile music players, mobile game players, mobile video players, mobile voice recorders, and mobile book readers. The problem with all this discussion about mobility is that those writing about this brave new world assume that everyone else knows exactly what they mean by "mobility." Unfortunately, this is not always the case, especially with a field as new and dynamic as mobile security. There may be a generally understood notion of what the industry calls "mobile data" or a "mobile device," but the precise definition of "mobile" can vary from person to person, from device to device, and from product to product. Until we clearly define and understand these terms, nothing else in this book will make much sense.

One of the things all security professionals learn early in their careers is that all security initiatives must start with one very basic question:

What are you trying to protect?

This may seem almost too obvious, but this simple question is often overlooked in the name of expediency, lack of foresight, or just plain carelessness. How many security programs or projects seem to career out of control or collapse under their own weight trying to satisfy too many requirements at once? Worse yet, many of those projects started with very simple-sounding objectives like, "Protect the network from hackers," or "Find out what information is leaking from the organization," or (a personal favorite) "Just keep us out of the headline news." These are all lofty and worthwhile goals, but hardly the type of concrete direction upon which a solid security program can be built. In short, none of these goals answers the basic question, "What are you trying to protect?"

The same can be said of current popular security (and marketing) mantras such as "protect mobile devices" or "secure mobile data." It is easy to understand, on an intuitive level, what these are intended to mean. In fact, many current information technology (IT) security projects are being based on little more than these phrases issued as proclamations from the highest levels of the organization. The risk many organizations face through mobile data moving around their networks or the mishandling of data on mobile devices is enormous, and without a concentrated effort to place effective controls on this type of data, the risk will continue to rise. However, many of these efforts are based on little more than the idea that there is some type of data out there called "mobile data," that it can reside on things called "mobile devices," and that somehow this "data" on these "devices" must be protected. Unfortunately, neither of these terms has a clear definition, and without those clear definitions, there cannot be a satisfactory answer to the question, "What are you trying to protect?"

The purpose of this chapter is to clearly define these two terms—*mobile data* and *mobile device*—not just giving them formal meanings, but also presenting a context for their use. In addition to their formal definitions, we'll also discuss how these concepts intertwine and interact. This discussion is essential because simply providing definitions for certain terms is, frankly, boring and fails to provide the deeper meaning these terms have with respect to the security and privacy of confidential data. Words have a context apart from their pure definition. So, in the case of mobile data and mobile devices, it's important to understand not just the factual definition of the terms, but also their broader meaning, why they are so important to us, and why they strike such fear into the hearts of information security people and business leaders everywhere. Going through this process will provide a much greater appreciation of how to use and address these issues throughout the rest of this book, and also lead to a clear answer to that basic question, "What are you trying to protect?"

Finding a Definition for Mobile Data

Security terms like *firewall*, *encryption*, or even *false positive* have clear, precise, and commonly known definitions, but terms like *mobile data* and *mobile device* do not. As a result, we will have to build one ourselves. Let's start with the word *mobile*, which *Merriam-Webster* defines as:

> **Mobile:** Capable of moving or being moved : movable[1]

The clarity and brevity of this definition should not come as a big surprise, but it is a starting point for explaining why mobility is such a problem when it comes to data.

From a security standpoint, stationary targets are generally much easier to protect than moving targets, but in our modern, networked business environment, movable data is quickly becoming the norm. Consequently, data that is "capable of moving or being moved" is much harder to protect than data that remains stationary.

Newton's Telecom Dictionary, the standard reference for technicians in the telecommunications industry, has a precise definition for mobile data. According to Newton's, mobile data is:

> **Mobile Data**: ...a generic term used to describe data communications through the air from and to field workers—from package deliverers, to car rental companies (to track cars), to field service personnel, to law enforcement officials checking license plates.[2]

This starts to get closer to a working definition that is useful for our purposes. In *Newton's* definition, mobile data is not just data that is moving around from place to place, but it is used by people in the normal course of their everyday work. Unfortunately, *Newton's* definition is too industry-specific to be useful for our purposes.

In some ways, all data is mobile, that is, it is "capable of moving or being moved." Data moves all the time within our computer systems, from permanent storage (disk or tape) to temporary storage (RAM) and back again. It moves along a data bus and it moves to peripheral devices like display monitors and printers. But this type of movement is not our primary concern because it is localized and confined to the internal workings of the system that is using or processing it. When data moves from the system bus to RAM and then off to the local hard disk, it never leaves the confines of the system where it originated. This, essentially, makes the data stationary. Understanding this aspect of internal data movement is important, but it ultimately confuses the definition we are trying to establish.

So the most important element of mobile data is, in fact, its *external* mobility. Mobile data is the end result of any process that moves data from point to point beyond the system from which it originated. This external movement is referenced indirectly in *Newton's* definition ("through the air from and to field workers"), but Newton bases his definition on the experiences of his target audience: telecommunications workers. For our purposes, we need a definition that will be applicable to a much wider audience. Mobile data moves not just over the air, but over wired networks and device connections as well. In short, mobile data becomes mobile the moment it moves outside a closed or contained system. At that point, we lose the ability to completely manage the environment in which it exists. It is no longer stationary and no longer confined in its constrained environment.

What we're concerned with, and what we'll spend the rest of this book discussing, is data that moves beyond the boundaries of your direct control. This is data that moves outside your systems and networks and travels—even temporarily—beyond the boundaries of your infrastructure. More specifically, we're trying to protect data that moves outside those boundaries through the use of a mobile device (which will be more clearly defined in just a moment).

Based on this additional information, we can now complete the official definition of mobile data for the purposes of this book:

> **Mobile Data**: Information that is intentionally moved beyond an organization's borders (physically or logically) by means of a mobile device.

Mobile Data Scenarios

To provide some concrete examples and clarify this definition of mobile data, let's look at several situations where mobile data can cause security problems for an organization and see how well this definition applies. We'll examine five different and very common data movement scenarios:

1. Copying a presentation file to a Universal Serial Bus (USB) flash drive
2. Posting company information onto a Web page or social media site
3. Synchronizing your calendar, e-mail, and contacts to a smartphone or personal digital assistant (PDA)
4. Taking pictures of coworkers and posting them to an online photo site
5. Copying the company's address book to a smartphone

Scenario 1: Copying a presentation file to a USB flash drive. This is clearly mobile data based on our definition. The information in this case is the presentation file (although you can easily substitute a financial spreadsheet, project proposal, or technical data in its place), and the data is moving from the closed system of the computer onto a device that can be transported almost anywhere with little control over that movement. This is the classic example of mobile data in action, and the one most often used as the scenario that launches an organization's mobile data protection efforts.

Scenario 2: Posting company information onto a Web page or social media site. This is not mobile data based on our definition. The issue of an employee posting sensitive company information on noncompany Web sites or forums is certainly a growing problem and is clearly a case of data moving outside the boundaries of the organization. However, the information is placed on the external service directly by the user without the use or need of an intermediary device. This type of data movement is the subject of a branch of information security known as Data Loss Prevention (DLP). DLP is currently a fast-growing concern among security and IT professionals, and it addresses a real and potentially damaging threat to the security and privacy of information. Data distributed (and disclosed) in this manner has many of the same risk and threat characteristics that mobile data possesses, and in some cases the ways to prevent this type of data loss mirror those used to prevent mobile data loss. The difference between this type of data movement and what we have defined as mobile data can be subtle, but in the effort to clearly define what we are trying to protect, it is important to make the distinction. We will discuss DLP and how it relates to mobile data in more depth in Chapter 7.

Scenario 3: Synchronizing your calendar, e-mail, and contacts to a smartphone or PDA. This is mobile data. The growing use of continuously networked PDAs and smartphones has been a productivity boost to modern workers. These devices allow users to keep in constant contact with what's happening both at work and in their personal lives. They also offer many productive tools, such as a calendar with scheduling capabilities, a contact list, document storage, and access to work and personal e-mail—all in a device that fits easily into a shirt pocket. Unfortunately, these devices often lack basic security controls to protect this sensitive personal and company information. Because the information is moving outside the boundaries of your organization through the use of the smartphone or PDA, this is classified as mobile data for our purposes.

Scenario 4: Taking pictures of coworkers and posting them to an online photo site. This is mobile data. While many of the photos posted to online photo sites like Flickr and Webshots contain images of family vacations and college parties, some people have used these sites to post images of coworkers, company facilities, project information, and even confidential documents. Because these images pass through a mobile device (i.e., the digital camera or camera-enabled phone), they are classified as mobile data.

Scenario 5: Copying the company's address book to a smartphone. This precisely fits the definition of mobile data and is a common scenario among workers who spend much of their time on the road. Having the corporate directory in your phone's address book is a convenient way to make calling and sending e-mail to coworkers much simpler. Unfortunately, if that phone is lost or stolen, the attacker will have the phone number and e-mail address of every employee in the company.

Other Factors to Consider

While these simple examples give a better understanding of what is meant by the term *mobile data* and how it will be used and referenced in the rest of this book, there are other factors to consider that provide a better context for understanding our mobile data definition. Two of the most prominent of these are that the data in question must be important to someone and that it is being moved on purpose.

The importance factor is one that cannot be overlooked. One of the basic axioms in all security is that the amount spent on security efforts (in time, effort, money, or people) should not exceed the value of the information being protected.

Therefore, the assumption is made that the mobile data must, in fact, be worth protecting. Preventing sensitive company documents from being downloaded onto an employee's PDA is worth the effort and expense because the value of that confidential information, should it fall into the wrong hands, is much higher than the value of the effort needed to protect it (such as adding encryption capabilities to the PDA or blocking such transfers altogether). Restricting the use of flash drives in a call center (where users may have access to millions of financial or health care records) is deemed worth the cost because the amount spent on protections like computer-port management or user-activity monitors pales in comparison to the financial, reputation, and litigation costs the company will incur if one of those call-center employees downloads those records onto a flash drive.

Likewise, there is some data whose importance is negligible and whose loss would hardly be noticed. For example, suppose the manager in charge of the company cafeteria copied the schedule for next month's menu selection onto a CD and placed it in her briefcase. Later that evening, her car is broken into and her briefcase stolen. Unless the recipes on that menu plan were award-winning culinary delights coveted by Iron Chefs the world over, hardly anyone would consider that lost data important, much less worth the effort or money to protect it. In another scenario, suppose someone in your marketing department takes all the company's current sales brochures and copies them to a floppy disk* for delivery to the local printer. From there, they will be printed and mailed to current and potential customers to entice them to buy more of the company's products. After the disk is delivered to the printer, it is somehow lost. Is this a cause for concern? Perhaps not. The act of copying company information onto the floppy and taking it out of the company is certainly of concern, but the risk to the organization due to the exposure of the copied information is relatively low. The disk contained sales brochures that were already intended for public distribution. There are no secrets lost when public information is disclosed. The data may be important to the marketing department in its effort to attract and retain customers, but there is no heightened value associated with its loss or disclosure. Therefore, it remains unimportant from a mobile data security perspective. The risk/benefit considerations and business value judgments around making such decisions will be discussed in more detail in Chapter 2, but for now the important point is that the mobile data that needs the most protection is the mobile data with the most significant value.

That value may be tangible—for example, the secret formula to a million-dollar-a-year product. If the formula is leaked and a competitor is able to duplicate your formula, you could lose up to a million dollars per year in revenue. Alternatively, the value may be intangible. For example, if your employee phone list was stolen, could you place a value on that loss? While that information does have value to your organization, can you determine the precise financial or operational cost that information represents? Assets (including data) with a high intangible value can be

---

* Yes, there are still some floppy disks in use, though they are rapidly disappearing.

just as important and can require just as much security protection as those whose value can be precisely derived, but determining the proper level of security for assets with intangible value can often be difficult.

In addition to the importance of the data, the second factor to consider is that the mobile data we are most concerned with has become mobile for a specific purpose, and that purpose may be either nefarious or benign. When considering this aspect, it is not so important to consider the value or sensitivity of the information that has gone mobile, but rather to consider why it has gone mobile in the first place. Who sent it on its way, and what was the reason for doing so? Data rarely moves by accident; its movement is almost always part of a larger process or activity. A personnel management system will move employee data back and forth between the application and the tables in an employee database. Online photo storage services will transfer pictures between a user's PC and the online system. Financial management systems may transfer account records or funds between banks on opposite sides of the globe. These are all predefined motion paths that applications take. Mobilizing data can be a part of that predefined path and a normal occurrence within a system's operation or process. Alternatively, mobilizing data can also take that information out of the predefined path to an alternate destination, usually at the instigation of a person interacting with the data somewhere along the path. Depending on the security controls surrounding and protecting the data, that path may be out of the organization's direct control.

As an important side note, the fact that data rarely moves by accident does not mean that the data owner is always conscious of its movement. Indeed, data often becomes mobile because someone takes it upon himself to set it along that path. This is often done with the best of intentions by someone trying to make the data more useful or more available to others, but it also occasionally happens because an attacker sets it in that direction for his own nefarious purposes. Data movement based on either of these scenarios is not the original intention of the data's owner, nor is it guaranteed that the owner will even know that the data has been set in motion and in a direction not originally intended. We will examine this type of ad hoc movement and its consequences in more detail in Chapter 3. Nevertheless, the data is now on its way and needs to be protected.

Defining a Mobile Device

Having a formal definition of mobile data begins to greatly clarify the scope of what we are trying to protect. However, this still leaves a gap in our full understanding of the mobile data problem. When business leaders and security industry personnel discuss the security of mobile data, they are often only considering half the equation—the data half. This is because they believe that the movement of the data, as well as the protection that data has (or, rather, the lack of it), is the root cause of their security problems. But there is another half to the mobile security problem that cannot be overlooked if we are to get a real understanding of both the problem and the ways that the risk of mobile data movement can be mitigated. The latter part of our mobile data definition reveals this other essential component: the mobile device.

It's impossible to take a thorough look at mobile data security without also looking at the mobile devices on which that data is transported. Mobile devices are explicitly referenced in our definition of mobile data, and the use of mobile devices, and their rapid ascendancy into the mainstream of technical and cultural use, has made them an inseparable part of the way we look at data movement and information flow in modern business.

At first glance, the definition of a mobile device would seem simple:

Mobile Device: A device that is mobile

As we did for the definition of mobile data, let's refine this definition into a form that allows us to specify what it is we are trying to protect. The first consideration is the form factor of the device. The most commonly used mobile devices—indeed, anything commonly using the term *device*—are typically electronic in nature. While we can conceivably classify standard paper file folders and leather briefcases as mobile devices, doing so doesn't help address the most pressing security problem, which is the ability for the mobile devices to connect seamlessly into infrastructures. It is also possible that an organization might see file folders and briefcases as high-risk information containers and seek to restrict or ban their use, but it is more likely that small electronic storage devices would present more of an immediate threat and warrant more direct action.*

The portability of the device is also an important factor to consider. If mobile data represents a risk because it is easily moved, the devices that enable easy movement must be considered risks as well. The devices that would fit our definition of a mobile device must excel in their ability to move from place to place easily without the need for special handling. Portable hard disks, flash memory cards, digital cameras, MP3 players, laptops and "netbooks," and optical media like CDs and DVDs are all easily moved from place to place in a briefcase, purse, or shirt pocket. While not indestructible, they generally withstand normal handling (and mishandling), and they can connect easily to a plethora of computer and communications equipment with little effort or configuration. In fact, most of the more popular electronic devices now come equipped with USB interfaces or adapters, making these devices even more universally accessible. Additionally, most modern operating systems have incorporated "plug and play" services into

---

* In most areas of security, a particular objects is itself neither "good" nor "evil." Briefcases can be used to protect sensitive documents as well as provide a cover for an attacker trying to steal them from a building. The same is true of folders, flash drives, and smartphones. The determination of the benevolence or threat of an object or device is usually based more on the use of that particular object for a specific task rather than the properties inherent to the object itself.

their architecture, making the installation and use of these devices accessible to even the most inexperienced computer users.

This has created a bit of a "chicken and egg" situation in the evolution of mobile devices and the use of mobile data. The desire to easily move large amounts of data between systems requires devices that are small, portable, and have a high storage capacity. This requirement drove the development of devices with precisely those characteristics. This, in turn, has led to an even greater capability (and accompanying desire) to move even more data onto these devices, which users have embraced enthusiastically. With continued advances in storage technology and mass-market availability of that technology, the cycle will continue unabated for the foreseeable future.

All these additional characteristics that define our need for, and use of, mobile devices allow for a much more precise definition for the purposes of this book:

> **Mobile Device**: A device, typically electronic in nature, that can store large amounts of information and may be easily transported from place to place without undue effort or cost.

To complete a common understanding of specifically what devices fit within this definition, here is a short—and highly incomplete—list of what are commonly understood to fall into the category of "mobile device":

- Laptop computers
- Cell phones and smartphones
- Personal digital assistants (PDAs)
- Portable media players
- Digital cameras
- USB-based storage drives, commonly referred to as flash drives
- Flash-memory cards, regardless of actual format (for example, Compact Flash, SD, xD, etc.)
- Recordable CDs and DVDs*

There are devices that fit some, but not all, of the definition's criteria for a mobile device and, therefore, can't fit neatly into the mobile device category based on our definition. For example, a modern mainframe computer is certainly smaller than its 1960s ancestors, but nobody would consider it portable. Record players and CD/DVD players can be used to play back the information on the media they use, but they are not, themselves, storage devices. Televisions can range in size from 60-inch high-definition behemoths to small 3-inch pocket TVs, but they generally only capture and present information, not store it. Finally, a desktop computer is an electronic

---

* Note that CDs and DVDs can also be regarded as "mobile media." However, because they are a primary transport mechanism for mobile data and fit within the criteria set by the definition, they will be classified as "mobile devices" for the purposes of this book.

device that can certainly store large amounts of information, but it is not easily transported. For something to be classified as a mobile device, its fundamental function and design must be based, at least in part, on its actual (and practical) portability.

None of these examples is, of course, absolute. There are televisions that come with storage for recording programs, CD players that can record and play media, and desktop computers small enough to fit in a (large) handbag. The point here is not to provide an exhaustive inventory of every conceivable type of portable device, but to give examples of the types of devices that probably will (and won't) be causing concern when it comes to protecting an organization's information. It is conceivable that, at some time in the near future, someone will produce a television with DVD writing capability and 64 GB of storage in a package small enough to fit in your hand. Mainframes, on the other hand, are not likely to be considered portable any time soon.

Distinct, but Intertwined

So there you have it: the definitions of *mobile data* and *mobile device* that will be used throughout the rest of the book. Keep in mind that changes in technology and our understanding of how to use that technology will mean that the definitions will have to evolve over time. Nevertheless, they will serve us well in the coming chapters. Based on these definitions, however, some very interesting relationships between mobile data and mobile devices start to become apparent that may not have previously been obvious.

The terms *mobile data* and *mobile device* are often used interchangeably, and incorrectly, in normal conversation. It's not uncommon to hear people talk about protecting mobile devices when they are really referring to protecting the data on those devices. In many ways, the two ideas are intertwined: Mobile data without a transportation mechanism is simply stationary data. A mobile device without content to transport loses its key functionality. However, it is critical to be clear about distinguishing these two ideas. The data that is transported is separate and distinct from the medium used to facilitate that transport, and it is important to understand the role that each plays.

Mobile data is independent of the technology that is used to store and transport it. Information can exist in many forms and formats, and can be transported by a variety of mechanisms. A spreadsheet file contains the same bits whether it's on a PC, burned to a CD, or copied to the data-storage volume of an iPod. Moving the file to a different mobile device does not change the contents of the data, nor does it have any effect on the utility of the data once it gets to its final destination. In addition, the file can exist outside the confines of the mobile device. In fact, most data originates on nonmobile devices such as PCs, mainframes, and servers and may live its entire life span without ever coming in contact with a mobile device. Clearly, data does not require a mobile device in order to exist.

Likewise, mobile devices themselves can exist without mobile data. When you purchase that shiny new memory stick, it has no prerecorded data on it.* A mobile device, however, needs data to be useful, and a mobile device can store many different types of data. A single flash memory card can hold presentation files, spreadsheets, photos, text files, movie files, and even application programs. The only limit is the storage capacity of the device. The mobile device does not even need to know how to interpret or use the data it is carrying. For example, when a PowerPoint presentation is copied to a flash drive, the flash drive does not need to understand what PowerPoint is, how the file format works, or how to interpret the bits in the file to display the presentation. It is simply acting as a carrier for the bits until they reach their final destination. The situation is analogous to the act of mailing a letter inside an envelope. The envelope does not know the contents of the letter, nor does it make a difference if the letter is in English, French, or Hebrew. The envelope simply acts as a carrier from the sender to the recipient. It is the recipient who must be able to understand the letter and interpret its contents.

The combination of the two elements—the content and the carrier—both contribute to the security of the information. Each element can have security controls added to it that make the data more secure. The data can be encrypted or password protected. It can be encoded in a format that only certain programs can read. Or it can be totally innocuous and unimportant to anyone who may intercept it. Likewise, the mobile device can have hardware or software protections that restrict access to the data. Or, if the data it is carrying is not at all sensitive, it can have no protections at all. The combination of the protection mechanisms applied to the data and the protection mechanisms available on the mobile device determines the overall security of the information during transit. The goal of an effective mobile data security program is to determine exactly what that combination must be in order to provide optimal security.

Movable Data, Movable Risk

Data moving along the mobility path can also have different risk profiles based solely on the characteristics of the device where it resides at any given point in time. A data file containing the personal medical histories of a hospital's patients is generally considered to be sensitive and confidential no matter where it is located. If the file is located on a file server in a data center—protected by all the physical and electronic access controls a modern data center can provide—it is much safer and harder for an attacker to steal. If the file moves to a desktop computer, it loses many of the physical and logical protections it enjoyed while in the data center, but it can still be considered a relatively low risk if the computer where it resides is in a secured area, the security features available in the desktop operating system

---

* The device may have some pre-installed utilities on it for data backup or security, but these are not considered "data" for our purposes.

have been enabled, and the user follows adequate security procedures (such as using strong passwords and locking the computer when she walks away from her desk).

Once that file moves from the desktop computer to a mobile device, the risk profile can change dramatically. Suppose, for example, a user copies the file to a flash drive and tosses it into his briefcase. By doing so, he changes the overall risk to that file. It loses the protections available from the PC and now relies solely on the protections available from the flash drive and the briefcase. On the flash drive, the user can encrypt the data or use some type of Information Rights Management (IRM) system to provide protection. As for the briefcase, there are not a lot of security mechanisms inherent in the average case, so only good physical security can reduce some of the risk. For instance, if he locks the case in his trunk, drives straight home, and brings it directly into his locked house, he might have a good chance of keeping the sensitive data safe. If he leaves the case in the back seat, stops at the mall for some shopping on the way home, and forgets to lock his car in the parking lot, the risk to that data remains high. Likewise, if he gives the briefcase to someone else to take home so he can pick it up later, he may have increased his risk because he has transferred the responsibility for securing the case to someone else but has no way to ensure that security is upheld.

The list of potential scenarios relating to the interaction between mobile data and mobile devices could fill an entire book, but the fundamental principles are the same in all cases. As data moves through various containers and transport mechanisms, it takes on different risk characteristics, and those risk characteristics are a function of both the ability to protect the data itself and the protection mechanisms available in the container. The protection any data has and, thus, its subsequent risk—particularly if it is mobile data—is dependent on the circumstances surrounding that data at any given point in time. We will cover the risks to mobile data and how to go about determining exactly what those risks are in much more detail in Chapter 2. The point here is to illustrate how the security of mobile data and mobile devices are interdependent, and this interdependence is highlighted by the changes in the risk profile of the data as it moves from container to container or location to location.

The fatal mistake that many organizations make when attempting to protect all things mobile is trying to focus on one form of data or device over another. Because mobile data and mobile devices are so intertwined, and their risks so dependent on each other, trying to address mobile data as a stand-alone project only addresses half the problem. Conversely, trying to limit the use of mobile devices without addressing and restricting the type of data that these devices can hold will inevitably leave you short of your total information protection goals. Both of these efforts are important and essential to the overall security of an organization, but to address one while ignoring the other will lead to endless frustration (at best) and duplicated effort or wasted time and resources (at worst). Naturally, the ultimate goal of any information security program is to protect the organization's information, including its mobile information. Because data mobility (as we have defined it) requires the data to move from device to device, you must at least consider the effect that those devices will have on the protection of that information.

Following the Path

One final idea to consider when understanding the relationship between mobile data and mobile devices is the transient nature of data on many of these devices. The mobile device where the data's journey begins might not be the same one where the journey ends, and not all storage along the path is long term. Let's take the example of a photograph taken with a typical cell phone camera. The photo is initially stored in the phone's local memory. From there, is can be attached to an e-mail message to the photographer's friend, who might, in turn, post it on her Flickr or Facebook account. Or, the friend might download the photo to her computer and, from there, to a CD full of other recent images. The CD is then taken to her place of work, where the images are reviewed by her coworkers, edited, then transferred to a flash drive where it will be … Well, you get the idea. The photo image, like many other pieces of mobile data, only resides on the various mobile devices on its journey for a relatively short period of time.

In some cases, that period of time may only be an instant. Suppose our photographer was, instead, a blogger trying to present live coverage of MoDevCo Inc.'s launch of its latest product, the Gadgetron, the latest and most innovative product to hit the market in years. The Gadgetron project has been shrouded in secrecy for months, and MoDevCo is both highly secretive and extremely protective of its marketing image and intellectual property rights. It has banned photographers and video cameras from the event, but our intrepid blogger wants to have an exclusive scoop. He plans to use the camera on his cell phone to secretly capture streaming video of the event and post it immediately to his blog site. From the site, users can download the video or still images of the Gadgetron as well as engage in a lively discussion of the product and the event.

The observant reader might see more than a few security issues with this scenario that fit well into this discussion of transient mobile information storage. To begin with, our blogger is using his advanced mobile device—in this case a cell phone with high-quality video recording capabilities—to capture MoDevCo's intellectual property and the likenesses of the event's participants. However, that device did not permanently store the data on that device. Instead, the data was immediately transferred over the local cellular network to an Internet-connected Web server, where users of the Web site can copy, transfer, retransmit, or alter the images as they see fit. Here we see mobile devices in use not as a data-storage mechanism, but rather as a data-transmission mechanism. The storage aspect of the device is secondary to its ability to transfer whatever data is captured instantly to another place. The phone may, or may not, store or cache the images as they pass through the device on their way to the Web site. In either case, the storage is ephemeral and lasts only as long as is needed for the device to process the captured images, place them in the transmit queue, and move on to the next set of images. Any security mechanisms or attempts to protect the data as is moves through the device need to account for this momentary storage capacity, including any remaining trace of the data once it has left the device.

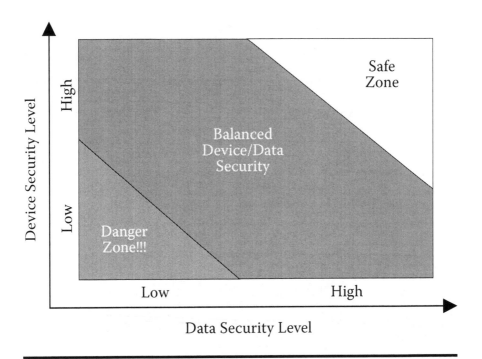

Figure 1.1 **Relationship between data and device security.**

Securing information as it moves through such devices can present numerous difficulties when trying to provide end-to-end security for that information. The transient nature of data transmission combined with the unknown state of security controls on any given device creates a mismatch between the security of the information and the security of the device. As the data moves from device to device, that mismatch can increase or decrease, depending on the nature of controls available through the new device.

Figure 1.1 shows a graphical illustration of this relationship between data security and device security. The figure shows how changes in the security levels for both data and devices affect the overall security of the data/device combination. As depicted in the figure, the worst-case scenario is the placement of data without any protection on a device without any available security controls. This is the "Danger Zone" in the lower left corner of the figure and should be avoided for all cases where sensitive data needs to be placed on a mobile device. Increasing the protection of either the device or the data moves you into the middle zone, where the right balance of device and/or data controls may be able to provide the required and appropriate level of protection against a finite pool of potential threats.

Adding protection controls to both the data and the device puts you in the "Safe Zone" in the upper right corner of the figure, where multiple types of controls offer the best protection against data loss or theft. This is a common security strategy called "defense-in-depth" that assumes that any single protection mechanism in your environment will fail at some point. When that failure occurs, there must be some additional, compensating, or complementary protection or control that can take up the slack and provide continuous security defense until such time as the original failure can be rectified and the original protection mechanism restored. Defense-in-depth is a fundamentally sound approach to all security architecture, engineering, and operations, and this holds especially true in the world of mobile security. Providing either data *or* device security can help protect data. Providing both data *and* device security not only puts up more barriers that an attacker must penetrate to get at the data, but also provides backup security should either the data or the device security fail.

Figure 1.1 seems straightforward at first glance, but further reflection of how data flows between mobile devices reveals the most alarming aspect of mobile security. The movement of information between the zones in the figure is alarmingly fluid, and on a single journey, data can move around to different areas of the chart as easily as it moves between devices and handlers. Sometimes that transition is within your control and can be managed so as to minimize risk to the information. The more common scenario, however, is that the transition from area to area will be initiated by events or actors over which you have no control and in environments where you do not have the ability to ensure that adequate protections are in place.

The Inverse Distance Principle

Finally, to make matters worse, the Inverse Distance Principle of mobile data security can have a profound effect on your ability to protect data as it moves from place to place:

> **Inverse Distance Principle**: The ability to enforce security protections over a piece of data is inversely proportional to the logical distance between that data and its origin.

Put another way, the further (logically) that data moves from its original source location, the less control the data owner can exert over its protection and security. For example, as data moves from an originating file server to a flash drive, then to a laptop, then to a CD, it is getting logically further from its original source (the server), regardless of the actual physical distance between all these devices. The natural tendency for data on the move is to lose protection as it moves from device to device. Like radio waves and network transmissions, the security exerted over mobile data tends to decay over time unless continuously reinforced. Unless the user or current custodian of the data takes active interest in maintaining the protection of information as it is moved from device to device, that information will tend to move from a more secure state to a less secure state over time in the absence of active security management.

To address this tendency, the ideal approach is to start out the data's journey with as much security protection as possible. This includes utilizing as many data protections as is feasible and utilizing devices that have as many security controls as possible. In this way, as the data starts hopping along the mobile device path to its final destination, shedding security protection as it moves along that path, enough of the original protections may remain to enable the data to maintain adequate security along its journey.

The Effect on Our Approach

Before moving along to cover the many security aspects of mobile data and mobile devices, we need to look at the entire mobile data and mobile device issue in its proper context and provide—some might say justify—the backdrop against which many key decisions must be made. Given the heightened state of awareness (and, sometimes, near panic) regarding mobile technologies and information movement, it would be very easy to assume that mobile data is inherently bad and that the best solution is to simply ban all mobile devices from the enterprise. This would seem to be the only clear way to avoid this problem altogether. Indeed, some organizations, such as the United States Department of Defense (DoD), have banned the use of flash drives.[3] This step was in response to a worm that infiltrated its network through the use of such a device. Given the nature of the DoD's business, and the threat it faces should such an attack infiltrate a large portion of its information network, its response may seem prudent. However, that is not an action that many organizations are willing or able to take, and the cost to the enterprise should it try to enforce this may be higher than it is willing to expend. In short, the idea that the mobile security problem can be solved by banning all such devices from the enterprise is just not viable in most organizations.

To begin with, banning mobile devices in the modern workplace is just not that easy. As we've already seen, the number and types of devices that can be classified as "mobile" are already large and getting larger by the day. As storage technology advances, units become smaller and their price continues to fall. It's not hard to imagine a time in the near future when nearly every device will have some sort of mass-storage capability. Endlessly adding these devices to the list of corporate contraband is not a viable solution. While organizations with clear and strict security needs (like the DoD) may be able to enforce compliance among their employees, most enterprises don't have nearly that level of control.

The second, and perhaps more significant, aspect of the mobile data/mobile device explosion is that the devices in use today to provide mobile data movement are extremely well suited to the task and very popular with employees. There would not be such a rapid rise in the adoption of these devices if people didn't find them useful and beneficial to both their professional and personal lives. The convenient and essential services provided by these devices enable modern workers to manage, collate, and transform more data than ever before. While the security concerns around their use are obvious and will be discussed in detail throughout this book, the beneficial uses of these devices are too numerous to ignore, and the organization that tries to ignore or suppress them will find itself in a never-ending—and losing—battle.

Consider, as an analogy, the common steak knife. With a serrated steel blade, this instrument can be used to slice through fish and fowl alike, and inflict deadly damage on even the toughest of meat products. When turned against a human enemy, the steak knife can inflict wounds that will maim or kill in an instant. In the hands of a skilled attacker, the steak knife can be one of the deadliest of combat weapons.

When described in that way, it's hard to imagine why anyone in her right mind would allow one into her home, particularly in an age when the safety of children is a major preoccupation of most civilized societies. Yet, steak knives have been in existence for thousands of years, and one can hardly imagine a modern restaurant, kitchen, or dinner table without them. Their utility and functionality are so ingrained into our culinary culture that nobody questions the need to restrict their use. They are sold in boutique shops and corner grocery stores alike.* While some states have laws banning the sale of steak knives to minors, and attempting to bring one on an airplane will likely lead to a long conversation with the security agent at the gate, nobody would think of mounting a serious effort to ban their use.

Yet, try to imagine if nobody had ever seen a steak knife before. If someone introduced it into the marketplace today and tried to sell it to homes and businesses, the calls for banning the device and cries for restrictive legislation would be deafening. Those seeking to ban them would cite their inherent danger, the inability to protect innocent citizens from its dangers, the ease with which children can access them, and their attractiveness to terrorists as a weapon of choice as fundamental arguments against its use. Despite its potential beneficial uses, in today's security-conscious and terrorism-averse society, any new device with potentially dangerous applications is looked upon with suspicion and resistance.

However, steak knives are not new. Having been around since the Stone Age, their uses are no less dangerous now than they have ever been, but we've learned to deal with them. We lock them away, keep them out of reach of small children, and teach proper usage of these tools. And, occasionally, we get cut by one or someone uses a steak knife to hurt or kill someone. In short, we have learned to understand, deal with, and manage the risks steak knives present in order to fully appreciate and take advantage of the benefits of their use.

Mobile data and mobile devices share a situation similar to the steak knife. There are those who are rushing out to implement mobile data solutions and increase the proliferation of mobile devices without giving much thought to the potential security and privacy ramifications of their efforts. These are what sociologists and

---

* In a comically ironic twist, Victorinox, one of the oldest and most respected knife manufacturers in the world and maker of the famous Swiss Army Knife, now manufactures a Swiss Army Knife that includes a USB flash drive.

marketing experts call the "early adopters." Early adopters will assimilate new technologies into their lives before anyone else. From a business and industry perspective, early adopters are important because they can help jump-start new technologies. Unfortunately, early adopters rarely stop to consider the security and privacy risks that a new technology may pose to themselves, their organizations, or the public. That's not their primary function.

That function falls to the group called the "laggards" (in sociological terms). Laggards are the ones who resist new technologies because they find them impractical, unimportant, dangerous, useless, or too expensive. They are slow to adapt and will generally resist new technology until it becomes clear that it will fill a need they desperately have or they are forced to change by circumstances or situations. The key to mastering change in mobile technology, then, is to find the middle ground between the early adopters and the laggards. Both groups need to continuously examine new mobile technologies as they become available, looking for those that will truly enhance our collective personal and professional lives. The best (and perhaps the only) way to find this middle ground is by promoting the usefulness of mobile technology (thus satisfying the early adopters) while creating a secure environment for its use (thus satisfying the laggards). Through the combined and balanced efforts of both these groups, those mobile technologies that are new and unique today will be the mainstream technologies we use tomorrow.

Conclusion

We cannot simply react to the proliferation of mobile devices and the rapid increase in the use of mobile data with panic and worry, bury our collective heads in the sand, and hope it will all go away. It won't. The key to effectively dealing with this issue is to understand exactly what we mean when we discuss mobile data and mobile devices, understand the benefits that such technology can provide to the lives and businesses of its users, and seek to understand how those benefits can best be put to use. We must also understand the potential risks of this technology and how those risks can be mitigated or eliminated. Whether through enhanced protection controls or modification of our behaviors and expectations as consumers of these new technologies, there are ways that mobile data and devices can be more safely integrated into our lives. New technologies become old technologies over time, and old technologies eventually become ingrained in our consciousness to the point where we can't imagine life without them. Such was the way with the steak knife, and it will be that way with mobile data and mobile devices. Only through a balanced approach of managing the benefits and risks of this technology can we hope to reach that state of ubiquitous pervasiveness that the steak knife currently enjoys.

Despite the long path toward their current popularity, mobile data and mobile devices have presented themselves as the next wave in data movement and management, and both business and security professionals alike are trying to make sense of it. To do that, you will need to use all the resources you have in your security and risk-management toolkit. You will need to analyze exactly what are your goals, needs, and fears when it comes to mobile data, and you will need to determine where your comfort zone begins and ends when it comes to the movement of your data.

There will be many questions that need to be answered, and many decisions to make that have no clear answer. If you persevere, in the end you will come up with an approach to mobile security that best suits your business and personal needs. To start you on your way, you now have a basic definition of mobile data and mobile devices, and you understand both the context of their common usage and the subtleties of applying those definitions to today's complex systems and networks.

And you now have the answer to that most basic of security questions: "What are you trying to protect?"

Action Plan

Each chapter in this book ends with an Action Plan. This will be a brief review of the theme of the chapter along with some items that you should consider as you work through understanding and managing the use of mobile data and mobile devices in your own organization.

This chapter has provided you with the basic definitions of *mobile data* and *mobile devices*. More than that, it has begun to set the context for their use and introduced some of the risk and business issues that organizations face in trying to gain real benefit from mobility while protecting against some of the security problems it poses. As a result of this information, you should now have a firm grasp of the following:

1. Understand the definitions of *mobile data* and *mobile device*.
2. Understand how mobile data and mobile devices are each independent entities and concepts, yet intertwined by their common use.
3. Understand that the security of each has an effect on the overall security of your information, and that changing the security of one will necessarily affect the security state of the other.
4. Start to determine where your organization's security interests in mobile data and mobile devices will start.
5. Begin to answer the question "What are you trying to protect?" for your own organization.

Notes

1. *Merriam-Webster's Collegiate Dictionary*, 11th ed., s.v., "Mobile."
2. *Newton's Telecom Dictionary*, 19th ed., s.v., "Mobile Data."
3. Angela Moscaratolo, "Military's ban of USB thumb drives highlights security risks," *SC Magazine*, http://www.scmagazineus.com/Militarys-ban-of-USB-thumb-drives-highlights-security-risks/article/121326/. The ban was partially lifted by DoD in February 2010 after the implementation of technology and operational procedures to help mitigate some of the risks. http://gcn.com/articles/2010/02/23/dod-flash-drives.aspx

Chapter 2

It's All about the Risk

Life is all about risk.

You may personally think it's about happiness, or reward, or success, or even security. You may also believe in the idea that all your actions have consequences: Good actions lead to good consequences; bad actions lead to bad consequences. What you probably haven't thought of, however, is that the basis for those actions is a continuous evaluation of risk. More specifically, it's based on a never-ending series of risk judgments that guide your every decision and shape your every action. From the moment you awaken in the morning to the moment you finally fall asleep at the end of the day, you run through a frighteningly complex series of risk decisions. Here are just a few of the more common ones:

- "Should I get out of bed or call in sick today?" (What is the risk of not going in to work?)
- "Is it warm enough to wear a short-sleeve shirt?" (What is the risk of underdressing?)
- "Will I eat the salad or the cheeseburger special in the cafeteria?" (What is the risk of not eating a healthy meal? Or getting food poisoning?)
- "Do I let my daughter play on the school's field hockey team?" (What is the risk of her being injured?)
- "Should I start to look for another job?" (What is the risk of losing my current job? Can I afford to be out of work?)
- "Can I fix the roof myself or should I call in a contractor to do the job?" (What is the risk of me doing the work myself? Will I break my neck in the process?)

We all make literally hundreds—perhaps thousands—of risk decisions each and every day. Granted, many of these decisions have minor consequences. You may be a bit cold or gain an extra pound from making an improper choice, but the long-term effects are negligible. But what if these decisions weren't so trivial? If you are habitually absent from work, calling in sick may get you fired. If you fall off the roof during the repair and have no insurance, the accident and lost time from work could place you in financial peril. Unfortunately, there is often no clear answer to these questions. Each decision takes you down a different path, which brings even more risk questions and risk decisions.

Life is all about risk.

Organizations also deal with a constant barrage of risk decisions that are often much more complex than those we face in our personal lives. They deal with financial risk ("Will we have enough money to cover the payroll?" "Will the money we spend on research result in profitable products?"). They deal with legal risk ("Are our products likely to injure somebody?" "Are we complying with the appropriate government regulations?"). They deal with market risk ("What if the economy continues downward?" "How can we make our products stand out among the competition?"). They deal with technology risk ("Can our network support our systems?" "Do we have the proper technology to operate effectively?").

Most important to us, they deal with security risk. If you peruse the headlines of any business or technical journal, you will see a continuous stream of stories about security risks of all kinds: endless tales of hackers, identity thieves, fraud, lost tapes, stolen laptops, breach disclosure laws, government regulations, and computer security vulnerabilities. These appear almost daily, warning us about the dangers of the Internet, the loss of privacy, the constant barrage of hacker attacks, and the ongoing threat of identity theft. In the face of this, companies are forced to make some very difficult risk decisions about how to run their businesses and work with their customers to limit the risks these threats pose. They ask a constant stream of questions designed to help guide them through both the confusion and the constantly changing security landscape, questions such as:

- Are we making our systems resistant to hacking attempts?
- Are we protecting our customers' private information the best that we can?
- Do we have the capability to respond to a security breach?
- Are we compliant with security and privacy laws?
- Is our security technology keeping up with the latest attack techniques?

In short, organizations deal with risk management on a daily basis. It's all about the risk.

In many ways, risk is all about perception. How risky something appears to be is highly dependent on the circumstances surrounding the decision. One of the primary considerations in all risk decisions is the potential reward to be gained in return for taking the risk. The underlying presumption is that if you perform the questionable action and assume the risks of that action, there is a chance—however slight—that the outcome will be favorable to you or your organization. Let's look at a real-world risk/reward example many commuters face every day. Suppose there are two ways to travel the 28 miles from your office to your home every evening. You can take the freeway most of the way which, without traffic, will take approximately 30 to 40 minutes. If there is heavy traffic along the way (which happens often), it may add an extra 15 minutes to the trip and also put you in a foul mood upon your arrival. Alternatively, you can take the back roads, a more scenic route and one that rarely has much traffic. However, the scenic route takes 45 minutes, which is 15 minutes longer than the fastest highway time. So every day you have to make the risk/reward decision; do you try to get home faster and risk hitting traffic (and a foul mood), or take the slower but more reliable scenic route?

That same approach to risk vs. reward needs to be applied when addressing the issue of mobile data security and the growing desire for employees to use mobile devices to enhance their work. Mobile devices have some incredibly helpful uses, and more are being discovered (or invented) every day. Like driving the route home on the freeway without hitting traffic, the appropriate use of mobile devices can be a big benefit to your organization. They also have some obvious (and some not so obvious) risks that need to be dealt with. Suffering a data breach through the use of a mobile device will put you (and your company) in a much worse mood than hitting a little traffic on your way home, but the relative effect is the same. It may be better for your organization to avoid the risk and uncertainty of mobile device use by taking the equivalent of the "science route": restricting the use of mobile devices and relying on more traditional forms of data movement. This will slow down your "journey" but give you a more reliable and secure result. The key to success in managing the security of mobile data and mobile devices is to understand not just the potential risks this technology brings, but also the benefits to the organization these devices may have and finding the right balance of risk and reward to match your organization's business and security needs.

The best place to start is by examining the risks of mobile data from a business perspective because the introduction or restriction of any new technology must first address business needs and be evaluated in terms of its potential risks to the business objectives of the organization. Many new technologies pose technical or operational risks to the organization but may not have the potential to have significant impact on the long-term success or failure of the business as a whole. With mobile data, however, there are some significant risks to consider when trying to achieve that risk/benefit balance. Chief among these risks are three that have the potential to significantly affect the long-term viability of an organization:

1. Loss or disclosure of data to inappropriate persons
2. Loss of money
3. Loss of trust or damage to your reputation

Loss or Disclosure of Data to Inappropriate Persons

The first risk on the list is the one that most people think of when they contemplate the risks of mobile data. The average end user understands and embraces the convenience of mobile devices but does not necessarily understand the sensitivity of the data under his control. This can create a relaxed attitude about protecting either the information or the device where it resides. To make matters worse, even if the user does understand the data's sensitivity and wants to take appropriate precautions to protect it, most mobile devices have little in the way of built-in (or easy to use) security features. Thus, it becomes the user's responsibility to establish the method and technology required to manage that level of protection. While this may not be complex to set up, most users won't even bother.

The end result of this knowledge gap is that we have unprotected data on a mobile device. The many ways in which this can be lost, stolen, left behind, or otherwise misappropriated are numerous, but some of the more common methods include:

1. Leaving it in an accessible area, subjecting it to theft
2. Copying the data to another computer to work on and forgetting to erase it when done
3. Dropping it out of your pocket when removing other objects
4. Leaving it in a taxi for someone else to find
5. Leaving it plugged into a laptop computer and walking away
6. Mailing it to someone and losing track of the package

No matter how the information gets lost, the end result is that the data is now beyond your control. For argument's sake, let's assume the worst case has occurred and your mobile data has fallen into the hands of an attacker. What could the consequences possibly be? For starters, the data is now his to do with as he wishes, and since we're in a worst-case frame of mind, let's assume he wants to use it for personal gain. This can result in two basic scenarios: he can sell the information to third parties or extort money from you for its safe return.* If the information is valuable enough, the attacker might try to sell it to someone else to turn his ill-gotten gain into hard cash. This might be the case if the information in question is a valuable commodity, such as personal information (including names, addresses, Social Security numbers, credit card numbers, or bank account information) or valuable business data (including "insider" information such as future merger and acquisition information, confidential contract or business plan memos, payroll data, or

---

* There is also a possibility that the person finding the data will use it himself to steal money or cause you other harm. However, because the finding or acquisition of mobile data is more likely a circumstantial event (rather than a deliberate theft), it is more likely that the "finder" will be unable or unwilling to directly use the information. Instead, he will seek to transfer the data to someone who will be able to use it.

product strategies). This information is certainly valuable to the company that loses it, but it can be even more valuable to the organization that purchases it.

Personal information is one of the hottest commodities on the stolen-information market today. Tops on the list are credit card information (including both account numbers and security verification codes), bank account information, and online account credentials (such as user IDs and passwords). Fraud and identity theft have been problems since time began, as proven by stories from the Old Testament.[1] So it should come as no surprise that the rise of online commerce and the rapid adoption of online banking by consumers and businesses alike should see a corresponding rise in both fraud and identity theft.

This rise can be attributed to three primary factors. The first is the growth and increasing sophistication of malware (primarily viruses and Trojan horse programs) that enable fraudsters and thieves to easily capture users' login information, including such multifactor credentials as token codes and challenge questions. The second is the rising incidence of large-scale data break-ins allowing the attackers to capture millions of data records containing personal information. The third, and most important to this discussion, is the rising incidence of data loss through the misdirection of mobile data and mobile media. News reports appear weekly with more stories about stolen laptops, missing backup tapes, lost flash drives, and other examples of mobile data gone astray. The data on these devices ranges from personal identity information[2] to financial information[3] to sensitive employee data.[4] In most cases, the data on these devices was left unprotected. It may also be the case that these devices were accidentally thrown away or picked up by an innocent bystander who (not understanding or caring about its contents) simply tossed them into the nearest garbage bin with no ill intent. But the fact remains that this data was removed from the control of its owner and, without proper protections to ensure its security, could easily fall into the hands of someone who knows what the data is, understands its value to either its owner or someone else, and is not afraid to act on that knowledge.

The value of lost mobile information should not be underestimated. Assume for a moment that you are in a very heated market competition with your biggest business rival. Both of you are working tirelessly on the newest version of your next product. Whoever gets to market first has a very good chance of taking a huge amount of market share away from the other. The stakes are high, fortunes could be made or lost, and the pressure is on both companies to produce the best product quickly. Now suppose that an anonymous caller contacts you and says they have gotten access to the feature set, market plan, and even the source code of your rival's product. Knowledge of that information could mean you would be able not only to match your competitor's product feature for feature, but you would also know your competitor's entire pricing and market strategy. Such information would be invaluable as you make your own plans for market domination. How valuable would that be to you and your company? Would you be able to resist the temptation? If the tables were turned, would your competitor be able to resist?

Loss of Money

This example shows us that the risk of information loss is very real and very tangible to someone trying to come to grips with the issue of mobile data protection. But information loss leads very quickly to the second of our primary risk points for mobile data: loss of money. While loss of data may be of concern to an organization, it is still a somewhat abstract idea. In fact, loss of data itself is often a difficult concept for some to imagine. After all, the data often isn't really lost. It's still there in your databases, on your computers, and available in your applications. You know exactly where it is, so it can't really be lost. However, from the standpoint of control of that information and the ability to know exactly who has it and what he is doing with it, the data is most certainly "lost."

Money, on the other hand, is a very real and concrete concept to most organizations. Money, after all, keeps them in business. Even not-for-profit organizations rely on money to help them with their social, charitable, or humanitarian efforts. Therefore, identifying loss of money as a real risk will be sure to grab the attention of most organizations. Therefore, making the transition from the abstract concept of lost data to the concrete concept of financial loss becomes an exercise in demonstrating that lost data *becomes* lost money. This is true even if the original copy of the information is still in your possession. Unfortunately, another exact replica of that information is also in the hands of someone else.

Let's start with the loss itself. In many situations, particularly where the lost data contains consumer information like health records or financial data, most organizations are required to report that loss to someone. As of July 2009, 45 states, the District of Columbia, Puerto Rico, the U.S. Virgin Islands, and numerous countries had enacted some type of breach notification law requiring organizations that lose consumer information to report the loss to the appropriate agency.[5] In addition, the organization may have to notify each data subject individually of the breach, describe what happened, and explain how the breach affects them. The cost of notifying several million people by mail (if that's what is required) can be significant.

That's just where the money troubles start. In some cases, there can be heavy fines and penalties for incurring such a breach. When the Bank of New York Mellon lost a box of computer tapes with approximately 12.5 million records of personal information in March 2008, it was required to pay the state of Connecticut $150,000. In February 2009, CVS pharmacies were found to be disposing of sensitive information in unsecured receptacles and settled with the U.S. Department of Health for $2.25 million.[6] These are just two of the larger penalties that have been imposed in the past few years. As the attention to this issue increases and state legislatures seek to both provide better protection for their constituents and make examples of those who they feel aren't adequately protecting their citizens' data, you can expect these types of fines to increase both in frequency and in severity.

Once the breach is disclosed, the inevitable lawsuits will follow shortly. In some cases, state attorneys general will try to hold the company accountable for the loss by charging it with criminal violations. Customers or data subjects may also want to hold someone accountable and sue the company for damages. Class action lawsuits in data disclosure cases are common and typically lead to settlements that include credit monitoring for a period of time (typically one to three years). The cost of monitoring is paid for by the company, continuing the financial cost of the data loss for several years. Finally, you can add the cost for all the lawyers to handle all this legal activity (and rest assured, there will be *lots* of lawyers).

These costs can be considered *external* costs, because they are financial losses paid to those outside the organization. However, an organization might also face many *internal* costs as a result of a mobile data loss. There will be the cost of investigating the incident to determine where the breach occurred and how the data was accessed, downloaded, or copied. There may be the cost to change internal processes and install new technology to monitor and restrict access to sensitive data. Finally, there will be a great deal of testing and auditing performed as the organization attempts to demonstrate its new-found respect and concern for protecting sensitive information.

For those keeping count, that adds up to no less than ten sources of financial loss potentially affecting the company in the event of a mobile data loss. The totals for a large event can easily scale into the millions of dollars. A 2009 report from the Ponemon Institute set the average cost of a data breach to $202 per record, or more than $6.6 million (on average) per breach. In addition, the report set the average cost of lost business at $4.9 million, or $139 per compromised record.[7] Even someone who can't easily relate to the abstract concept of "lost information" should be able to easily grasp the very real prospect of losing millions of dollars due to the loss of that information!

What if the data lost on that mobile device was not consumer-based information, but rather internal and sensitive company information? In many ways, the financial impact will depend on the specific data that is lost, but we can make some general assumptions. If the information contains financial data about the company—perhaps financial forecasts or market projections—those could be used to determine the company's future growth and market potential. As we saw before, such information would be extremely valuable to someone trying to undercut the company's position in the market or make stock market trades based on this inside information. Large swings in the company's stock price as a result of lost data could lead to large losses for the organization. If that lost data contained intellectual property about the company's products or services—perhaps technical specifications for its latest product or market expansion plans for a new line of business—that might result in more losses to the company. In the hands of a competitor, that information could be used to build a competitive product or alter its own marketing plans, potentially resulting in lost income or market opportunity for the victim company.

Finally, an attacker may use the lost data directly against the organization. She may attempt to blackmail the company into paying her substantial amounts of money to prevent the release of the stolen information to the authorities, competitors, the media, or others who may be interested in using it. As with other forms of blackmail, companies facing this type of threat must tread carefully when it comes to complying with the blackmailer's demands. Because digital information can be easily copied there is no guarantee that another copy does not exist, even if the attacker returns the information.

Loss of Trust or Damage to Your Reputation

If your organization can survive the financial burden that a mobile data loss incident can bring, it may be faced with an even greater challenge. While it may be true that money makes the world go 'round, business are built and lost based on their long-term viability and the reputation they build with their business partners, the financial community, and their customers. For example, drug companies build trust that their products are safe and reliable. Airlines rely on the trust of the flying public that their planes are safe and won't randomly fall out of the sky. Food product companies build trust among the food-consuming public that their products won't poison consumers. Banks build trust among their customers by ensuring that their money will be safe. The type of trust these businesses enjoy is hard won and not to be taken for granted.

But what happens when that trust is lost and that well-earned reputation is in jeopardy? Just ask ChoicePoint, a company that provides information used in personnel background checks. In February 2005, identity thieves established themselves as ersatz businesses and used ChoicePoint's services to steal personal data about more than 160,000 individuals. Once the fraud was uncovered, ChoicePoint found itself facing a public relations nightmare, and was eventually forced to pay out over $25 million in lawsuits and penalties.[8] ChoicePoint's stock fell more than 18% in the weeks after the disaster as a result of the breach.*

You can also ask Heartland Payment Systems, the Princeton, New Jersey, company that processes credit card payments and other financial transactions. In January 2009, the company discovered malicious software on its systems that was capturing card data as it traversed Heartland's network. The total number of affected accounts continues to be revised, but it is estimated that the attackers had access to approximately 100 million records per month. Immediately after the announcement of the breach, Heartland's stock fell 42%. To date, over 650 financial institutions have claimed that they were affected by the breach, and the company is facing more than 31 separate lawsuits.[9]

Along with the financial hardship these companies have suffered, they also share the loss of brand loyalty, customer affinity, industry reputation, and market position. When the stock price starts to tumble and the news reports repeatedly cast your

---

* Although ChoicePoint's stock regained much of its value in the weeks following the breach announcement, the episode sent a clear signal to businesses that such breaches might have a significant impact on a company's market value.

company as the one unable to protect its customers' private data, it can be a devastating blow. One need only look at CardSystems Solutions, whose loss of 40 million customer records led to the suspension of its processing privileges by American Express and Visa,[10] the sale of a substantial portion of its assets, and the eventual filing of Chapter 11 bankruptcy reorganization and a Chapter 7 liquidation case for the company.

You Are Not Immune

As you read through the case histories of these data breaches, two things might quickly gain your attention. First, you might notice (and gain some comfort from the fact) that all these incidents were cases of break-ins to systems and networks where the data was stolen. While system break-ins, network hacking, and stolen credit cards are certainly interesting from a security perspective and troublesome from a business perspective, none of these is an example of lost mobile data or attacks on mobile devices. The second thought you may have is that these cases may be sensational examples of the worst consequences a data loss may bring, but that they are the outliers. These are the worst-case scenarios that demonstrate the point in the extreme but are not the common or standard examples that companies experiencing a data loss will probably see.

You would be wrong on both counts.

To get a better perspective on this issue as it relates to mobile data, it is helpful to examine the list of information breaches kept by the Privacy Rights Clearinghouse (PRC).[11] This list contains a running account of breaches of personal information since 2005 and is an excellent resource for researching the history and ongoing details about specific data security incidents. Figure 2.1 summarizes breaches of mobile data based on the PRC's research.

The information from the PRC's research is eye-opening. From 2005 through October 2009, incidents involving mobile data or mobile devices account for at least 18% of all data breaches annually, and more than 25% of *all* breaches in that nearly five-year period involve mobile data or mobile devices. In 2006 alone, mobile data breaches accounted for nearly one-third of all data breaches! This should dispel any misconceptions that mobile data protection is a minor problem or somehow less important to address than other information-protection issues. In addition, as you peruse the names of the organizations on the PRC's incident list, you will see that it is a problem shared by organizations both large and small. This should refute the second source of false comfort: that the big-name companies and large-scale data losses on the list are outliers and not typical (or common) examples of the risk of mobile data loss. Every incident of data loss, even though it may not receive national headlines or lead to congressional hearings, could happen to anyone and can easily be bigger and more devastating to the company involved than the ones that make national headlines. Suppose, for a moment, that it was your company involved in one of

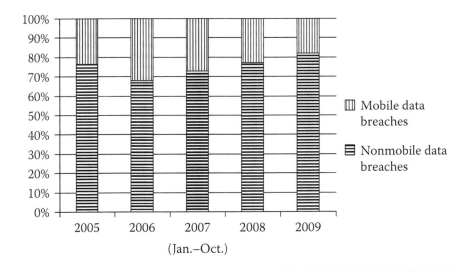

Figure 2.1   Mobile vs. nonmobile data breaches, 2005–2009.

these incidents. Would you be able to manage through the crisis? Would your company's financial or market stability suffer? Would your customers forgive and forget, or just forget you?

Reviewing these incidents plays an important role in defining the true risks and determining the overall goals surrounding the protection of mobile data. In many ways, they contribute to the "what are you trying to protect" question. In this case, what we're trying to protect is the organization itself, and we're doing so by protecting its data. This, in turn, helps protect the organization's financial well-being, its reputation, and its credibility. Each of the incidents described here demonstrates the effects that data loss can have on these three areas, and can be considered the primary risk points in an organization's program to protect mobile data.

Risk, Threat, and Value

To get a better understanding of the actual risk your organization may face from mobile data, you need to first understand the relationship between four basic security concepts: risk, threat, vulnerability, and countermeasures. When trying to understand the real risk you may face in any particular situation, there is a basic formula that can be applied to any number of risk scenarios. The formula is:

$$\text{Risk} = (\text{Threat} \times \text{Vulnerability}) - \text{Countermeasures}$$

In plain English, the level of risk to a particular asset is a function of the threats to that asset and the vulnerability of the asset to those threats. The overall risk level is then reduced by any countermeasures that may be taken to counteract those threats and vulnerabilities. For this discussion, we will assume the "asset" to be a piece or collection of mobile data and any device(s) that may contain such data.

The first thing to understand is that the formula is useful for understanding the relationships among threats, vulnerabilities, and countermeasures. Independently, each element of the formula can stand alone as an important consideration of the overall risk an asset might face in any given situation. However, it is the interaction between the components and their relative assigned weight that makes the formula useful as an analytical tool. The point is to see how changes in the threat landscape, the vulnerabilities in the environment, or the countermeasures you put in place all affect the risk of a particular action or program.

Given this basic methodology for identifying the general risk of an issue, it's time to examine more closely specific risks related to mobile data and analyze the potential threats and vulnerabilities that affect each risk. Specifically, we'll review the following risks commonly associated with mobile data:

1. Lost or stolen mobile devices
2. Inability to secure devices to the desired level, granularity, or uniformity
3. Access to internal information from uncontrolled devices
4. Introduction of malware into the environment from unprotected mobile devices
5. Information loss due to uneducated, inattentive, or uncaring users
6. Lack of compliance with the legislation du jour

Risk: Lost or Stolen Mobile Devices

This risk is the "poster child" for the mobile security issue. Whenever a discussion on the security problems of mobile data starts, the first—and most prevalent—issue is the potential for the data to be acquired by unauthorized parties through accidental or intentional means. This is also the risk most organizations focus on exclusively, and therefore it gets an inordinate amount of attention from both the media and security professionals alike. The consequences of data loss (such as loss of information, financial penalties, and reputation damage) were discussed at length earlier in this chapter, so there is no need to repeat the discussion here other than to summarize the main point: This would be a bad thing.

The fundamental purpose of mobile devices is to exploit their mobility for professional or personal benefit. Therefore, the very fact that these devices are moving around, often in less than ideal conditions, increases the threat of their loss or illicit appropriation. Whether or not this has a negative impact on an organization is based partly on how the organization has decided to deal with the mobile device issue. For example, if your company has taken the extraordinary step of banning the use of all mobile devices on its systems and networks (as some organizations have done), this threat would be low, since there would be fewer devices containing sensitive information to steal or lose. Even if an employee possessed one of these devices, she couldn't attach it to a company system, so the damage incurred if the device is lost would be minimal. If, however, your company still allows the use of mobile devices to store company data, the chances are good that one of those devices will contain valuable data and someone out there is willing to go to some lengths to get it. Even if the device is accidentally lost through the actions of the user (and not intentionally stolen by an attacker), there is a good chance that the person who finds it might gain access to the information, understand what it is and (more critically) its value, and try to act on that knowledge for his own gain. It is therefore easy to conclude that the threat of losing a mobile device—based on the number of ways that the device can "go missing"—is relatively high.

If the user ensures that the device is secured at all times, its vulnerability to theft or loss is greatly reduced. This includes locking it away in a safe place when not in use and keeping it in a secured location while traveling. A locked cabinet in your home or office is a much safer location than your briefcase, but storing it in a cabinet would negate the benefits of the device's mobility. When you do travel with the device, a locked safe in a hotel room is a better storage location than your suitcase because of the higher level of security the safe provides. How many people on the hotel's staff have the ability to open the room safe? The number is probably far fewer than the number who have the ability to discover the combination to your suitcase's 3-digit lock. Likewise, the locked suitcase is safer than your purse because the number and motivation of people who would try to break into your suitcase is less than the number and motivation of people who might try to steal your purse or opportunistically look through its contents should you forget it somewhere. Finally, the purse is safer than your shirt pocket because you are more likely to notice your purse is missing or that someone is trying to steal it than you are likely to notice if the device accidentally falls out of your pocket. Your vulnerability to the threat of a lost or stolen device is therefore directly related to the physical protections you can provide the device which, in turn, is the result of balancing convenience of access and availability of the device with the physical protections afforded by its location.

Once you have identified the physical vulnerabilities to the mobile device, you can then turn your attention to the exploitable logical vulnerabilities of that device. Recalling the defense-in-depth approach, if the physical protections you have placed around the device fail (and you must assume that they will eventually fail), you need to supplement those with logical protections to ensure the continued security protection of the information on the device. Unfortunately, many mobile devices provide little in the way of built-in logical controls. The more sophisticated mobile devices, such as portable computers and personal digital assistants (PDAs), do offer protections like encryption, authentication, and access controls to limit who can access the device and what they can do with that access, but the majority of mobile devices (such as optical media, memory cards, and audio players) have few effective protections. Your vulnerability to this threat, then, rests in the availability of such protections on the device of your choosing, either built into the device or as an add-on with third-party tools.

Unfortunately, many mobile device users are not sufficiently proficient or comfortable with technology to either use the built-in protections or add them. The more effort and complexity that is required to provide sufficient protection against this threat, the less likely it is that the average user will take advantage of it.

Applying this information back into the risk formula, the threat of a lost or stolen mobile device is sufficiently high to warrant concern. The vulnerability to the threat is variable based on the physical protections placed around the device, the availability of built-in logical controls to protect the information, and the sophistication and diligence of the user to activate or install the appropriate protections on the device. Because of the variable interaction between all these vulnerability components, we must make the assumption that the average user will be unable to understand what protections are needed or take the appropriate steps to enact all the required protections. This leaves a high threat level and a high vulnerability level, ultimately resulting in a high risk level. According to the formula, some highly effective countermeasures must be applied to reduce this overall threat level.

Risk: Inability to Secure Devices to Desired Level, Granularity, or Uniformity

The next notable risk to mobile data is the inability to provide the specific protection controls that an organization desires because of limitations in technology or the negative impact such controls might have on the user community. For example, a team of auditing consultants might have a few laptops and flash drives that team members share. The devices are only used for field work, and team members don't need them when they're in the office, so this practice saves the company the cost of buying team members individual pieces of field equipment. These devices contain financial and legal data from the clients that the team members are working with at any given time. However, the team wants to ensure that the information on these devices is protected not only from hostile outsiders, but also from team members themselves, because the company has strict rules against sharing client data, even among employees.

The threat on which this risk is based is very similar to the threats encountered in the "lost or stolen device" example discussed previously. In this scenario, however, there is the added dimension that a group of authorized people will all have access to the same devices, meaning that unless access control and information protections are implemented properly, they will be able to see one another's work despite the requirement to keep them separate. The threat of information theft or leakage to knowledgeable insiders is the additional wrinkle in this scenario.

The level of vulnerability to this additional threat is based entirely on the ability of each device to enforce the separation of information between team members as well as the (previously defined) need to keep information out of the hands of unauthorized outsiders. This will require a combination of good access-control mechanisms and information-protection mechanisms. The laptops the team members are using will most likely have an operating system (such as Windows or Linux) that enforces separation of user spaces on the device. If, however, the team is using the shared flash drives, they are much more vulnerable to the threat of information leakage. Some flash drives come without any built-in authentication features, and those that do have an "all or nothing" authentication approach. In other words, once a user authenticates himself and unlocks the device, that whole device is available to him, including any data that may have been left there by previous users. In this case, the vulnerability to the threat of intra-team information leakage is high and needs additional countermeasures to help reduce the overall risk.

The device may have both strong access-control and information-protection capabilities but lack the granularity to protect just the portions of the device the organization is concerned with. Such is the case with many smartphones currently in use. These phones allow their users to store contact information, appointment calendars, documents, and e-mail for both professional and personal use. This may all be considered company confidential information that an employee may take with her when she leaves the organization, share with her new employer (perhaps a competitor), or use for personal gain. Likewise, anyone who finds the device will also be able to access the information it contains. An organization's vulnerability to this threat is often directly related to the ownership and management of the device. If the organization purchases all the IT (information technology) equipment its employees need (including computers, laptops, and even smartphones), then the company has the ability to dictate when and how the device gets erased, and there is little the employee can do to prevent it.

However, some organizations are beginning to allow employees to purchase their own devices as a way of reducing overall IT costs. While a 4-GB flash drive may be purchased at Walmart for just a few dollars, a fully loaded smartphone may cost several hundred dollars plus the ongoing costs of the service plan. For an organization that needs to purchase hundreds of these devices, the costs quickly add up. Budget-conscious organizations are beginning to shift that cost to their employees and requiring them to purchase their own technology.

The employees then connect these personally owned devices to the company's infrastructure to synchronize their e-mail, calendars, and contacts. They also put their own personal information, e-mail, music, photos, ringtones, and Web applications on the same device. When the employee leaves the organization and the device must be erased, it's often difficult to distinguish between company and personal information. Wiping the device means wiping the *whole* device, not just the corporate data. This makes users (who have spent a great deal of time and, in some cases, money personalizing their devices) very upset, especially when they feel it is their device, not the company's. The vulnerability is created because companies are unable, or unwilling, to erase a device they do not own without the owner's permission.

Risk: Access to Internal Information from Uncontrolled Devices

Although smartphones can often be centrally deployed and managed, a majority of the devices used to store and transport mobile data have no such central management capabilities. In this category we find the plethora of flash-memory cards, tape units, media players, and PDAs. These "second tier" devices are often just as capable as their premium cousins and just as capable of storing and moving large amounts of data. Their biggest drawback is that they are (for the most part) unmanaged within the environment, configured and supported by end users themselves, and largely unaccounted for in official enterprise inventories. Flash drives can now be purchased from almost any retail store, audio and video media devices are fast becoming ubiquitous in the consumer consciousness, and PDAs of all sorts can be configured to synchronize e-mail, calendar, and contact data directly from the end user's computer without the need for connection to an enterprise service. The threat that these devices brings to the environment is their use to bypass centralized enterprise controls and mobilize data at will without any corporate oversight. When users are left to their own judgment to determine the proper security controls that are needed to protect information, the majority of them will underprotect the information.

There are several vulnerabilities that amplify this threat and enable the unfettered flow of unmanaged data to unmanaged devices. The most common vulnerability is users' ability to connect any device to their computers without restriction, including peripheral drives, memory cards, music players, and smartphones. Some of these devices require additional software to install and manage, and some use the operating system's "plug and play" features, but few of them can be managed centrally by the organization, assuming the organization is even aware of their existence. By allowing such a large array of unmanaged devices to attach to (and exchange data with) the company's infrastructure, the organization leaves itself vulnerable to data loss and misuse without the ability to track who is accessing the data, where (or to what device) it is being sent, or ensuring that the device has the appropriate protections in place to secure that information while it is in transit.

The second vulnerability that contributes to this risk actually has two components that work together against the organization. First is the general lack of strong access controls on enterprise data. Companies naturally want their employees to have access to all the data they need in order to be good, productive workers. Most organizations, however, don't segregate their information well enough. Some may have specific data stores or shared drives that are restricted to a particular work group or project team, but almost all have some type of general directory or file server where users from across the company can store and retrieve files without restriction. When two employees from different parts of the company need to share information and neither can get to the other's group directory, they'll turn next to one of these open directories to exchange that data. These directories tend to perpetually grow in size because users place information in them but rarely go back to clean up after themselves. The IT department managing the directory may occasionally clean out the directory to save disk space, but until that happens, there is a virtual treasure trove of sensitive data available to anyone with access to the drive. You can argue that this type of file sharing allows workers and groups to exchange data quickly, but it also makes the data available to those outside of the group or collaboration chain who do not have a need or reason to access that data. Given the ease of movement to portable devices that most organizations allow, this leaves the data much more readily available for theft and disclosure to unauthorized persons.

Now add on top of that the second component of this vulnerability: the lack of control over what type of data can be moved to a mobile device. Even in the most security-conscious of organizations, once data makes its way down to the end user's system, there are few controls that prevent that data from moving to a peripheral device, especially in the hands of a determined attacker. This is directly related to the inability to secure devices to the desired granularity, as unmanaged data moved to improperly secured devices leaves a gaping vulnerability in the organization's ability to protect that information.

Risk: Introduction of Malware into the Environment from Unprotected Mobile Devices

Much of the discussion around mobile security centers on the movement (and associated loss) of data flowing outward from an organization. As the major point of concern for businesses, the loss or theft of confidential information can consume a large portion of an organization's information-protection program. However, a related risk from the proliferation of mobile devices comes from outside the organization and concerns threats coming into the infrastructure from external sources. The risk of malicious programs (such as viruses, Trojan horse programs, keystroke loggers, worms, and other forms of malware) infecting systems where mobile devices are attached continues to grow as a concern, and several recent malware outbreaks have used this specific attack vector to spread from system to system.

There are a number of scenarios that demonstrate how this works and how it can rapidly spread:

- An employee needs to give a presentation at a conference and transfers the presentation to a flash drive for easy portability. Upon arriving at the presentation room, the flash drive is inserted into the laptop computer provided by the conference facility. The laptop is infected with malware that recognizes the new device and copies itself to the flash drive.
- An employee allows his child to use his flash drive to copy files from the school's computer to work on at home over the weekend. The computer at school is infected with malware that copies itself to the flash drive when it is inserted into the school's computer.

■ A customer needs to send an employee some files too big for e-mail. The customer burns them onto a CD and mails the disk to the employee. The customer's system is infected with malware that copies itself to any CD that is written on that computer.

What happens next holds the key to the threat. In each of these scenarios, when our well-meaning employee places the infected device back into her computer, her system likewise becomes infected. That malware can then use her system to gather information, record keystrokes, spread to other systems on the company's network, and generally do all the evil things that malware is infamous for doing. This threat scenario is both highly plausible and a common way that malware spreads.

As we know, threats need to be coupled with vulnerabilities in order to become a credible risk, and there are several common vulnerabilities that allow this threat to occur. The most prevalent vulnerability is the general promiscuity that users demonstrate with respect to their portable devices. The highly interoperable nature of most mobile devices makes this an easy vulnerability to exploit. Additionally, many mobile devices allow the random reading and writing of information to the device without the ability to write-protect the device and prevent malware infection. Mobile devices sometimes have a switch to prevent writing data to the device, but it is inconvenient to use and relies on the user to know it is there and understand how (and when) to use it. As a result, this feature is ignored by most users in the name of simplicity and expediency. Once again, we see that protection of information on mobile media often falls to the knowledge, skill, and diligence of the end user to enable the mechanisms that provide that protection.

A companion vulnerability that compounds this problem is the inadequacy of malware controls on many systems. While most corporate IT departments do their best to keep their managed systems up to date with the latest antimalware defenses and configuration files, most home, educational, and small business systems are woefully undermanaged when it comes to antimalware defenses. Many home users never upgrade their antimalware defenses after their initial system purchase, and the staff of small offices and educational institutions are often more concerned with keeping their systems and networks operational on a tight budget than they are about keeping up with the latest security threats. Finally, systems located in public or semi-public venues such as Internet cafes, conference kiosks, or presentation rooms are often left alone with minimal security updates or patches. As a result, they become breeding grounds for malware that easily spreads to whatever systems or devices connect to them.

Even well-run and well-managed corporate systems sometimes fall victim to inattention or configuration errors. All major antimalware products have the ability to scan incoming or newly opened files for malware. Unfortunately, this setting is sometimes overlooked in favor of on-demand manual scanning or weekly systemwide scans, or it is disabled in the belief that using this feature will negatively affect system performance. As a result, these scenarios can work to infect company systems despite the belief that the organization's antimalware controls are in effect.

Risk: Information Loss Due to Uneducated, Inattentive, or Uncaring Users

One of the basic axioms in all information security is the notion that a great deal of an organization's security rests in the hands of the organization's people and the extent to which they take the security of the organization and its information seriously. It's common to believe that information security is primarily a technological discipline and that most security issues can be solved by the suitable application of the appropriate technology. Nothing, however, could be further from the truth.

In many respects, security is a behavioral discipline. It's about human behavior, how people treat the assets with which they are entrusted, and how they will alter their behavior to obtain the assets they covet. It's also about their attitudes and motivations. "Good" people will try to uphold security practices (to the extent they don't interfere with other factors that motivate their lives), and "bad" people will try to subvert those same practices. That's why security practitioners always place such a heavy emphasis on security knowledge, awareness, and policy reinforcement in addition to establishing effective security processes to back up the policies and training. Technology is a valuable tool to help reinforce policies and practices or provide control where policy or practice is insufficient to ensure good security— that's defense-in-depth. Technology itself is not a goal.

This is why organizations dealing with the risk of mobile data and mobile devices have such a difficult time making progress. Their first tendency is to purchase the latest and greatest mobile security technology in the hope that its use alone will help reduce the risks. However, they fail to understand how important people—both inside and outside the organization—are to the overall information security effort.

The threats regarding how people interact with information are very straightforward. People create the information, manage it, manipulate it, and analyze it, and they are the ones that ultimately see the need to make it portable. If employees do not understand (or are not made to understand) the value of the information they are managing and the security issues surrounding its portability, then all other security efforts—policies, procedures, and even technology—are doomed to failure. In addition, many users don't understand their role or responsibility in the information-protection chain. Many believe that protecting information is not their responsibility; it's the job of the IT or the information security departments. Only a well-educated and continuously reinforced user population has a fighting chance of maintaining good mobile data security.

A key point to remember is that users generally act in ways that they believe are appropriate and proper for the work they are trying to do. Setting aside the conduct of malicious users (who will act against the organization no matter what policies, procedures, or technologies are in place), employees are generally doing what they need to do to get their work done. They see mobile devices and mobile data as a means to the end of getting that work accomplished in an efficient and expedient manner. Unless the organization has an outright ban on the use of these devices, employees will use them to benefit the organization, the customer, and ultimately themselves. They have access to the data, so they reason that they should be able to use and transport that data as best benefits the company, including using devices that can have a clear benefit to their productivity. Moreover, because many organizations' policies on mobile data and devices are vague and indirect (at best), they see no real deterrent or reasonable argument against their use.

The vulnerability to this threat manifests itself in a number of different ways. The primary measure is the extent to which an organization's education and awareness programs focus on information-protection methods in general and mobile data issues specifically. Organizations that have an awareness program—and many do not—tend to focus on core bread-and-butter security issues: password strength, locking workstations, shredding documents, social engineering, acceptable use, and clean desks. These are key security issues and need constant reinforcement with employees to ensure that the security message is retained and followed. However, more effective programs also emphasize topics specific to the mobile data threat, such as the policies surrounding the use of mobile data, protection of company information on mobile devices, and the legal ramifications to the company and the employee for inappropriate use of mobile data. Employees need to understand how they have a direct impact on the security of mobile information.

A measure of the extent to which this vulnerability is already present in the environment is the number of security incidents an organization has experienced related to mobile data. Even a moderate number of incidents (whether they are headline-making breaches or internal data misplacement) can be a signal that employees either do not understand their responsibility for managing mobile information or they are intentionally circumventing policies and procedures despite their knowledge. If this trend is left to continue, it will only be a matter of time before the organization becomes the next big data-breach headline. No company wants to be put in that position, especially for an issue that it has the ability to preemptively address and mitigate.

An organization's culture and work ethic can have a large impact on the employees' attitudes toward mobile data protection. Some organizations, particularly those that deal with military or government information, have a very prevalent security culture. Employees are forced to understand the value of good security practices because it is a basic part of their job description and pervades all aspects of their jobs and daily routine. For most other organizations, however, security is not emphasized as a core job requirement. It may be important, and the organization may continually emphasize its value to the company and its employees, but it's an add-on support function secondary to the organization's primary goal of serving customers. In such a company, customer service often wins over enforcing tight security. If a salesperson needs to send out a contract and pricing schedule to a client to win a critical bid, she may not stop to consider whether she should encrypt the e-mail or the file. If a telephone-support engineer is being measured on the number of problems resolved on the first call as well as the number of calls taken per hour, the quickness of issue resolution takes precedence over strongly authenticating the person on the other end of the phone before giving out sensitive information. When a busy executive needs to work on sensitive internal information while he is traveling, he may not think twice about reading those documents in a crowded airport lounge or airplane seat where others will be able to see the information.

All these scenarios point directly to a company's culture when it comes to dealing with sensitive information, and this directly affects employees' attitudes about mobile data protection. Most companies have a "customer first, at any cost" attitude about their work. There is nothing to fault with this approach to business, and many of the most successful companies have become successful precisely because they back that attitude with superb customer service and value. The problem starts when that attitude takes a back seat to protecting the information needed to support that customer-focused attitude. As has been mentioned before, security decisions almost always involve trade-offs between protection, cost, and convenience. When a company repeatedly chooses cost and convenience over protection, it is on the path toward a major security event.

An organization's attitude toward the consequences of mishandling mobile data speaks directly to its ability to effectively protect that data. Most companies' security policies say something like this:

> Failure to comply with security policies will result in disciplinary action
> up to and including termination of employment.

The exact wording and consequences may vary, depending on the company, local labor laws, and other cultural differences, but the intent is the same. Break these policies and bad things will happen to you. Unfortunately, bad things rarely happen. For many companies, the extent of penalties for breaking security policies varies widely from incident to incident. While there is always room for variation in discipline based on the circumstances of a particular incident or infraction, an organization that consistently underpenalizes employees that break or ignore security policies sends a clear message to the employee population: Security is not important.

Finally, the user community, and the effect that mobile data controls will have on them, will have an enormous amount of influence when it comes to establishing and enforcing mobile data security within an enterprise. Many security teams seeking to implement mobile data protection programs start out with lofty and well-meaning goals about restricting access to data and restricting specific devices. They may even go so far as to craft new restrictive policies and research expensive device-blocking, data-tracking, and encryption technologies to thoroughly protect the organization's information. However, when the team begins socializing the program around the company, some very interesting things happen. First, senior management will begin to hear the message that the new program will block access to some mobile devices, severely restrict access to others, and generally require more data restrictions than the organization has previously experienced. The leadership will challenge this, because they fear that employees will not be able to get their work done as effectively or efficiently as they did without the new controls. If the project is able to survive an executive review, the next stop will be the internal help desk, because that is the team who will take the calls from end users whose existing functionality for working with mobile data will no longer work. The help-desk staff will look at the proposal and start calculating how many extra support calls this project will create, and how much longer each call will take. They will also ask how employees can get exceptions or exemptions from the policy, because when the user gets too angry, the help desk will want to be able to pass the caller off to some higher-level authority for review. Help desks are measured in throughput: how many calls they can process in a given period, how many callers hang up before getting an agent, how many issues are resolved on the first call, how satisfied callers are, etc. The reward system for call centers is entirely motivated by high throughput. Any initiative that will reduce that throughput will be looked upon with disdain.

The end users themselves may raise their collective voices in protest to any new restriction or control on mobile devices. When security controls are reasonable and the effort required to comply with them does not present an undue (in the user's opinion) burden, users will be more likely to comply with the policies and restrictions. However, when the policies are unreasonable, require too much effort to comply with, require extensive changes to the established work process, or prevent employees from doing what they perceive is necessary to perform their jobs, they will actively reject the control, complain loudly, and make life miserable for both management and the security team. In some cases, users will go out of their way to avoid or bypass the control, often expending more effort bypassing the new controls than compliance with the control would take.

The bottom line to all of this is that, if you want your organization to take your mobile data policies and controls seriously, you will need to include them and their perspective in your planning, technology development, deployment, and communications to ensure their approval (or at least their grudging acceptance) of the changes and the reasoning behind them.

Risk: Lack of Compliance with the Legislation du Jour

There is not a business leader or security professional anywhere who will tell you it's not important to protect sensitive company and customer information. It's considered an essential part of business life. We do it because protecting this information helps the continued viability and success of the organization. We do it as a service to customers to help protect their privacy. We do it because doing so prevents financial and business loss due to leaked or stolen information. We do it because it's the right thing to do.

But most of all, we do it because someone tells us we have to.

Government and industry regulation is one of the fastest growth areas in information security. The number of laws directly or indirectly requiring protection of private and consumer data is growing constantly, not just in the United States, but across the globe. Most of this legislation pertains to general information protection without specifying mobile data as a specific issue. Nevertheless, data is data, and compliance with these laws (and the business, financial, and security risk of noncompliance) is a major concern of modern enterprises.

The risk of noncompliance with specific laws is straightforward: Comply with the regulation or face the penalty. The penalties for noncompliance vary greatly, depending on the particular legislation or regulation being violated, but some of the more common include:

- Financial penalties
- Criminal liability
- Civil liability
- Loss of permission to manage a particular type of data (for example, credit card data)
- Loss of permission to service a type of customer (for example, government contracts)
- Loss of customers due to the inability to maintain compliance certification

Any of these penalties by themselves would be a cause for concern to any organization, but noncompliance often results in more than one type of sanction, leading ultimately to the potential failure of the business. Given that background, it's clear why organizations take compliance so seriously. Because the threat is so clear-cut, the vulnerabilities within the organization that lead to a noncompliance situation are equally simple to enumerate. To start with, the organization must be aware of which regulations it is required to comply with. This is much easier said than done. With some laws, it's easy to understand whether or not your company is affected. For example, if your company's stock is traded publicly in the United States, you are subject to the Sarbanes–Oxley Act.[12] If you are a bank, you are subject to the Gramm–Leach–Bliley Act.[13] If you are in the health care industry, you may be subject to HIPAA regulations.[14] If you are managing personal information in the European Union (EU) or transferring such data from an EU company to the United States, you must follow the EU Data Protection Directive.[15]

Those are easy examples, and companies directly affected by those laws generally know that they are affected. However, many regulations often affect companies that are not directly aligned with the "audience" for the regulation. For example, would a credit card payment processor know if it is subject to new HIPAA regulations? Would a company in Milwaukee know that it was required to follow a Nevada data-protection law? Knowing what laws are on the books can be challenging, and determining if your organization is affected by those laws is a daunting task. However, an organization that doesn't make the effort to determine the laws with which it must comply is risking the same penalties as those that know they need to be compliant and ignore the requirements nevertheless. As lawyers say, ignorance is not a positive defense. An organization needs to make the effort to determine the scope of its compliance needs using either internal resources or hiring outside legal consultants to guide it.

Once the organization's compliance needs are determined, many organizations develop a passable compliance program to meet those legal or industry requirements, including getting the required examinations or certifications from the appropriate regulatory or oversight body. The effort to get the program established is often managed under a tightly compressed time frame, and the overriding emphasis is on establishing the minimum set of controls required to pass the certification. While this may allow the organization to achieve its compliance certification, it often leads to bigger security problems further down the road. Taking a "minimum necessary" approach to compliance forces the creation of control procedures to fit the current set of compliance requirements as interpreted by the organization's internal staff or an expert consultant. As techniques, experience, and technology changes, the interpretation of provisions within a regulation will change as well. The organization that takes a "minimum necessary" approach risks falling behind as those changes lead to new ways of approaching compliance.

No organization wants to overspend its money or overallocate its resources in any area, and information security is one area where cost considerations are a constant point of contention. However, the organization needs to determine not only what is required by a specific regulation, but also whether (and how) the proposed controls and processes required to achieve compliance can be extended or modified to help achieve a broader, and ultimately more sustainable, compliance program. For example, many U.S. companies were affected by the passage of the California Information Practice Act (better known as SB 1386), which became effective in July 2003. SB 1386 requires:

> Any agency that owns or licenses computerized data that includes personal information shall disclose any breach of the security of the system following discovery or notification of the breach in the security of the data to any resident of California whose unencrypted personal information was, or is reasonably believed to have been, acquired by an unauthorized person. The disclosure shall be made in the most expedient time possible and without unreasonable delay, consistent with the legitimate needs of law enforcement, as provided in subdivision (c), or any measures necessary to determine the scope of the breach and restore the reasonable integrity of the data system.[16]

This is a fairly common requirement by today's standards, but it was the first of its kind in the United States and was considered radical and unprecedented for its time. It also sent companies into a panic, wondering if they were affected by the new statute and how they would comply. Some took the "minimum necessary" approach, only encrypting the data they managed about California citizens and establishing notification procedures to be enacted only if data about Californians was breached. Companies who took this approach may have satisfied the letter of the law, but found themselves consistently changing their procedures as state after state began implementing similar laws.

What the more forward-looking companies did in response to SB 1386 was to develop better overall information-protection services and more robust notification practices. Rather than just encrypting data about California citizens, they chose to encrypt all personal information in their systems. Instead of beefing up their data protection to segregate California information and give that data special protection, they elected to enhance their overall data-protection programs. Instead of creating notification procedures in the event of a California data breach, they created general notification procedures that would be applicable to a wide variety of security incidents. Enacting these more general security-program improvements did not cost these organizations much more time, money, or effort, but it better prepared them for the future in the anticipation that other states or the federal government would enact laws requiring similar procedures. The moral of this story is that the "minimum necessary" approach to compliance will get you past the certification and perhaps allow you to maintain compliance with the legislation du jour, but taking a broader approach will position your organization to better anticipate and accommodate tomorrow's compliance requirements as well.

Evaluating Your Risks

The list of risks we have just reviewed is by no means exhaustive, but it does highlight some of the more common risks an organization will face when dealing with the mobile data issue. In order to help consolidate your thinking and allow you to formulate your own approach to identifying and analyzing the risks of mobile data and mobile devices, Table 2.1 summarizes the risks, threats, and vulnerabilities related to mobile data and mobile devices that we have reviewed. This list should be the starting point for your own organization's discussion on how to manage and protect mobile data. Use this list as a starting point, but by no means should this limit your thinking. Each organization's risks are slightly different, and even two organizations that share the same general risk may feel quite differently about their level of exposure to that risk and the ways in which they wish to address that particular risk. As the saying goes, your mileage may vary.

The key to successfully navigating the waters of mobile data risk is to identify all the mobile data and mobile device risks that can potentially affect your

Table 2.1   Risk, Threat, and Vulnerability Summary

Risk	Threat	Vulnerability
Lost or stolen mobile device	Devices are inherently mobile	Protection is dependent on physical location and environment.
	Potential for loss is high	Many devices have few built-in information protections. Users are not knowledgeable or proficient in security techniques or technology.
Inability to secure devices at acceptable levels	Devices do not adequately protect information	Limited controls available on many devices.
	Multiuser devices may allow access to all data by all users	Inability to separate or segment data. Protection controls are not granular enough.
	Personal ownership of device can lead to data leakage	Users commingle personal and corporate data. Users take corporate data with them when they leave the organization. Installation of nonstandard applications can lead to unauthorized access, data leakage, or data corruption.
Access to internal information from uncontrolled devices	Unmanaged devices can provide unauthorized access to internal networks and applications	Many mobile devices cannot be centrally managed. Unmanaged devices can bypass established access controls or data restrictions. Unmanaged devices rely on user judgment and action to enforce security. Inability to block data flow to unmanaged devices.
Introduction of malware into environment	New malware specifically targets mobile devices as infection vector	Many OSs automatically load and execute programs on attached mobile devices. Some antimalware systems do not automatically scan mobile devices. General user promiscuity regarding attaching mobile devices to multiple systems.

(Continued)

Table 2.1 Risk, Threat, and Vulnerability Summary (Continued)

Risk	Threat	Vulnerability
Information loss due to uneducated users	Inattentive users will not apply proper data controls	Users do not have proper knowledge for protecting systems.
	Organization may experience more mobile data incidents due to lack of employee knowledge	Users do not apply known controls due to perceived expedience or convenience.
	Company culture may emphasize "customer service at all costs"	Many awareness programs do not emphasize mobile data security issues.
	Employee and management resistance may block efforts to implement effective controls	Employee and management unsympathetic to specific mobile threats.
Lack of legislative compliance	Financial, civil, and business penalties	Company does not understand all its compliance requirements.
	Loss of business or reputation	Company takes a minimalist approach to compliance.

organization. Using Table 2.1 as a starting point, this should include as many risks as you can think of, both big and small. To make your list as complete as possible, do not concern yourself at this point with how likely it is that a particular risk will affect your organization. In other words, don't worry about the applicable level of threat or vulnerability. Your goal is to make the list as complete as possible. This exercise should be done as a team in conjunction with others in your organization that have an interest in protecting mobile data, such as your legal department, human resources, IT, the help desk, and anyone else who may have a stake in protecting mobile data.

There may be a tendency during this exercise to automatically dismiss some of the risks identified as trivial, inconsequential, or unlikely to affect your organization to any degree. It is important that you keep these risks on the list anyway, even if you later decide not to address them with your risk-management plan. The reason for including them in your initial analysis is that you need to be able to explain to an auditor, regulator, customer, or lawyer who will later ask you (and someone eventually *will* ask) how you developed your mobile data management program, and what risks you considered necessary to address in that program. You need to be able to show that you did a thorough analysis of all the potential risks before determining which were critical enough to warrant follow-up action.

How Valuable Is Your Data?

There is another component to the risk-assessment process that should be an important consideration when determining the organization's risk and the determination of how much effort, time, or money should be placed into enabling appropriate protections. This last component is the concept of *value*. Every asset in an organization—a computer, a piece of furniture, an employee, a building, or a bit of data—has a value to the organization, both in monetary terms and in terms of the contribution each makes to the success and growth of the organization. Sometimes the value is easily calculated—for example, the cost of the hardware and software within a computer system, or the construction and maintenance cost of a building. Some values, however, are less tangible and harder to define. For example, what is the value of a company's information network? The initial cost of the cables, switches, and network-management services can be calculated, but there is also the value of the efficiency and business opportunities a well-run network can bring to the organization. What is the value of an employee? One can easily calculate the salary and benefits cost of "maintaining" an employee, plus any operational overhead (such as office space and insurance, generally known as the "loaded rate"). However, those costs are not the sole measure of an employee's value to the organization. Employees bring knowledge, skills, and energy to the organization. They can help move the organization forward to overcome difficult business obstacles, and the best of them can motivate others to propel the organization past the competition to become the leader in its marketplace. Most would agree that such an individual would be considered a "high-value" employee.

Likewise, the information a company works with every day has value. Whether it is next quarter's financial projections (arguably a highly valuable target) or today's cafeteria menu (a decidedly low-value target), each piece of information in the company's possession has a value that must be determined in order to provide it with the appropriate level of protection. Information with high value is worthy of a considerable amount of protection. This might include product-planning documents, pricing schedules, salary information, legal contracts, merger and acquisition information, and customer personal data.

The value of an asset is closely related to our evaluation of risk because high-value assets tend to be those with the most direct threats against them and for which we need to pay closer attention to vulnerabilities. Suppose, for example, the asset in question is a database of credit card information. This is an asset with a high value to both a company and to attackers alike. Attackers would be highly motivated to try to steal that information, thereby increasing the overall risk level. Conversely, it's important to remember that not all information consists of classified state secrets. Suppose the asset in question is next Thursday's starting lineup for the company's softball team. This may be highly interesting to team members, but the value to the rest of the world is negligible. The information's vulnerability is generally high (after all, nobody puts this type of information under lock and key), and the opposing team might be considered a threat who might try to steal the lineup information, but the value of the information is sufficiently low as to warrant little expenditure of effort or money to protect it.

Therefore, value is an important consideration to the risk equation, but one that is separate from the notions of threats, vulnerabilities, or countermeasures. For this reason, let's add value to the risk formula:

$$\text{Risk} = (\text{Threat} \times \text{Vulnerability} \times \text{Value}) - \text{Countermeasures}$$

With this change, value is now included in the overall risk formulation, and an asset with a sufficiently low value can effectively negate the effect of the threat and vulnerability factors.

Value is determined in two complementary ways. The first is the amount of time, effort, and money your organization is willing to expend to protect that information. This is called *internal value* because it is a reflection of the net worth the information has to the organization and its internal uses. Companies place a high value on intellectual property and other internal bits of information that, if improperly disclosed, could have an adverse impact on the company, its customers, its financial position, or its market prospects. That same information, however, may also be valuable to those outside the organization. This *external value* is the amount of time, effort, or money someone else is willing to expend to acquire that information or its value to her if she should somehow acquire it through other means. If the information is important to you, it's easy to imagine that someone on the outside recognizes its value as well.

When going through your risk evaluations and calculations, you will need to carefully consider the internal and external value of the asset at risk. There are no hard-and-fast rules for doing this, because value is highly subjective and dependent on circumstances. However, assets with a high value are usually considered to be bigger targets and, subsequently, will have a higher threat value. Therefore, you will need to lower that asset's vulnerabilities or increase your countermeasures to lower the overall risk to the asset.

What about Countermeasures?

You may have noticed that there is one component of the risk formula that has not yet been discussed: countermeasures. Countermeasures are the policies, processes, and technologies that you enact to counterbalance the risk, threat, and value components of the equation, all of which have a direct influence on the overall level of risk for any given area or activity. The primary goal of risk management is to reduce the level of vulnerability that a particular asset has to a given threat. Unfortunately, such direct reduction of vulnerability may not be possible if the asset in question does not allow for direct modification of its operating or environmental parameters.

For example, suppose the asset in question is a smartphone, and the risk you are most concerned with is the disclosure of sensitive e-mail if that phone is lost. The phone is vulnerable to that risk because it does not provide any built-in controls that would prevent this threat from occurring, such as data encryption. In the absence of such built-in controls, you might consider establishing a countermeasure such as the use of a password to gain access to the phone. The countermeasure reduces the overall risk, since knowledge of the secret password is now required to view the data. The risk does not go away completely, but the presence of the countermeasure has provided some mitigation.

The full discussion of countermeasures is omitted from this chapter on purpose. They are of such importance—and their implementation is so critical to the effective mitigation of mobile data and device risks—that they've been given their own special treatment. Chapters 6, 7, and 8 will discuss the use and implementation of various mobile security controls (another term for *countermeasures*) at great length.

Conclusion

This discussion of risk has been a long, but it is absolutely necessary before moving ahead to the chapters that follow. The fundamental concepts in this chapter bear repeating:

1. Everything in business involves some level of risk, including the use of mobile devices and data.
2. Each organization understands and treats risk differently.
3. Risk is a function of *threats, vulnerabilities, value*, and *countermeasures*. You must understand these four elements of any activity before you can understand the overall risk of that activity.
4. In general, high-value data has higher levels of risk and requires more protection than low-value data, but circumstances may require you to approach data protection differently.

As you go through the risk assessments for your mobile data concerns, there is one final thought to keep in the back of your mind that may prove helpful. That thought is the "Secret Sauce" of risk assessment: All risk assessments ultimately come down to an opinion.

This may not be a great revelation, but too often this simple fact gets lost in the hundreds or thousands of data points a detailed risk assessment can entail. There are so few definitively quantifiable data points when dealing with risk issues that the levels of threat, vulnerability, value, and countermeasures usually come down to a relative opinion and consensus among the "smart people" in the organization as to the precise influence each of these will have on the organization's overall risk profile. While the smart people may be very knowledgeable, many of the issues and facts surrounding mobile data protection and how to address its risk within an organization are open to intellectual disagreement, especially when it comes to determining the threat or vulnerability a particular asset or area may be facing. While there may be some general consensus on the boundaries of acceptable and unacceptable levels of these parameters, smart people disagree, and often for good reasons. There is often no right or wrong answer during a risk assessment. The ultimate goal, then, is to come to some generally agreed-upon understanding of the level of risk the organization faces and what the organization needs to do to address that risk.

This chapter has given you many of the tools and considerations to factor into your mobile data risk assessments, and provided a potential path to follow for performing that assessment. You may determine that your organization has an entirely different set of risks from mobile data or that your approach to addressing the risks presented here is different from the discussion provided. That's okay, and taking such a path shows that you truly understand your own organization and your own environment. No one set of rules, guides, or examples will fit every situation, nor should they.

This chapter started out with the idea that life is really all about risk. By now, you should understand that mobile data is just one risk among thousands that your organization must deal with on a regular basis. Its importance to you may be elevated, but it's just one issue among many. By clearly and systematically understanding the threats, vulnerabilities, values, and available countermeasures, you can quickly come to an understanding on how to deal with this risk and start enacting your plans to better secure your mobile environment.

Action Plan

Based on the discussion in this chapter, there are several actions you can take to evaluate the risk of mobile data and mobile devices in your organization. The outcome of these activities will identify the largest and most potentially harmful of the risks you face. Those risks will then constitute the start of your mobile security plan.

1. Determine if there are any additional categories of mobile risk (other than the ones presented in this chapter) that your organization must address.
2. Determine which of the identified risk areas have the greatest impact on your organization.
3. Review your company's security awareness program to determine if your employees are receiving adequate communication concerning the use of mobile data.
4. Review your company's compliance program and determine the extent to which mobile data security affects your ability to comply with applicable government and industry regulations.
5. Complete the risk, threat, and vulnerability chart from Table 2.1 for the specific elements of your company's mobile data environment. Use this as a guide for ranking the most important risk concerns.

Notes

1. Genesis 27:1–40.
2. In February 2007, a portable hard drive was reported stolen or missing from the VA Medical Center in Birmingham, Alabama. The drive contained personal information for nearly a million physicians and VA patients. (Privacy Rights Clearinghouse, www.privacyrights.org.)
3. In October 2008, a laptop computer containing sensitive personal and financial information on 84,000 University of North Dakota alumni, donors, and others was stolen from a vehicle belonging to a UND vendor. (Privacy Rights Clearinghouse, www.privacyrights.org.)
4. In June 2009, the names, addresses, and Social Security numbers of nearly 3,000 current and past employees of six large corporations were on a flash drive stolen from the car of a Florida Department of Revenue employee. (Privacy Rights Clearinghouse, www.privacyrights.org.)
5. Nation Conference of State Legislatures, "State Security Breach Notification Laws," http://www.ncsl.org/Default.aspx?TabID=13489.
6. Privacy Rights Clearinghouse, "A Chronology of Data Breaches," http://www.privacyrights.org/ar/ChronDataBreaches.htm.
7. Ponemon Institute, LLC, "2008 Annual Study: Cost of a Data Breach," February 2009.
8. There are many interesting articles on the ChoicePoint incident, including:
   Jon Brodkin, "ChoicePoint Details Data Breach Lessons," *PCWorld*, June 11, 2007, http://www.pcworld.com/article/132795/choicepoint_details_data_breach_lessons.html.
   Privacy Rights Clearinghouse, "A Chronology of Data Breaches," http://www.privacyrights.org/ar/ChronDataBreaches.htm.
   Sarah Scalet, "ChoicePoint Data Breach: The Plot Thickens," CSO Online, http://www.csoonline.com/article/220341/ChoicePoint_Data_Breach_The_Plot_Thickens.
9. There are many interesting articles on the Heartland incident, including
   PGP Corporation, Cybercrime Grit & Grime Blog, "Heartland Demonstrating Just How Costly Data Breach Can Be," http://blog.pgp.com/index.php/2009/05/heartland-demonstrating-just-how-costly-data-breach-can-be/.

Anthony Freed, "Another Payment Card Processor Hacked," Information Security Resources, http://information-security-resources.com/2009/02/14/another-payment-card-processor-hacked/.

10. There are many interesting articles on the Card Systems Solutions incident, including
   Robert McMillan, "Troubled CardSystems to Be Sold," InfoWorld, http://www.infoworld.com/%5Bprimary-term-alias-prefix%5D/%5Bprimary-term%5D/troubled-cardsystems-be-sold-462.
   Arizona Daily Star, "Credit Card Company Facing Liquidation," http://www.azstar-net.com/sn/business/212858.php.

11. Privacy Rights Clearinghouse, "A Chronology of Data Breaches," http://www.privacyrights.org/ar/ChronDataBreaches.htm.

12. Public Company Accounting Reform and Investor Protection Act (U.S. Senate) and Corporate and Auditing Accountability and Responsibility Act (U.S. House of Representatives), Public Law 107-204, 116 Stat. 745.

13. The Financial Services Modernization Act of 1999, Public Law 106-102, 113 Stat. 1338.

14. The Health Insurance Portability and Accountability Act of 1996, Public Law 104-191.

15. Directive 95/46/EC of the European Parliament and of the Council of 24 October 1995 on the protection of individuals with regard to the processing of personal data and on the free movement of such data.

16. California SB1386, amending civil codes 1798.29, 1798.82, and 1798.84.

Chapter 3

The Many Faces of Mobility

Modern mobility means many things to different people. Earlier chapters made a distinction between mobile data and mobile devices, and whether you look at these two components separately or together, how they're used and how people interact with them varies greatly from application to application and from person to person. From laptops to flash drives, portable hard drives to music players, optical disks to floppies, mobile data continues to integrate itself into all aspects of modern business life. Think about your own work habits, and try to imagine all the places where your work relies on, or at least intersects with, mobile data or mobile devices. Now try to imagine doing the same job without the ability to move data from place to place or the convenience of taking data with you wherever you go.

Of course, you could manage somehow. Many readers of this book will be able to remember a time before BlackBerries, before e-mail, before fax machines, even before voice mail. Those of us old enough to remember the early days of technology were somehow able to struggle through a day's work, but today's tools make that work much easier. The advent of mobility in all its forms has led to great advances in productivity, information flow, and personal and commercial benefits for those who are able to take advantage of these tools. Yet, as a result, the distinction between different types of data has become blurred, and along with it has gone the ability to understand how each type differs in risk and protection needs. As a way of understanding those different needs and how the different forms of mobility change the security and risk considerations for protecting mobile data, it helps to develop some general categories of mobility and highlight the differences behind each category. The goal of this chapter is to present concrete examples of mobile data and mobile devices, and illustrate how each fits within the definitions established in earlier chapters. In addition, we'll look at various examples of mobility and discuss the implications for an organization's ability to control and protect the data and devices it must deal with on a daily basis.

Following the Bits

It all begins with the data file. The data file is the fundamental unit of information that most people deal with on a regular basis. Data files come in many forms and formats, but at their most basic level, they are ultimately nothing more than electronic ones and zeroes (known in computer parlance as bits) strung together to store information for later use. The data can be humanly readable (for example, a text file with your favorite apple pie recipe), or it can be readable only through the use of some application program (for example, a digital photo that requires an image editor to open and translate the bits into a human-viewable format). Data file formats are as numerous as the number of applications that are available to use them, and most applications define their own file formats based on their own requirements for data storage. Nevertheless, every single data file has one thing in common. Each of them, from the smallest text file to the largest multi-terabyte decision-support database, consists entirely of electronic ones and zeroes. That doesn't sound so exciting, does it?

But there *is* excitement to be found within those ones and zeroes. That excitement comes from the way those bits are moved in and between systems, the way different systems and applications treat those bits, and the way those bits can be protected, lost, or manipulated by users (both good and evil) that come in contact with them. As the creators and consumers of those bits, we humans take particular pleasure in manipulating them to fit our will and needs of the moment, and those same bits can fill multiple purposes, depending on our own requirements. Let's look at an example of how this works.

To make the example more meaningful, let's assume that the data file in question is a project report for the new Gadgetron product MoDevCo is developing as its next big breakthrough. The owner of the document is Sylvia, the product manager. We will assume that the file was created, and is being maintained, in Microsoft Word (or substitute your own personal software of choice). Sylvia created the document on the PC in her office, and updates it weekly in order to be ready for presentation at a weekly product managers' meeting.

As part of her weekly status update, Sylvia decides that she needs to get updates for her report from members of the product team. The first person she contacts is Marc, the head of development. Sylvia sends Marc an e-mail requesting the information she needs and attaches a copy of the report to the e-mail message. The project report, once at rest on Sylvia's computer, is now officially mobile. It will be the first of many mobile trips this data takes. In addition, there are now two copies of the report: the original on Sylvia's PC and the copy now sitting in Marc's e-mail inbox.

The e-mail trip to Marc's computer is uneventful, arriving in his inbox almost instantly. What Sylvia is unaware of, however, is that Marc's e-mail is configured to synchronize automatically with his smartphone so that everything sent to his corporate e-mail address—attachments and all—is also forwarded to his phone. Now the report is in three places (Sylvia's PC, Marc's inbox, and Marc's phone), only two of which Sylvia knows about. Marc looks at the document in question, makes his edits and comments, and sends the result back to Sylvia directly from his phone. Sylvia receives his reply, blissfully unaware that her report has begun to circulate out of her control.

Sylvia also needs information from the lead programmer, Julie. She's concerned about the software interface between two of the Gadgetron's biggest components—the Heisenberg Compensator and the Flux Capacitor—so she sends the project report to Julie along with some additional questions. In order to give Sylvia a complete answer, Julie decides that she needs to consult with her programming team. The members of the programming team are very visually oriented, so rather than just forwarding Sylvia's original report, Julie decides to create some PowerPoint graphics to illustrate the problem using the information from the original report. This puts the same information in a different format and creates a second file with the original information, an action of which Sylvia is again unaware. To complicate the situation further, Julie needs to present the slides to the team in another building, so she copies the PowerPoint file to a CD rather than carrying her whole laptop with her. Now the data has moved to yet another mobile device. Sylvia is still unaware of its continued movement.

Sylvia also needs to consult with Dena, the head of marketing, on the Gadgetron's marketing plan. She e-mails the project report and questions to Dena. Dena works all day on the changes, but needs to leave the office before she has a chance to finish. Dena copies the document to a flash drive she keeps in her briefcase so she can work on it at home. Once at home, she loads the file from her flash drive onto her home PC so she can finish her edits. After a full evening of work, Dena needs to e-mail the file back to Sylvia. Unfortunately, Dena doesn't have the ability to connect to the company's e-mail system from her home PC, so she uses her personal Web mail account to send the file.

Finally, Sylvia needs to discuss pricing for the Gadgetron with Juan, the head of business development. Juan doesn't need the entire document, but Sylvia has some specific questions about some of the information in the report, so she contacts Juan with an instant message (IM). Juan answers the IM (conveniently from his smartphone), and the two executives discuss the pricing strategy for Gadgetron's rollout next month. During the course of the conversation, Sylvia cuts and pastes several passages from the report into the IM conversation for Juan to review. At one point, Juan feels he needs to confer with Dena on a particular strategic approach, so he sends her a text message with the information he needs her to comment on. Dena replies with a return text, and Juan and Sylvia conclude their discussion. When all this conversation, e-mailing, texting, and IMing are completed the next day, Sylvia compiles all the resulting information, finalizes her changes to the project report, and delivers it just in time for the product managers' meeting.

In case you had a hard time following the data flow from this example (which was, really, sort of the point), Figure 3.1 shows how it all went.

All seems well and good, at least from Sylvia's standpoint. She was able to use all the modern communication tools at her (and the team's) disposal to get the information she needed. However, as Figure 3.1 shows, what started out as a simple activity—getting input on a report from multiple sources—quickly became a mobile data free-for-all as the recipients of that data decided to manipulate and repurpose the data to suit their needs. In the end, Sylvia's original report ended up in the following places:

- Sylvia's computer (the original location)
- The corporate e-mail inboxes for Sylvia, Marc, Julie, and Dena
- Marc's smartphone
- A PowerPoint file on Julie's PC
- A CD for Julie's presentation
- Dena's USB flash drive
- Dena's home PC
- Dena's personal e-mail account

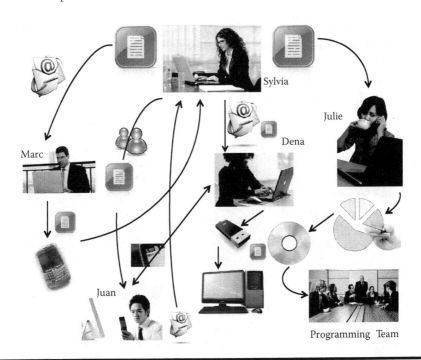

Figure 3.1   Gadgetron report data-flow diagram.

- Sylvia's and Juan's instant-message logs (assuming the company maintains logs of IM chats)
- Juan's phone (saved as part of his IM conversation with Sylvia)
- The text message and IM logs for Juan and Dena

This "simple" transaction (getting input for a project report) involved moving data to more than 15 different locations and included translation of the document (or selected information from the document) into e-mail (corporate, smartphone, and personal), Word and PowerPoint documents, IM conversations, and SMS (Short Message Service) texts. Watching this scenario unfold illustrates a number of important points.

The first and most obvious point is that the data in this scenario (the project file) moved quickly and freely from point to point as different people in the communication chain developed different needs for the data. Some needed the data in e-mail, others needed it in a format suitable for presentation, some discussed it in IM and text messages, and others just used its original format on a different computer. Each of the participants manipulated the data to suit his or her individual needs at the time. Marc worked on the file using his smartphone. Julie converted the information to a PowerPoint format for further presentation, then (presumably) translated the results back into Word for delivery back to Sylvia. Dena needed the data on her home PC and thought nothing of moving the bits to a flash drive. All this mobility was initiated quite simply and with little effort, because the manipulation of bits is something that computers (and their users) do very well.

The second point to note in this scenario is that much of this data mobility happened without the primary data owner's knowledge or consent. While it may be argued that all the participants in this drama had Sylvia's implied consent (after all, she did send them the information in the first place), none of the participants checked with her first to determine if it was acceptable to move the data to a PowerPoint file, flash drive, smartphone, or CD. They executed these transformations on their own accord, without regard to Sylvia's intentions. This is a classic example of the Inverse Distance Principle in action: the further data moves from its original source location, the less control the data owner can exert over its protection and security.

This example illustrates this problem perfectly. What if Sylvia did not want the data forwarded to a smartphone or edited on a home PC? She might have prefaced all her original e-mails with a warning saying, "Please do not copy or forward," but she didn't. This left the recipients free to interpret her request (assumed to be, "Please read this and respond with comments") as they pleased and do whatever they felt was necessary to comply with that request, including moving the data from device to device.

None of the participants thought twice about reforwarding or repurposing the information they received, nor did they consider taking any added precautions to protect the data in their possession as it moved from place to place. There may be mitigating security facts that are not evident in the brief description presented here. For instance, Marc may know that his phone encrypts all its data, Dena may be using an encrypted flash drive, or Julie may have driven to the team meeting in an armored car. However, it is more likely that none of these mitigating factors was in existence at the time each of the participants decided he or she needed to move the data to a new place. In Marc's case, he didn't even choose to specifically send that particular e-mail to his phone; his e-mail service automatically forwarded the original message to the device. Even if Sylvia had asked that recipients of her original e-mail not forward the information to other people or devices, it would have had no effect in Marc's case. He could not have complied with Sylvia's request even if he had wanted to.

This scenario thoroughly demonstrates the many faces of mobility. Some of these are more permanent (files on a laptop or flash drive), and some are more ephemeral (e-mail attachments, IM notes, SMS texts), but they all fall into the category of mobile data. However, the mobility of this data changed instantly, without notice, and in unanticipated directions. In order to try to protect all this data, it helps to understand some of the basic mobile data and mobile device forms to gain an appreciation of the security considerations each form has. As you gain this understanding, your ability to protect mobile data as it changes form and direction will improve.

We've already seen how a data file can change and migrate from place to place, which makes protecting it that much more difficult. The data file may be the basic unit of information storage, but that basic unit gets transformed in many ways as it makes its journey from person to person and device to device. Not only does the location of the data change as it makes this journey, but the ease or difficulty of protecting that information changes as well. To get a better understanding of what these protections might be, let's take a look at some of the more common mobile data and device technologies and see how each has its own challenges in these areas. To make the process more uniform, each category will be examined in terms of two basic characteristics:

- Ease of *intentional* mobility: How easily can an authorized person move the data from one place to another?
- Ease of *unintentional* mobility: How easily can an unauthorized person take the data and move it to another place?

Portable Storage Devices

There was a time, not too long ago, when adding storage to a computer was a very big deal. Disks were expensive, difficult to install, and had limited ability to move from machine to machine. In contrast, today's storage options are cheap, plentiful, and (most important) extremely portable. Hard disks have standard interfaces to make movement between systems easier, and they can store huge amounts of data for a fraction of the cost of the storage seen even a few years ago.* For the ultimate in portability, Universal Serial Bus (or USB) storage drives are now available with large capacities (up to several gigabytes) in a package the size of an adult thumb (hence their common nickname, the "thumb drive"), often for less than US$50. Flash-memory cards—portable solid-state devices small enough to fit inside a cell phone or digital camera—provide the ultimate in small storage. A MicroSD memory card measures just 11 mm × 15 mm × 1 mm and can hold gigabytes of data. Other formats, such as SD, CompactFlash, and MemoryStick, have similar properties.

All these devices are perfect for moving documents between systems or carrying important information around for later use. Most modern operating systems already have built-in drivers for these devices and can recognize them as soon as they are attached to the computer, making cross-platform use a snap. They are quickly becoming standard equipment on newer systems, and inexpensive card readers are available for older systems. Most important from a security perspective, portable storage devices represent the biggest source of fear and anxiety among security and data-management professionals. Because of their near-universal interoperability, small size, and inexpensive price, portable storage devices have become the data-transport medium of choice among computer users.

Portable Storage Devices: Intentional Mobility

Portable storage devices create a plethora of options for intentional mobility of business and personal information. They can hold an entire music or video library for use at multiple locations (employees, for example, can enjoy their personal music library both at home and at the office†). Photographers can use flash drives and digital cameras instead of traditional film cameras to eliminate the need for carrying and developing rolls of film. Home users can use a portable hard drive to back up important documents from their home computer and take the drive to a safe deposit box for secure off-site storage. Employees can copy important documents they are working on to a flash drive so they can use them at home or at a remote location. The amount of available storage is limited only by the user's budget. Standardized connectivity between devices and computer systems (typically via USB, Firewire, SATA, or eSATA interfaces) ensures the "plug and play" utility of these devices.

It is specifically these characteristics that make the use of portable storage devices so troublesome for organizations wishing to protect their sensitive information.

---

* A quick search of a major online retailer can find a 1-terabyte (1 billion bytes) portable hard drive the size of a thick paperback book costing less than US$100.
† Examples of mobile device usage may involve behaviors that may, or may not, be appropriate in a business or professional setting. Whether this use is consistent with a particular organization's policies is left for each organization to determine for itself. They are presented here as an activity that can—and does—happen in real environments.

Because movement of information to these devices is easy and the devices themselves are so portable, users see them as a natural extension of their computing environment and view portable storage as just another tool at their disposal. Because the price is so low and the devices are readily available, employees can purchase them on their own without the need for the company's procurement organization to get involved. This leads to information moving freely between devices to which the organization has no visibility and over which it has no control. Without the proper set of security precautions, this data is highly vulnerable to loss, theft, or misuse.

Portable Storage Devices: Unintentional Mobility

Some of the very characteristics that make portable storage a great candidate for intentional mobility also make it highly susceptible to unintentional mobility. The risks of portable storage are plentiful (just ask any security manager), but fall into several basic categories. The first major risk is that the devices themselves are small, lightweight, and cheap, making them easy to lose, temporarily misplace, or steal. The person who finds such a device can suddenly find himself sitting on a treasure trove of valuable information. The honest person finding such a device may seek to return it to its rightful owner, which may involve viewing the contents of the device to find identifying information to assist in the search. Such an examination might reveal confidential, sensitive, or embarrassing information that the finder should not see. The dishonest person finding such a device will skip right past the "good intentions" part of the discovery and seek to extract information from the device for personal or commercial gain. Either way, a lost or stolen storage device can lead to information quickly getting into the hands of the wrong people.

Most portable storage devices do not have any built-in data protection or access-control mechanisms, making the extraction of information from the device a simple matter. Modern operating systems have built-in support for USB-based data drives, so anyone finding or stealing one of these devices will have an easy time extracting its information. Recognizing the growing demand for protection of sensitive information, some drive manufacturers have begun selling models that have password control and encryption built into the device's hardware. Without the proper password to decrypt the device, the data is unavailable for extraction. This extra protection comes at a price, however, with hardware-based encrypted units costing significantly more than their nonencrypted counterparts.

For a less costly implementation, many software-based encryption products also operate well on portable storage devices. The user (or the user's organization) installs the encryption software on either the user's PC or the device itself. When the user needs access to the device, she runs the encryption program, supplies the proper access credentials, and the device is unlocked. When she is done with the drive, she closes the encryption software and the device is once again locked. The licenses for software-based encryption products can be less expensive than buying hardware-encrypted devices for all an organization's users, but the installation, maintenance, and support of the additional software must be factored into the organization's cost/benefit analysis to determine the best approach.

The small size of most portable storage devices also makes them easily concealed within a briefcase, purse, or even a shirt pocket. From a user perspective, this enhances their usefulness and portability, since specialized containers and packing are not needed to transport the device. However, this also makes it easy for attackers to conceal the data they have stolen from the organization. Prior to the advent of electronic miniaturization, a thief wanting to steal a cabinet full of documents from an organization had to copy the documents at a local copying machine (and hope nobody noticed him copying huge amounts of paper), then somehow hide the information in a briefcase, folder, or box as he left the building. Carrying large reams of paper documents out the door might make the guard staff suspicious, so it might take many such trips over an extended period of time to extract all the information he wanted.

Compare this with how the modern attacker might operate. To steal an equivalent cabinet-sized amount of data she will need to purchase a small USB-based portable hard drive and plug it into any computer connected to the company's network. The data she is seeking is no longer in a filing cabinet but in a directory located on the company's file server. The attacker simply copies the data from the network directory onto the portable drive in 15 minutes (more or less, depending on how much information she is stealing). Once the transfer is complete, she unplugs the drive from the computer, slips it into her briefcase, then walks out the door with a device full of company secrets. Far-fetched? Not really, and this scenario is plausible in most office environments today. The main issue is the new ease with which portable devices now facilitate the extraction and concealment of data in a manner unheard of five years ago. Unless the organization physically searches every person leaving a facility, there is no way to detect a portable hard drive or flash drive in their possession when they walk out the door.

The final attribute of portable media devices that facilitates unintentional data mobility is the inability to centrally track and manage these devices. The first rule of asset management is that you must have an inventory of the assets you are trying to manage. However, many of these devices are either purchased by individual employees with corporate charge cards (they're inexpensive enough not to raise any suspicion with those who check expense reports), or they are purchased by employees using personal funds. In either case, they are invisible to system and end-user support teams without extensive and regular device inventories—a time-consuming and expensive proposition. Without such oversight from an authoritative body, employees feel free to attach these devices to their computers at will, with little fear of discovery and even less fear of recrimination. This leaves the organization with no way to understand what devices are attached to its infrastructure and, by extension, what information is being moved to those devices.

Tape Storage

Before there were flash drives, before there were portable hard disks, and even before there were floppy disks, there were magnetic tapes holding digital information for storage and backup purposes. The history of magnetic tape use for data storage goes back to the 1950s, but tape as a medium for mobile data storage got started in the late 1970s, when ordinary audio cassettes were used for program and data storage on the earliest personal computers. Although tape cartridges are still available for personal computer system backups, they are primarily used today as a backup medium for data-center systems and databases.

Tapes: Intentional Mobility

Despite the fact that they are no longer as common for personal storage as DVDs or portable hard disks, tapes are still well within the definition of mobile device because of their ability to store hundreds of gigabytes of information in a small, portable package. As a result, their intentional mobility factor is very high. Tape backup systems are a fixture in modern data centers, and backup processing is a major responsibility for IT and data center staff. Backups of both programs and data are typically made on a set schedule, and tapes (or copies of them) are often sent off-site to ensure their availability in the case of a natural or human-made disaster. Tapes are ideally suited to this task because they cost less per megabyte than any other media, are easy to manage and maintain, and are easily transported to other locations for production use or archiving purposes. They are, in short, perfectly suited to their assigned duties.

Tapes: Unintentional Mobility

The potential for unintentional mobility is a huge concern when tapes are in use. News stories exposing yet another instance of lost tapes and the information they contain—financial information, health records, or credit card data grab the most sensational headlines—are common. In fact, it may appear that tapes go missing on an alarmingly regular basis, though the reasons vary from incident to incident. Some are lost during transit by commercial carriers such as UPS and FedEx. Some are stolen while in transit by internal personnel moving tapes from location to location. And some get lost through mislabeling, misfiling, or just plain lack of attention to their handling while in a company's possession before they even get transported. Unfortunately, because of the public's heightened sensitivity to identity theft and their mistrust of data collectors in general, every additional story of lost tapes becomes a publicity nightmare for the company involved.

Magnetic tape is not as commonly available or in use by consumers as optical media or flash drives, and it requires special equipment to read and write the tapes. The equipment is not particularly difficult to obtain—a quick Google or Amazon search reveals several USB DAT tape units for less than US$100—but it's not an item that the average consumer or opportunistic thief would have available. Thus, its susceptibility as a target of information theft is limited to those attackers who have such equipment or are willing to spend a little effort or money to obtain it. Additionally, tapes used in large data centers for backup and off-line storage may require even more specialized equipment. This raises the ante a bit for the attackers but, again, does not raise the required level of effort above the realm of possibility. Nevertheless, one would suspect that the cases where corporate backup tapes are lost are more likely a case of the tapes being in the wrong place at the wrong time (in the back seat of a car that was broken into, in an "interesting" looking package moving through a warehouse, or loaded on the wrong cart and sent to the wrong location) than being specifically targeted for theft. However, since definitive statistics and case history in this area are hard to come by, one must assume for safety's sake that the tapes were specifically targeted and stolen.

Regardless of that assumption, however, the bottom line for any company to face is that no matter how a tape containing sensitive information goes missing—intentional or not—it is gone, along with the sensitive information it contains. The prudent course of action (and the action prescribed by many breach-notification laws) is to assume the worst and begin executing whatever data-loss response plan the organization may have in place.

Dual-Use Devices

As the variety and capabilities of available consumer devices increase, so does the demand for (and the use of) devices that provide some type of business or entertainment function along with data-storage capability. These "dual-use" devices* are becoming more commonplace in both professional and personal settings. A good example of a dual-use device is the modern digital music player, more commonly referred to as an MP3 player (named after the most common digital music format in use today). Despite its name, the digital music player is not just for music alone; it can store and replay hundreds of gigabytes of music, movies, television shows, and network-based radio programs (often called "podcasts" or "netcasts"). A descendant of a long line of personal entertainment devices (including the portable audio cassette recorder and the portable CD player), the modern digital music player brings a special twist to the technology; it is essentially a hard disk or flash drive with specialized software to translate its data files into entertainment. The hard disk portion of the device functions the same as the drive in a personal computer, with the ability to store files of any format (not just digital

---

* This is not to be confused with dual-use technology, a term used to describe a technology that has both military and civilian applications. The irony between the two definitions is duly noted.

entertainment content). Specialized software on the device is used to translate those files into a usable form, and also provides the ability to search, retrieve, organize, and run applications from the files stored on the device. Think of it as an intelligent data drive, because that's how it is designed and how it functions.

Other examples of dual-use devices include digital cameras, digital voice recorders, smartphones and PDAs (to a degree), and even nonentertainment devices like remote presentation controllers. The storage is generally used to maintain the files used by the device itself, but it can also be directly accessed by plugging it into a computer's USB or Firewire port. Once connected, the computer will see the data storage area as another drive attached to the system, and it will read and write data files directly to the storage area. This is an easy way to move large amounts of digital media to and from the device, and also an easy way to move confidential information covertly.

Dual-Use Devices: *Intentional Mobility*

The devices themselves often serve useful and valuable business purposes. Digital cameras are helpful for those whose work is based on the availability of visual images, such as photographers, real estate agents, and graphic artists. Voice recorders are useful for taking notes in business meetings or technical lectures. Listening to music in the workplace has varying degrees of social acceptance, depending on the office environment. All of these examples (and many more like them) show that these devices are not just a frivolous distraction in the work environment; they provide services and work assistance that their users can employ to the benefit of their work.

As such, intentional mobility is a primary consideration for providing storage capabilities in digital devices. The thought behind this feature is that a single device can provide multiple benefits to users. It also makes sense in other cases. For example, many remote presentation devices have a receiver that plugs into the computer's USB port and receives signals (such as "next slide," "previous slide," or "blank screen") from a remote control held by the presenter. That receiver also contains flash memory for storing the presentations the presenter is going to make, preventing the need for the use of additional media (like CDs or flash drives) for storing the presentations. This is a combination that makes sense, but for other devices, the thought processes seem less clear. (For instance, do you really need to store documents and spreadsheets on your iPod?) Nevertheless, the storage is there and made available to users for holding arbitrary data.

Dual-Use Devices: *Unintentional Mobility*

This readily available data storage capacity also makes unintentional mobility and the surreptitious exfiltration of sensitive data much easier for attackers. Copying large amounts of data onto a flash drive and walking it out of the building may be easy to do, but the perpetrator risks getting caught if the building's guard staff has been instructed to search all people leaving the building for flash drives. What better way to conceal your evil plan than to hide that trove of confidential data on your MP3 player or digital camera? Even if the guard was savvy enough to ask about the contents of the device you are carrying, you can just show them the very innocent-looking music or photos stored on the device. Very few security guards would consider hooking the device up to a computer to check the data portion of the device.

Smartphones and Personal Digital Assistants

Perhaps the most striking example of the advance of technology and the convergence of multiple digital capabilities can be seen in the modern mobile phone. In a single device, one can utilize the services of a mobile telephone, electronic calendar (synchronized with the user's corporate or personal calendar), e-mail (also synchronized with corporate or personal e-mail accounts), electronic contact lists, text messaging, Internet Web browsing, personal productivity applications, a digital music player, a digital image and video camera (with better-than-average resolution), and built-in storage capacity, all in a package roughly the size of a deck of playing cards. Such devices have so many useful and advanced features that they even have their own category—the "smartphone." It's a marvel of modern engineering and personal productivity, and a feat of technology only dreamed about by science fiction writers not so long ago. It's the ultimate portable computer, and it has led to a revolution in communications and personal connectivity that has changed the business and social landscape forever. But it's not perfect—at least, not from a security point of view.

Many of the security problems that plague the various mobile devices discussed in this chapter also apply to the mobile phone and its close cousin, the personal digital assistant (or PDA, essentially a smartphone without the phone component). It can hold lots of internal and sensitive company information. It is easily lost or stolen; users often don't configure it properly; it may be susceptible to malware attacks; it's too easy to leak information from the device, etc. To rehash these security shortcomings risks sounding redundant, given what has already been discussed.

Smartphones and PDAs: Intentional and Unintentional Mobility

However, what is slightly different is the ease of both intentional and unintentional mobility of these devices and the information they store. All the benefits of intentional mobility and the pitfalls of unintentional mobility that are found in portable storage devices and dual-use devices also hold true for smartphones. In fact, the smartphone can easily be seen as an extension of the dual-use device—call it a multiuse device—and that's where the data-mobility difference lies. With the other types of devices, if the device is lost or stolen, all that is lost is the single type or form of data the device carries: e-mail, photos, music recordings, presentations, or data files. The loss is limited in scope and potential damage. With smartphones and PDAs, however, the loss includes *all* the different data types the device contains, including:

- *Corporate and personal e-mail:* The attacker can find out a great deal about current business dealings, reports and presentations under review, and other internal discussions that are carried out over e-mail on a daily basis. In addition, the attacker can learn a great deal about the user's social network and current topics of interest. This information can be very valuable in a social-engineering attack.

- *Calendar and scheduling information:* Who is the phone's owner meeting with? What are the subjects of those meetings? Who are the attendees? An attacker can find out a lot about current project plans, corporate events, and potential business deals from reviewing the owner's calendar.

- *Contact information:* Who are the owner's personal contacts? What are their business titles, phone numbers, and addresses (both business and personal)? What comments does the owner have about them? The average smartphone contact list contains everyone the owner converses with on a regular basis as well as her circle of friends and influences. Like e-mail data, this information is invaluable for a social engineer trying to talk her way through getting information from company personnel, friends, or associates.

- *Other social circles:* Does the owner have social network accounts? Many smartphones contain applications or Web-based access to social network accounts such as Facebook, Twitter, and LinkedIn. If the owner's phone can access these accounts, the attacker can learn even more about the owner's personal life. He may even be able to impersonate the owner on these accounts and send messages, adjust security settings, or gain access to other applications based on this access.

- *Data files:* Because most smartphones allow flash memory cards to be inserted to provide additional data storage, the user may have stored important business or personal information there as well.

In summary, the information on a well-stocked smartphone or PDA provides a jackpot for the successful device finder or thief. When combined with the general lack of security controls available (or the presence of controls that are not enabled) on most smartphones, this can lead to a large loss of sensitive data or intellectual property for the company.

Optical Media (CD and DVD)

Optical media are often overlooked when discussing mobile data security and risk within the enterprise. This is understandable, since devices like flash drives, MP3 players, and smartphones usually grab the spotlight as the biggest threats to corporate data. However, optical media—the old-fashioned, everyday, ordinary writable CD or DVD—can present just as big a threat when it comes to data loss. Optical media can hold gigabytes of data (depending on the format), making it ideal for archiving and transporting large amounts of information, both intentionally and unintentionally. However, its use characteristics make it slightly different from the other forms of mobile devices.

Optical Media: Intentional Mobility

Optical disks are typically used in situations where archives, backups, or temporary storage of data is required. The most common use of optical media is to act as a backup mechanism for important files or as a storage mechanism while transporting files from one location to another. Because of their small size, large capacity, and nearly universal availability on most computers, optical disks are a natural choice for performing backups of files, drives, or even entire systems. They are also much more resilient than tapes and can withstand more abuse during handling and transport, increasing their desirability as long-term storage mechanisms. This durability is helpful when fulfilling their role as transport mechanisms, because users often throw their disks in their pockets or briefcases or leave them exposed to the elements in their offices, homes, and cars. Single-use disks are more commonly employed than rewritable disks, in part because the process for erasing an optical disk is cumbersome and time consuming, and in part because the low cost of blank optical media makes the extra effort to reuse disks less attractive to busy workers.

Optical Media: Unintentional Mobility

Unintentional mobility is a particular problem with optical media because of this proliferation of low-cost single-use or disposable disks. In addition to the usual problem of lost and stolen media (sufficiently covered previously in this book), once a disk has fulfilled its purpose and is no longer useful to its owner, most people simply throw the disk in the garbage. This is in sharp contrast to media devices such as flash drives, which easily allow for multiple cycles of erasure and reuse. This leaves a large amount of confidential and sensitive information sitting in trash bins and garbage dumps. Although not as thrilling or flashy as network hacking or social engineering, dumpster diving—rummaging around in trash bins and garbage heaps looking for confidential information—is still actively practiced by information thieves and can yield a large amount of data. Finding system backups or data files on discarded optical media can be quite a find for a successful diver.

Portable Computers

Portable computers (also referred to as laptop computers) represent the best and worst of all possible worlds when it comes to the perils of mobile data protection. Despite the problems of securing portable computers and their susceptibility to loss and theft, the uses and benefits of portable computers are so ingrained in the public consciousness that laptop sales have now overtaken sales of traditional desktop computers, according to a 2009 Reuters report.[1] Understanding the data storage, processing, and mobility capabilities of portable computers does not take a huge leap of the imagination, so a complete discussion of these capabilities here would not serve any educational purpose. However, for those whose imaginations need a bit of prodding, picture all the capabilities of a typical desktop computer, including data and document creation, mass storage, graphics and media processing, networking capabilities, and application usage. Now, shrink that computer down to the size and weight of a half-ream of paper, and you're left with the average portable computer. Many models (notably, the newer netbook computers) are considerably smaller and lighter, presenting even more potential for mobility and on-the-go usage.

Portable Computers: Intentional Mobility

From an intentional-mobility standpoint, portable computers provide the ultimate in data mobility and usage. Laptop users can essentially keep their entire office (minus the pens and stapler) with them when they travel. In fact, for many on-the-road workers, their laptop *is* their office, including all their applications, documents, network connectivity, and phone service (through the use of IP telephony). Given the widespread availability of mobile network connectivity, portable computers allow a user to find a network to connect to almost anywhere, at any time.

Portable Computers: Unintentional Mobility

What may be news to those whose primary goal is to get their work done (rather than spend time worrying about the security of their computer) is that this always-on, always-available computer and network capability also opens the portable user to a potentially continuous stream of hostile activities from the networks to which they attach. Most corporate desktop systems connected within a company's internal network are protected by the company's security infrastructure, which should include (at a minimum) firewall and antimalware protection. Many companies also have intrusion-detection and/or -prevention services on their networks to detect malicious activity. In contrast, many mobile users do not have access to this protective technology while they connect to the world from Internet cafes, hotel access points, and airport terminals. While many systems now have antivirus protection, fewer have PC-based firewalls or intrusion-detection software activated. This makes a portable computer an extremely vulnerable environment. That, combined with the wealth of data found on most workers' laptops, leads to a highly valuable target for would-be attackers, and the risk of unintentional data mobility (through both physical and network-based attack) substantially increases for portable computers.

An attacker who gets physical access to the portable computer will certainly have access to all the data stored on that system, but that's only the beginning of the unintentional data-mobility problem. Portable computers make a very attractive target because they are small, light, and easily concealed if stolen. The attacker can try to guess the laptop's password or simply remove the hard disk from the machine and examine its contents on another system (an easier and more likely scenario). Gaining access to the information on a portable computer not only opens up a wealth of corporate secrets and confidential information, but may also allow the attacker to gain access to the company's internal data network through any virtual private network (VPN) or other connectivity software that may be installed on the laptop. This assumes that the attacker can get through any authentication or access-control systems in place on the computer, but for many systems this is not a difficult exercise. If successful, the attacker can access the user's e-mail, network data drives, and applications. Even if network access is not possible (or desirable) from the laptop, the information found on the computer can be extremely valuable to the attacker or an information broker.

Electronic Mail

Electronic mail (more commonly referred to as e-mail) has been around since the 1960s, but the meteoric rise of the Internet in the 1990s catapulted e-mail into the de facto method of communication in the Internet age. When e-mail first became common, the data it managed (the e-mail messages themselves) was stored primarily on the mainframes and minicomputers where the e-mail services were run. This allowed for central management of both the e-mail system and the storage required for e-mail messages. As computing power moved from centralized systems to end-user-based computers (such as PCs and laptops), e-mail clients began to utilize local (PC-based) storage to manage e-mails either completely or in conjunction with storage availability on the e-mail server itself. Finally, as computing has become more distributed and e-mail clients have become available on phones and PDAs, personal e-mail storage has moved onto these devices as well.

In a typical e-mail model, a central server (such as a corporate Lotus Notes or Exchange server or a commercial service such as Gmail) manages the routing of e-mail as well as storing messages that are received, sent, or in transit. Once processed by the server, e-mail is placed in "mailboxes" for individual e-mail users. E-mail users then launch an e-mail client program (such as a Notes client, Outlook, or a Web browser) to access their mail box on the server. Depending on the configuration of the client, the client program can either:

1. Read mail on the server and leave it there
2. Copy e-mail down to the local system and also leave it on the server
3. Copy e-mail down to the local system and remove it from the server

When sending e-mail, there is a similar set of options, again depending on the configuration of the e-mail system

1. Send the e-mail but leave a copy on the local system
2. Send the e-mail without keeping a copy on the local system
3. Send an e-mail and leave a copy on the server

Keep in mind that this description only covers what happens on your local end of the e-mail communications. The person on the other end of the e-mail link goes through a similar process. As a result, the location where e-mail messages are stored is highly dependent on the e-mail system in use and the configuration options that e-mail administrators and end users have selected. From a mobile data perspective, however, the only part of the process that affects a mobile device is the local device storage used for received or archived e-mail. While the e-mail data stored on the server is important from a general information-protection perspective, it should be protected by the organization's normal physical and logical security controls surrounding its data-center environment.

E-mail: Intentional Mobility

Data stored by the e-mail client—the mobile data piece that's the focus of our discussion here—comes in two forms. First, there's the e-mail message itself. E-mail content generally does not have a fixed agenda or format.* It's often ad hoc and off the cuff, and people often put little thought into its content or presentation. While the message itself may contain confidential, sensitive, or private information, the thought that goes into collecting and distributing that content is often fleeting, at best. E-mail is the modern equivalent of the casual conversation. This is ironic, considering that e-mail is often used as an official forum for communicating actions, thoughts, and intentions in many business and personal settings. These two aspects of e-mail—an ephemeral medium used for official communication—seem incongruous, but it's specifically that incongruity that leads to the problem of securing e-mail when working with mobile devices.

Because most users take a casual approach to e-mail, even if the information they are conveying is formal or official, their attitude about the protection of that

---

* The content does not need to follow a specific format or layout (i.e., the words and arrangement of the content of the message). However, the layout of the data bits within the e-mail message have a very strict format and must conform to well-defined Internet standards in order to be interoperable with the multitude of e-mail systems on the Internet.

e-mail—more specifically, where that e-mail is going and what protections it will have when it gets there—is also casual. Thus, when employees use their smart-phones to access their corporate e-mail, they think little about the security of the devices, concerned only that the devices facilitate their ability to communicate. Does the smartphone encrypt the e-mail coming in and out of the device? Does it allow the downloading of attachments? Does it prevent forwarding of e-mails to other users? Users will know the answers to these questions only as much as it enables or prevents them from getting their work done.

The second form of data that most e-mail clients manage comes from attach-ments: those ubiquitous extra pieces of data connected to e-mails that add additional content, meaning, and value to the main message. The attachments—documents, slide presentations, video files, and photos—are often the main purpose of the e-mail, with the message body serving merely as the "gift wrapping" for the attach-ment's important content. Because the attachment stands out from the rest of the message, typically separated from the body with its own icon and file name, users get a visual cue that this piece might be important and worthy of separate protec-tion. Consider the following e-mail example:

From: Thomas Takeover <tom@modevco.com>
Date: Fri, Dec 11, 2009 at 2:52 PM
Subject: Acme Takeover Deal
To: Arthur Accountant <art@modevco.com>

Art,

It looks like the proposed purchase of Acme Enterprises is almost finalized. Their board fought long and hard, but finally agreed to a $13.75 share price. The deal is supposed to be approved and announced by next Friday.

Attached are the final figures. Please review them ASAP and get back to me with any comments by tomorrow afternoon at the latest. Also, please keep this data confidential, as we don't want word getting out on the street before the official announcement.

Thanks,
Tom
Attachment: ACME Takeover Financials.xls

When Art receives this e-mail, it's likely that his attention will be immediately drawn to the attachment, both because it visually stands out from the rest of the message and the fact that Tom wants him to keep it confidential. What Art will most likely fail to realize is that the most important part of the message (the price of the deal and the timing) is right there in the body of the message itself. Those who might wish to steal actionable information don't need to go to the trouble of finding and stealing the attached spreadsheet; all they need to do is read the e-mail body itself. This is the dual nature of e-mail information, and the one most often over-looked when trying to analyze how to protect e-mail as it moves outside the confines of a closed, in-house e-mail service. In order to secure data on mobile devices, you need to pay attention to both the e-mail content *and* any attachments.

E-mail: Unintentional Mobility

When it comes to the ease of both intentional and unintentional mobility, e-mail is perhaps the most mobile form of data in common use. For authorized users, intentional mobility of e-mail data is a snap: just click Send in the e-mail program and off it goes. However, as has been noted previously, the further the message gets from the original sender, the less control the originator has over its contents. So, an attacker trying to gain access to an e-mail message has several options:

1. *Break into the e-mail server that processes the message.* Not impossible, but he must get past whatever technical, physical, and administrative controls protect the server. Depending on how well the system administrator maintains the security of the server, this may be more or less of a challenge, but it represents the most difficult avenue of attack.
2. *Steal the mobile device used to access an e-mail account.* This will give the attacker direct access to the victim's e-mail account and the ability to view her e-mail, but it also requires direct personal risk to the attacker, who must get close enough to the victim to be able to steal her device.
3. *Find a user's lost mobile device.* This is much easier than stealing it directly, but it is also dependent on random chance to occur. It is not a very practical attack, but a boon to opportunistic information thieves who know how to capitalize on the misfortune of others.
4. *Monitor the e-mail transmission from somewhere along the communications path.* This requires access to the network transmission equipment between the e-mail server and the end user's mobile device. This is a highly probable scenario for someone inside the victim's organization who has access to the server or the network equipment. Monitoring the transmission from outside the organization requires the ability to tap into the phone company's or ISP's network, either with help from an insider or by breaking in to the network. While this is certainly not impossible, it does require a fair bit of technical skill and some expensive equipment.*
5. *Become a recipient.* This takes advantage of the Inverse Distance Principle applied to e-mail. In order to have access to the message and any attachments, you only need access to someone included in the communications chain. The more people who read, copy, forward, and reply to the message, the greater the chances are that someone in the chain will disclose the infor-

---

* And it's illegal in many jurisdictions.

mation to an unintended recipient. An astute attacker can combine this with some social-engineering skills to insert himself in the communications chain. For example:

"Hey, Art, Tom was supposed to send me his thoughts on the Acme deal but he must have forgotten. I can't seem to get hold of him, so can you send me his message so I can take a look?"

or

"Mr. Accountant, this is Frank Faker from the Securities and Exchange Commission. We're investigating some improper accounting in the estimates for the proposed Acme takeover. Can you please send us whatever information you have so we can include it in our investigation?"

Don't laugh too hard; social engineering is a surprisingly effective method of gathering information.

None of these is a perfect scenario. They all require a certain combination of skill (either technical or social), opportunity, and chutzpah, but they all serve the purpose of gaining access to mobile e-mail communications.

Instant Messaging and Text Messaging

Very closely related to e-mail are the twin technologies of instant messaging (IM) and text messaging (texting). These two technologies allow the establishment of multiway conversations between people in real (or near-real) time. Like e-mail before them, IM and texting have become standard tools used by businesses around the globe, and have become one of the primary methods of communications for younger people in school or those just entering the work force. Unlike e-mail, however, IM and texting are available on a wide variety of mobile devices, making the information sent over these channels easily available from any mobile device with an Internet or cellular connection. In addition, because IM and texting are so casual and conversational in nature, many users do not associate their behavior on these systems with proper (and protective) corporate attitudes about information protection and disclosure.

Like e-mail, the text of IM chats may contain sensitive financial, business, human resource, and technical information exchanged between IM users. If this information were to leak out, it could be very damaging to the organization. Such was the case in 2001 when the text of several IM conversations from the CEO of eFront were stolen from his PC and published on the Internet. The messages cast a very negative light on eFront's business practices and led to a very public scandal for the company.[2]

IM and Texting: Intentional Mobility

Intentional mobility comes naturally for both IM and texting. They were designed specifically to establish and maintain ad hoc and spontaneous conversations with a wide variety of people in unknown locations. Unlike e-mail, with its general presumption (however erroneous) that the recipient is sitting at her computer, reading and responding to e-mail messages, IM and (particularly) texting make no such assumption. Text messages can be sent from almost anywhere one can get a cellular signal, and while IM has traditionally been associated with desktop-bound clients, the new breed of mobile smart devices have built-in IM clients, allowing for continuous conversation no matter where the sender and recipient happen to be located. When combined with the conversational nature of IM and texting, this allows for nearly continuous conversation, no matter where the parties may be. IM and texting users see this as a boon to quick and efficient communications. Many organizations, however, might classify this as "unintentional mobility."

IM and Texting: Unintentional Mobility

For both IM and texting, much of the conversation occurs where an organization has no ability to monitor, record, or track messages sent and received. One of the biggest risks of these technologies is the ability for users of IM clients to transmit and receive files, making the spread of malware or illicit material a potential issue with IM systems. Because these conversations do not typically pass through the organization's malware defenses, this can be a potential avenue for infection into the enterprise.

IM clients also have very little in the way of strong user identification or authentication. For most public services, users can select their own user name, and authentication is managed through the use of a basic password (without any complexity requirements). For IM services that an organization establishes for internal use, user IDs may be based on some predetermined format (or based on their network login ID), but there is still no mutual user authentication required when a conversation starts, making social engineering much simpler to accomplish. Because of this lack of user-to-ID validation, it becomes easier to converse with an unsuspecting user, potentially obtaining confidential information through that exchange. Texting systems typically use a person's mobile phone number as their ID, but a person receiving a text from an unfamiliar number with the message, "Hi, Alice, it's Bob," is likely to believe Bob to be the actual sender and enter into a conversation with him, a conversation in which "Bob" could use social-engineering methods to try to get sensitive information from Alice.

Many employees use publicly available IM systems (such as AIM or Yahoo! Messenger) to converse with customers and business partners. The information shared in those IM conversations may be proprietary, sensitive, or otherwise internal to the company, and the content of the messages can be recorded by the IM or texting service provider. As a result, an insider at one of those providers could potentially use that information for evil purposes.

Finally, there is precious little logging saved from IM and text conversations. Information sent via IM and texting is stored locally on the device for an indeterminate amount of time, the length of which is variable and dependent on the default configuration of the device (in the case of users who don't change their default settings) or for an amount of time determined by the will of the user (for those who do). In addition, some IM and texting clients allow the text of conversations to be saved for archiving purposes. Others keep the messages only until they run out of storage space (deleting them on a first-in–first-out basis) or until the user decides to delete them. All this adds up to a general lack of consistent controls for information management and protection with IM and text messaging.

For internally deployed systems, the company may have the ability (depending on the IM technology in use) to store the full text of all IM conversations. This may be a requirement for some organizations in order to be compliant with various laws and regulations pertaining to record keeping. For example, if IM is used in the maintenance or operation of any financial reporting for a public company doing business in the United States, the company may be required to keep all records of those IM conversations for Sarbanes–Oxley audit purposes. Companies that manage the trading of stocks or other securities must record all IM messages used during those dealings and ensure that those logs are secured and available for audit or discovery purposes. These laws and regulations recognize that IM use is becoming as common as e-mail and the telephone for communicating, and seek to hold it to similar standards for tracking and monitoring. It's important to remember that once these logs are created—particularly if they contain the full text of all IM traffic—they need to be secured with the same protections that are used for other sensitive information.

Finally, text messages are difficult to log because the provisioning and operation of the text-messaging service is managed by a third party, such as the local phone or cellular service provider. Those carriers keep records of text message events (such as the date and time of the text as well as the names of sender and recipients), mostly for billing purposes. However, service providers rarely keep the full content of those text messages for more than a few days, primarily to ensure message delivery. After that, they delete them.

Conclusion

This chapter has been an exploration of the different categories of mobile devices in common usage today. However, it should not be thought of as an exhaustive or comprehensive inventory, because new devices are being introduced every day, and new uses for old devices continue to emerge as the way we think about mobility changes. When you look back to the basic definition of a mobile device—a device that can store large amounts of information and may be easily transported from place to place—the basic categories discussed in this chapter don't even begin to catalog the breadth and depth of the mobile devices one can use. However, these categories will help you formulate the ways in which your organization can structure the various policies, procedures, and technical controls that you will need to begin addressing the security issues surrounding mobile devices and mobile data in your environment. Whether you're worried about e-mail, tapes, smartphones, flash drives, or portable computers, there are things that can be done to protect an organization and its employees from the security issues—and the unwilling mobility—inherent in their use.

In this chapter we've merely catalogued the uses—good and bad—of these different technologies. Uses, however, are only half the issue. What is left to explore are the various methods for protecting yourself and your organization against the problems of unintentional mobility that we've identified here. Do not fret. These solutions—as well as the implications and ramifications of implementing them in a modern, complex enterprise—are still to come.

Action Plan

As you can see from the discussion in this chapter, mobility in the modern enterprise has many faces. In order to effectively plan the best way to address the mobile security issues you will face, you need to start identifying the faces of mobility in your own organization. Some of these—flash drives, laptops, and smartphones—will be obvious. Others, not so much. Think about multiple e-mail systems, instant-messaging services, customized mobile applications, Web 2.0 services, and cloud computing facilities all starting to encroach on mobile data as they wind their way through your systems and mobile devices.

To start you on your journey, begin to think about the faces of mobility in your environment using the following guidelines:

1. Identify the types of mobile data most prevalent in your organization. Are you concerned with data movement through flash drives and writeable CDs, or do smartphones and text messaging worry you more?
2. Once you have identified your areas of concern, review the potential intentional and unintentional mobility scenarios where data can move to and from your organization. Some scenarios will be more likely than others, so don't get too carried away. It's possible that a secret agent with a laser scope can read the vibrations from your smartphone to eavesdrop on your conversation, but that may not be the most realistic scenario or one that you are willing to invest a great deal of resources in to protect against.

3. Apply the first part of the risk equation—Risk = (Threat × Vulnerability × Value)—to evaluate the overall level of risk to those areas you identified based on the various unintentional mobility scenarios you have identified.
4. As you did in Chapter 2, begin to rank these risk areas in order of most concern, based on your evaluation of the overall risk. This will allow you to concentrate your resources on the most critical areas that also carry the largest amount of risk.

Notes

1. Kelvin Soh, "Is It the End of the Desktop PC?" Reuters, January 7, 2009, http://www.reuters.com/articlePrint?articleId=USTRE50601320090107.
2. Paul Festa, "ICQ Logs Spark Corporate Nightmare," *CNET News*, March 15, 2001, http://news.cnet.com/2100-1023-254173.html.

Chapter 4

Data at Rest, Data in Motion

To this point, we've been discussing the problems that are encountered depending on where data moves or resides. Now we will look at how data gets from place to place and the changing security issues it will encounter along the way. News stories involving information loss from mobile devices (like laptops and flash drives) tend to take a skewed view of the mobile data issue, focusing on the sole fact that mobile devices were involved in the data loss and portraying mobile devices (and the data they contain) as a general security menace. What these stories almost always fail to address—and the heart of the mobile data problem—is that the data had to somehow navigate its way on to the mobile device in the first place. It didn't just magically appear there; it was put there. Why was it put there? Where did it come from? Who was sending it? Where was it going? In short, these stories are rarely based on the motion path of the information, focusing instead only on its location when it went missing.

It's All a Matter of Physics

In this chapter we are going to look at both mobile data in motion and mobile data at rest. There is no better place to start than with one of the greatest pieces of scientific literature ever published: Isaac Newton's *Principia Mathematica*.

Corpus omne perseverare in statu suo quiescendi vel movendi unifor-
miter in directum, nisi quatenus a viribus impressis cogitur statum
illum mutare.

[Every body persists in its state of being at rest or of moving uniformly straight forward, except insofar as it is compelled to change its
state by force impressed.][1]

Translated again for the purpose of describing mobile data, data at rest will
stay that way unless put into motion by an external force (typically an information
user). Once set in motion, that information will stay in motion unless acted upon
by another external force (typically another information user or a device along the
data's motion path) that prevents its further travel.

This classic law of physics describes not only the movement of planets in the
solar system, but also the basic security problem with mobile data. Data at rest (in
storage, on a disk, or in memory) will stay there unless forced into mobility by an
outside force. Once mobile, that data will tend to stay mobile as long as such mobility is desirable to—and managed by—the data's users. The "managed by" part is
critical to ensuring the continued security and privacy of the information during
its journey. Once the desire for the data's mobility has waned, an outside force must
again act on the data to move it back to a resting state.

More Definitions

As has been our practice to this point, there can't be a discussion of "data at rest"
or "data in motion" without first defining those terms. Unlike previous chapters,
however, there isn't much theory or background required to understand the context
for these definitions.

> **Data at rest:** Data that has a fixed location (physically or virtually).
> Any interaction with that data is based on accessing the data in the
> place where it is stored.
> **Data in motion:** Data that does not have a fixed location (physically or
> virtually). Data in motion travels along one or more media paths on its
> way to another (temporary or permanent) resting place.

The relationship between these states of data existence is simple and dictated
by Newton's law; data at rest and data in motion will maintain their natural state
until acted upon by an outside force. Newton may not have realized it in the 17th
century, but his laws of motion still rule in the 21st century, and in areas he probably never dreamed of.

When it comes to mobile data, there is often confusion about whether it is considered "at rest" or "in motion." Clearly the term *mobile data* implies a certain level

of motion. Even our definition of mobile data from Chapter 1 ("information that is intentionally moved beyond an organization's borders [physically or logically] by means of a mobile device") indicates that the data is in motion. However, the generally accepted definition of data at rest includes data that is resting on a mobile device, even though that device may itself be in motion. For example, suppose you copy a presentation file to a flash drive to bring to a customer site for a sales meeting. To you, the data is in motion. It's not in a fixed location and is traveling from your office to the customer's location in your pocket (or your briefcase, or attached to your key chain). But from the data's viewpoint, it is at rest. It is in a fixed location on the storage device and (based on Newton's law) will stay there until it is acted upon by an external force, namely when a user or program copies it from the storage device and sends it somewhere else. While this may seem a bit counterintuitive, it really does make sense. The data is not what's in motion; the data's *container* is in motion. The data is just along for the ride. Therefore, data on a mobile device is deemed to be data at rest.

The two concepts may seem to represent opposite sides of the same idea; however, the protection mechanisms for each are surprisingly similar. Data—whether at rest or in motion—has no inherent protection and must rely on additional mechanisms to protect it wherever its current location may be. Data at rest must rely on the protection mechanisms provided by its container. Data in motion—whether it's moving over a network over a wireless connection, or over a direct-wired connection between two systems—must likewise rely on additional security measures to protect that communications channel. Both forms rely on outside agents to encapsulate the data and provide security against attack. Where the two forms differ, however, is in the scope of the required protections.

For data at rest, the protection mechanisms are concentrated at the point of data storage, such as a disk drive, backup tape, or personal digital assistant (PDA). Because the data isn't moving anywhere, we have the opportunity to build fortifications against attack (in the form of security controls) that can stay in place and ward off any interlopers. These controls are effective because the environment in which they have to work is fixed and well defined. Therefore, the protection mechanisms within these environments can likewise be fixed and well defined. Without the requirement for mobility, fixed fortifications can be as elaborate, sophisticated, and all-encompassing as the data owner requires.

In contrast, data in motion cannot rely on fixed-point defenses to protect the data. By definition, the data is moving along a communications path, so any protections must be able to maintain the security of the data along the entire length of that path. This can be accomplished by one of two basic methods. The first is by adding security to the communications path itself. The most common example of this is to encrypt the communications channel while the data is in motion. Many users experience this when they conduct financial transactions over the Web. Most Web sites use Secure Socket Layer (SSL) or Transport Layer Security (TLS) encryption to protect the communication channel between the Web browser (where the user sits) and the Web server (where the transaction is taking place). When this encryption is in effect, any data sent between the browser and the server is protected from eavesdropping along the entire communications path. If the communications path consists of multiple network devices linked together, the encryption must be able to protect the data through all of those links in order to ensure the end-to-end security of the information.

The second general method of protecting data in motion is to assume that the communications channel can't be secured and protect the data itself against compromise. This might be the case if the channel you are using does not support any end-to-end protections (like encryption) or you believe that the channel may already be compromised by attackers and don't want to send unprotected data through it. By encrypting the data itself or using a technology that encapsulates the data inside a container requiring strong authentication before allowing access, the information can be secured no matter what the communications medium. This applies whether the communications link itself has any built-in protections, or whether or not there are hostile forces along the communications path.

Protecting Data at Rest

Data at rest has a number of inherent risk factors that make it particularly inviting for an attacker. This is certainly the case when the data is at rest in a traditional location, such as a PC hard disk or a file server in a data center, but it is even more vulnerable when the data is resting on a portable media device that may not enjoy the luxury of physical and logical defense-in-depth. To illustrate this point, let's take a look at the various risk factors affecting data at rest, and distinguish how the data's location and mobility will factor in to those risks.

The most important point to remember when protecting data at rest is that the environment that protects that data is largely under your control. As long as you have possession of the device or location where the data resides, you have the power to ensure that it has the proper physical or logical protections in place to keep the data safe from prying eyes. How well you apply those protections will ultimately determine whether the data ends up in the wrong hands, and if it does, the fault is yours to bear. The moment that data moves into someone else's hands (either physically or logically), you lose that absolute control. The key, then, is to ensure that the data and (potentially) the storage device have all the appropriate protections in place before they go wandering into hostile territory.

Physical Protection Methods

Taking a standard defense-in-depth approach, the first place to protect data at rest is to consider the physical environment. The physical protections you provide your data are your first line of defense and have the most profound effect on the overall security of that data. This starts with the most basic of physical protections:

the location of the device where the data is located. If it's located in a building you or your organization own or maintain, the building's infrastructure can provide multiple protection layers. Lobby guards, badged access, locked cabinets, and restricted-access areas of a building all contribute to the physical barriers a site can provide to protect information.

However, when the data moves outside of that location, the need for physical protection of the data does not end. In fact, it increases because mobile data is, well, mobile. That means that any physical protections in place inside the controlled location must be mobile as well, or new physical protections must be provided to compensate for those available at your location. You may not be able to carry a locked filing cabinet with you when you leave the office, but you can lock your briefcase and make sure your briefcase is in your possession at all times.

This example is a great illustration of how the physical protection of mobile data needs to adjust to the physical surroundings of the data and of the devices where it is moved to. Because you can't carry buildings and cabinets around with you and most likely do not have the services of an armed escort at your disposal, you need to be more creative and diligent in providing the physical protections used to safeguard your mobile data. The most basic protection is to maintain physical possession of the data and devices at all times. Maintaining physical possession helps ensure that the proper physical security protections are in place.

In addition to physical possession, there are a number of other physical protections that can be used for mobile data. Some of these are a bit more practical to employ than others, but all are possibilities to consider, depending on the sensitivity of the information and the likelihood that the information will be lost or stolen while in transit:

- Keep the storage device hidden
- Split the data onto multiple devices
- Use a locked container
- Use tamper-proof or tamper-evident containers
- Use a special courier
- Use obscurity to your advantage

Keep the Storage Device Hidden

This may seem obvious, but it's a surprisingly simple way to protect information, whether it's on a flash drive or printed on paper. Unless you are actively working on the data, it is always a good idea to keep the device it's stored on hidden out of sight in an envelope, folder, briefcase, or some other obfuscating device. Displaying your information openly, or failing to conceal obvious data-carrying devices, allows casual onlookers in hotel lobbies, airport waiting areas, restaurants, or even on the street to observe your information and potentially use it to their advantage or your detriment. Just ask U.K. assistant commissioner Bob Quick, who in 2009 walked past a group of journalists and photographers on his way to see the British prime minister while holding documents marked "SECRET." The documents contained plans of an impending raid on suspected al-Qaeda members. Enlargements of the photos allowed the reporters to see the contents of the secret documents, nearly ruining a months-long investigation.[2] Even pulling a portable hard disk or flash drive from your travel bag may present enough of a temptation for an opportunistic thief to grab it and run, stealing your data in the process. If you have secret information, you need to take every precaution to keep it secret by keeping it under wraps and out of sight whenever you are not using it.

Split the Data onto Multiple Devices

One way to limit the amount of damage that lost information can inflict on the organization is to limit the amount of data that can be lost at any one time. Splitting the information onto multiple devices and sending each device along a different path to the final destination means that the loss of any one of the devices does not mean the loss of the data set as a whole. For example, suppose you need to send a file with 10 million health care records on a DVD to a service provider and you want to reduce the potential for that information to be lost during transport. You can split the single large file into multiple files with half a million records in each file, then burn the smaller files onto separate DVDs for transport. Once you have the DVDs created, you send them to the service provider via separate routes (for example, mailing them from separate post offices or sending them with different people traveling to the service provider's location). In this way, if one of those disks should get lost or stolen, the amount of information lost (as well as the subsequent damage to the organization) is limited to only the information contained on that lost disk.

Splitting up information onto multiple devices is also effective in situations where all the pieces are required for the information to be useful, such as a secret formula. The attacker may only be able to obtain one or more parts of the formula, but not all of them. Without all the parts, the formula is useless, the attacker has not gained anything, and (most important) the owner of the formula has not lost anything. The splitting of the data multiplies the work the attacker needs to perform to obtain all the information and divides the amount of damage that the loss of one of those pieces will have on the organization. Unfortunately, keep in mind that splitting the data in this manner also increases the complexity and cost of managing and tracking that data through the multiple paths it will take to its destination. The organization will have to weigh the benefits of increased security against the cost of the additional complexity.*

---

* The astute reader will already have surmised that encryption will solve this problem (and many others) in an easier and more manageable way. Good work. We'll cover encryption in much more detail in Chapter 6.

Use a Locked Container

In situations where more robust physical protection is a requirement, the use of a locked container should be considered. A locked storage container serves as a physical deterrent to the theft of the information inside the container, and the type of container used will depend on the level of security required, from a simple lockbox to a sophisticated sealed, multiple-lock container. When selecting a container to transport mobile media, both the lock and the container should be resistant to breakage or destruction. Using a state-of-the-art lock is of no use if the container it is protecting is made of light plastic or wood. Of course, the use of a locked container begins to stretch the notion of "mobile" and "portable," as the container itself begins to get bulky and difficult to transport. However, if the data under consideration is valuable enough and other forms of physical or logical protections do not measure up to the security requirements for protecting that data, a locked container may be the best bet to help ensure its safe passage between points.

Use Tamper-Proof or Tamper-Evident Containers

A locked container may be able to secure your mobile devices, but in some cases it's also important to have visual warnings or indications that a container has been tampered with. To fill this need, you can use a tamper-proof or tamper-evident container to store the device during transport. A tamper-proof container will prevent an attacker from getting the contents of the container without destroying either the container or the contents in the process. Tamper-proof containers can be difficult to design and use in practice, but if your data protection needs require absolute assurance that the data will not be acquired by unauthorized persons, this may be an option worth exploring. In the most extreme example, the container could be rigged to destroy itself and its contents if tampering or forced entry is detected. Depending on the method of destruction (perhaps through explosives or incineration), this could present an extreme safety risk to those handling the container. A more benign design might physically destroy the contents by immersing it in a corrosive compound or colored dye that renders the information useless to an attacker.

All these scenarios would serve the purpose of keeping the contents of the container away from prying eyes, but their practical uses are limited to the most sensitive of data for which security is of the utmost concern. Moreover, tamper-proof containers are expensive to develop and produce, and the cost of their implementation may be beyond the resources and security needs of many organizations.

In electronic applications, tamper-proof mechanisms are often implemented as virtual "self-destruct" features. Devices with tamper-proof mechanisms are designed to electronically destroy their data and system code if the component is opened, disassembled, or otherwise used in a manner inconsistent with its normal operation. These types of tamper-proof mechanisms are commonly found in cryptographic processing and storage systems, where attackers might attempt to disassemble or reverse-engineer the electronics of the system to discover the cryptographic keys used to protect the system's data. If the system detects such tampering, it is designed to destroy the keys to prevent such a compromise. Such tamper-proof designs can be an effective protection if the goal is to absolutely protect the contents from disclosure or compromise.

An organization may be more concerned with knowing whether its data has been accessed or tampered with than with absolutely keeping it away from prying eyes. For example, suppose you needed to transport secret encryption keys between locations or groups. Because these are new keys that have not been used for any previous communications, their interception by attackers would not compromise any existing secrets, but an attacker who gets them will be able to decode all future communications between sites. The organization will want to know if the keys have been intercepted and viewed by an unauthorized party so that they can discard those keys and generate a new set. To create a tamper-proof transport container for the keys may not be practical or cost-effective. In this case, all the organization really needs is a way to know if the data container has been tampered with. For this purpose, it doesn't need a tamper-*proof* container; it needs a tamper-*evident* container.

Tamper-evident packaging has been a part of security design since ancient times. Kings often used sealing wax dripped on private or important documents and imprinted with their personal design etched onto a royal ring. If the seal was removed, the king (or the recipient of the document) knew that it had been opened in transit. Because forging a duplicate royal ring was expensive (and against the law) the seal provided a reasonably secure method (for its time) of document protection.

In the late 1970s and early 1980s, consumer-product manufacturers began experiencing threats and actual incidents of product tampering, affecting both their businesses and their reputations in the eyes of their customers. Because it was impossible in many cases to create packaging that was completely impervious to tampering, they turned to tamper-evident packaging for their products. Jars of food were fitted with "pop-up" lids that would indicate if the lid had been removed, and pill bottles began using special seals that could not be replaced if broken. If consumers saw these indicators, they would know not to use the products. These new types of packaging gave consumers a visual indicator that the product had been opened prior to its purchase, benefiting both the consumer and the manufacturer. They saved the manufacturers the cost of developing completely tamper-proof packaging (if such was even possible); they provided prior warning to consumers that something was potentially wrong with the product (preventing countless cases of illness or death); and they protected the manufacturers from the potential legal liabilities should a consumer use a tainted product.

For mobile data protection, a tamper-evident container or seal serves the same purposes. Tamper-evident packaging is a perfect solution for situations where the knowledge of potential data tampering is equally or more important than the actual prevention of such tampering. One of the most common methods is a special sealing tape that leaves a design or mark on the container's surface if removed. Once the tape is lifted and the mark appears on the container, the tape cannot easily be reattached without displaying tell-tale signs of its removal. Other potential containers include special bags that, once sealed, cannot be opened and resealed without leaving an indication of entry, and containers with special sealed lids that break apart upon opening and cannot be reattached.

Use a Special Courier

Sometimes the best physical protection for mobile data is to use a special service to move the data from point to point. Such services are designed specifically to move important or valuable items (including data) and have specialized procedures for protecting their cargo. Depending on the circumstances and value of the cargo, these services may include armed guards or armored cars to provide even more protection. This may be overkill for most mobile data needs, but it may be necessary in some situations where the data or device is valuable enough and its loss or compromise is unacceptable.

When considering the use of a courier service, be sure to research the service thoroughly to ensure that they are trustworthy enough for your needs. All reputable courier services are bonded, meaning that they are backed by insurance that will cover you (and them) in the case of a problem during the transportation of your cargo. The bonding process serves as a certain measure of the trustworthiness of the service, since the insurance company would presumably not cover the service if it was unreliable or prone to losses. This is not foolproof, however, as even well-insured cargo sometimes gets lost or stolen in transit, or the insurance company may have performed a poor analysis of the company's risk profile. In addition, the insurance may not be sufficient to cover the financial or reputation damage that can result from a lost-data incident. These factors must all be weighed when deciding whether a courier service fits your data transportation needs.

Use Obscurity to Your Advantage

In security circles, the reliance on "security through obscurity" is one that security professionals try to avoid. Security through obscurity is based on the notion that the less that is publicly known about a security mechanism, the more secure that mechanism will be. For instance, most companies do not reveal details about their system and network security procedures for fear that revealing such detail would give potential attackers information that might allow them to breach those networks. Security product companies often withhold information about the inner workings of their product for fear that publishing those details would allow hackers to develop specific attacks that can compromise the product. In short, the point of security through obscurity is to prevent attackers from breaking the security by withholding information that would allow them to understand how it works. This makes intuitive sense, but in reality it rarely works well.

The reason is that security through obscurity relies on secrecy to protect the security of the system. That secrecy, unfortunately, is difficult to maintain. Reverse engineering, design and functional analysis, or inadvertent disclosure of the secret mechanisms by those who know the secret are all ways that can be (and have been) used to defeat security through obscurity. As such, it should not be relied upon as the sole security mechanism protecting highly sensitive information.

However, there are circumstances where obscurity can work in your favor, particularly when it comes to transporting highly valuable goods or information. Today's information security environment has become a technology-dependent discipline, and security professionals and engineers often look first to highly technical and complex methods of protecting information, often overlooking the obvious and simplistic methods we use every day to protect things. The world is full of goods and information moving from place to place, and hiding something inside that constant stream of movement can be just enough to ensure its safe passage.

For example, in June of 2008, the American Numismatic Society (ANS) needed to move its collection of 800,000 coins, bank notes, medals, and other artifacts 22 blocks through downtown New York City. However, it feared that providing the amount of security worthy of such a treasure—including armored cars, helicopter escorts, and a large police presence—would attract too much attention and invite robbers to attack the convoy, in addition to raising the cost of the move to astronomical proportions. So instead, ANS decided to pack its treasure inside ordinary moving crates and disguise the endeavor as an ordinary office move, a typical and daily occurrence in downtown Manhattan. Secrecy was paramount. Only a very small circle of insiders knew what was really being moved, and not even the moving company was informed of the real cargo until the morning of the event. Although there was a police escort for the caravan, the operation was decidedly, and intentionally, low key. As a result, the move went off without a hitch, and 12,000 metal trays worth hundreds of millions of dollars blended in effortlessly into the stream of New York City traffic unnoticed and undisturbed.[3]

Suppose you needed to apply this same concept to the movement of data from one place to another. If you have a large cargo of backup tapes with sensitive information to transport to an off-site facility, you might consider packing them in containers that are labeled anything but "sensitive backup tapes" and shipping them via a standard courier service. If you have optical disks that you need to carry with you on a trip, include them among a pile of ordinary music CDs or movie DVDs that you carry with you as well. The idea is that the cargo holding the sensitive information should be as inconspicuous as possible and blend in with the surroundings of its environment so as to not draw undue attention or bring on heightened risk. This may be enough to allow you to transport the cargo (i.e., your data) past the watch of potential thieves and attackers.

Be forewarned, however, that this type of security through obscurity is *not at all foolproof.* Packages go missing all the time, and briefcases get lost and stolen regularly, so this should not be considered a primary security protection under any circumstances. However, given the *right* set of circumstances, the appropriate cargo, and the right amount of proper planning, security through obscurity might just be the way to move sensitive data from one point to another in the most expedient, cost-effective, and least troublesome way possible.

Physical Protection Summary

In this review of the potential physical protections available for mobile data on mobile devices, all of the methods have followed the same basic theme: Place the device inside some obscuring container and protect the container as it is transported from one site to another. The container can be an envelope, a lockbox, a briefcase, or a moving van, but the idea is still the same: to ensure that the protective container provides enough resistance to attack to adequately protect the data it contains. Alternatively, the container could provide enough evidence of a compromise that the device (or its data) should be considered unusable. However, there is a practical limit to the amount of physical protection that can be afforded to mobile data. While lockboxes, moving vans, and special couriers are all possibilities for transportation, they begin to stretch the credibility of the term *mobile*, at least as much as we understand that mobility of data implies the ease of transport for that data. Nevertheless, in a true defense-in-depth approach, all the various forms of physical protection for mobile devices must be considered when trying to protect data at rest on those devices.

Logical Protection Mechanisms

Once you have considered the physical protections that can be applied to your mobile device, you can then turn your attention to nonphysical (or logical) protections that may be available to protect your data. Unlike physical protection, with its need for an encapsulating container, logical protections work within the confines of the mobile device itself and do not have the physical bulk and limitations of the physical protections described earlier. The selection of potential logical controls available for a particular set of mobile data will be dictated primarily by the capabilities of that device. The three most common logical protections available on popular mobile devices are

- Authentication
- Access controls
- Encryption

Authentication

Authentication is the process of proving one's identity, and the most common authentication mechanism available on mobile devices is the use of passwords or personal identification numbers (PINs). Mobile phones, PDAs, and even some flash drives have incorporated password protection to restrict access to the data stored on the device. More sophisticated devices, like laptops and smartphones, allow the user (or the organization's administrator, if the devices are managed centrally) to set the required complexity of the password. For example, the policy might require that all passwords be at least eight characters long and contain a mix of uppercase and lowercase letters, numbers, and special characters (like %#!*&^%, for example). These are typical settings for general-purpose computing environments and are considered "industry-standard" settings.

The reason these complexity rules are in place is to prevent against "brute force" attacks. Brute force attacks are attempts to guess a password by trying all possible combinations of characters in the password. For example, if the password consisted only of four digits, there would be 10,000 potential passwords for that device ("0000" through "9999"), and an attacker trying to use brute force to guess the password would be able to find it, on average, within 5,000 tries and definitively within 10,000 tries. If the password consisted only of four lowercase letters from a to z, the total number of potential passwords would be 456,976 (which is 26^4). By increasing the complexity requirements to eight characters and requiring the use of letters, numbers, and special characters, the potential number of possible passwords becomes so great that a brute-force password attack becomes much less practical to execute.

Because such complexity rules have become standardized as a good security practice recommendation for general end-user access control, many organizations simply use these same settings when developing standards for mobile computing environments like smartphones and PDAs. However, these may not be the appropriate settings for mobile environments.

Consider the case of the smartphone. We have already seen how these devices have many of the same computing and storage capabilities of their larger laptop cousins, so it stands to reason that organizations would want to use similar password complexity standards to provide an equivalent level of security. Unfortunately, the use characteristics of these devices are much different than their larger counterparts. On the typical desktop or laptop computer, users have full use of both hands for data entry, and their full attention is paid to the device when they are interacting with the machine. The same is not true of the smartphone environment. Users of these devices are typically doing something else while they are interacting with the device, like walking to a meeting, talking on the phone, or even driving a car. The user's attention is divided between the task they are engaged in and their interaction with the smartphone. In addition, the user rarely has both hands freely available to interact with the device, especially when engaged in an activity like driving a motor vehicle. Setting aside the lack of good sense exhibited by operating a smartphone while driving a car, it happens nonetheless, and organizations need to take this behavior into consideration.

Finally, many mobile devices contain keyboards that are much smaller than their desktop or laptop counterparts. Single keys are often used for multiple characters, and special characters require multiple keystrokes to enter into the text stream. As a result, the use of the standard eight-character/alphanumeric/special-character password-complexity rules begin to add significantly to the users' password-entry burden and, in some cases, may increase the risk to their personal safety.* For these reasons, organizations need to make informed judgments on how to apply or modify their password-complexity requirements to accommodate the complexity of key entry on each different type of device.

This decision will follow closely with the organization's overall approach to security and end-user responsibility in general. Some organizations will hold the security value of a highly complex password above the perceived user benefit of ease of entry and usability. Others will understand that, human nature being what it is, complex password requirements on mobile devices are an impediment to user productivity and will seek to reduce the password-complexity requirements for these devices. While this may seem to go against common notions of standard security practices, it is nonetheless completely in line with the organization's responsibility for determining the overall risk of mobile data and devices: not just the risk to the data but also the risk to employee productivity and safety.

While this position may seem to subject the organization to an overall lower standard of security, the use of a defense-in-depth approach can reestablish a comfortable security position for such devices. For example, many phones and PDAs have the ability to lock the user out of the device after a certain number of invalid password entries. This prevents the user from accessing the information on the device even if she subsequently enters the correct password. If this number is set to lock after four or five attempts, the device will lock quickly enough that a password with a lower complexity requirement (for example, four or five characters) might provide sufficient protection because a brute force attack against the user's password would be unsuccessful. Other devices have the ability to completely wipe the information on the device after a certain number of invalid password attempts, typically set to around ten. If the user (or, more likely, an attacker) tries ten times unsuccessfully to enter the proper password for the device, all data on the device will be wiped out and the device will return to its factory-delivered state. While this renders the device itself usable to the attacker, it does prevent him from seeing any of its sensitive data, which is, in fact, the organization's primary concern.

Passwords and PINs are not the only authentication method for protecting mobile devices and their data. In particular, they are of no use on devices that do not have any input mechanisms to enable password entry. For such devices, other authentication methods will be required. The most common of these methods is the use of biometric authentication, most typically involving fingerprint scanning. Devices that utilize fingerprint authentication have a fingerprint reader built into

---

* In a highly litigious society, it is not difficult to imagine an employee suing his employer because he got into a car accident while trying to type "aCD%#$45" to gain access to his smartphone.

the device. Fingerprint readers use a registration process to capture the fingerprint of the user that has the authority to access the device. Once the authorized fingerprint is captured, the device is locked. To access the information, the proper user must press the correct finger against the sensor plate on the device for scanning and analysis. If the finger on the plate matches the one stored in the device's list of acceptable prints, access is allowed and the user can use the data stored on the device.

Another popular access method that does not necessarily require passwords or keyboard entry is the use of a smartcard for user authentication. Smartcards are credit card-sized devices that have on-board memory and processing capacity, and the device requiring authentication must have a proper smartcard reader built in or attached to it. Because of the physical size of the card and scanning device, this solution is typically found on larger devices like portable computers or laptops. Smartcards can store digital certificates for use during the authentication process. The certificates can be tied to a legitimate user, and only the presence of the proper card in the reader will permit the user to access the data on the device.

Of course, smartcards can be stolen by attackers who can use them just as easily as everyone else to provide authenticated access to a system. To provide enhanced authentication, smartcards are typically used in conjunction with a password or PIN that is memorized by the user and must be entered with the smartcard. In this way, the user is required to *know* something (the password or PIN) and *possess* something (the smartcard) in order to complete the authentication process—a process commonly known as *two-factor authentication*. Two-factor authentication is much more difficult for an attacker to break, as she must not only steal the smartcard, but she must also know (or be able to guess) the user's password or PIN.

Access Controls

More than any other type of data protection, access controls provide the ability to fine-tune the way data on a mobile device is made available to its users. The term *access controls* refers to (a) the mechanisms used to control who can access specific information and (b) the procedures for making that determination. Access control can be implemented in a variety of different forms, depending on the type of device in use. In general, as the complexity of the device increases, so does the number of available access controls.

For example, general-purpose desktop and laptop computers have a wide variety of access controls available as part of the computer's base operating system. These controls are based on the user identity presented during the login authentication process. Depending on the operating system in use (typically either Windows, MacOS, or Unix/Linux), access controls can be set at the file, directory, or program level and can specify who has the ability to read from, write to, or execute certain files on the system. Access controls on end-user computers can get quite complicated (for example, allowing the creation of specific groups of users and assigning read, write, modify, create, and execute permissions based on that group membership), but most organizations tend to reserve complicated access control restrictions for their servers and network-based data-storage areas.

End-user access control is based only on individual user spaces. When a user logs in to her laptop, she is assigned a particular file space for personal use. She can read files from that space and write files to that space, but she cannot read or write files from any other user's file spaces (unless that user gives her specific permission to do so). Likewise, other users of the system (with different identification and authentication credentials) cannot access this user's files or directories unless the user specifically allows this type of access. As a method of protecting mobile data on these computers, this method of access control presents a good compromise between protection of data, ease of administration, and ease of use.

Keep in mind, however, that even operating system–based access controls are effective only as long as that operating system is managing access to that device. If an attacker is able to remove the drive from the computer and load it into another system—or boot that same system with an alternative operating system for which he has administrative privileges—he may be able to bypass those access controls and access the data directly. This is another reason why good physical security is an essential part of all information-security efforts.

For devices such as flash drives, optical media, cell phones, and portable music players that do not have the granular, user- and file-based access controls seen in general-purpose computers, the ability to provide effective access control becomes more problematic. In some cases, the use of a password becomes the sole method of access control, barring access to those who do not know the proper password or PIN. However, such control is an all-or-nothing affair; once you supply the password and gain access to the device, all the data stored on that device is at your disposal.

Encryption

Perhaps the most effective form of at-rest data protection available for mobile devices is the use of encryption. Encryption is the process of scrambling information through the use of a mathematical algorithm in such a way that the data is not usable unless the user employs a specific key—a special password—to unscramble (or decrypt) the data. Encryption incorporates both authentication and access control into a single process. The authentication comes from the knowledge of the decryption key. Only authorized individuals should have access to the proper key (or keys) to decrypt the data, so the ability to properly perform the decryption serves as proof of their identity. This assumes, of course, that the secret key has not been discovered by an attacker and used surreptitiously to decrypt the data. This, however, is a problem with authentication schemes in general and not a problem particular to encryption.

Encryption can also provide access control by sharing the decryption key only with authorized individuals, thus restricting unauthorized people from accessing the data. Alternatively, some encryption methods allow the use of multiple keys, one for each person authorized to access the data. This ensures that if one person's key is compromised, only that key needs to be changed, making administration of keys easier.

Encryption is such an important topic, and its proper use and deployment are so critical to effective mobile data security, that an entire chapter of this book has been devoted to its description and use. Chapter 6 covers encryption in the mobile world in greater detail.

Effective Data Management

Aside from authentication, access control, and encryption, there is a fourth method to protect sensitive information from the perils of mobile device use: effective data management. The most important point about effective mobile data management can be condensed down to a single basic idea: *If it doesn't need to be stored on a mobile device, don't store it on a mobile device.*

While this simple idea may sound intuitive, it is surprising how many users fail to follow this single protection control. In this age of always-on Internet connectivity, ever-expanding hoards of files and data, and unlimited availability of cheap storage, the idea of "taking it all with you" is a reality to many. When people travel, they like to have all their files with them, whether or not they will actually need them during their travels. Likewise, end users stock their hard drives with every file they have ever created (such as documents, photos, music, movies) without ever stopping to clean out old or unneeded data. Unfortunately, that hoard of files makes quite the inviting target for an attacker. Even if the attacker doesn't know what is on the device or disk when he steals it, think of the vast amounts of information that he will find when he surveys his take. Was all that data really necessary to store on such a vulnerable device? Probably not.

To find out if you are violating this simple rule, take a look at the mobile device you use the most often and answer these three simple questions:

1. How many of the files on the device do you use on a regular basis?
2. If the device contains a phone book or contact list, how many of those contacts do you converse with regularly?
3. How much past and future calendar information do you store on the device?

If you are only using a small percentage of the files or contacts, or if you have past and future calendar information that you rarely refer to, you may be in danger of having too much information on your portable device. While it may be functionally easier just to synchronize everything you have on your desktop system to the mobile device ("just in case I may need it while I'm out of the office"), having so much data not only threatens the security of your company's sensitive information, it may also threaten the security and privacy of your personal life or that of your friends and family. Keep as much of your valuable and sensitive information as possible *off* the mobile device in the first place! Then apply the appropriate authentication, access control, and encryption protections as needed to protect whatever is left.

The Problem of Heterogeneous Information

There is one last point about data at rest that is important to consider and will have a bearing on how you approach protecting mobile data. Data at rest is rarely homogeneous, meaning that different types of data are usually stored together in the same storage area. As proof, consider the hard disk on your main PC. It's likely that you have business documents, a few spreadsheets, some personal files, a collection of photographs, some music files, personal contact files, and calendar and schedule data stored on the same system. That's just the information you manage yourself. There are also data and storage that the operating system manages on your behalf, such as temporary files, Web-surfing histories, and trash/recycle bins. Most smartphones and PDAs have many of the same types of data on them, with perhaps a greater emphasis on contact and calendar information. Finally, the average flash drive will contain a mix of whatever data you needed to work on in the past few weeks or months. In practice, flash drives and portable hard drives tend to accumulate data until they become full and need to be cleaned out.

It is nearly impossible to examine the average computer drive, PDA, or portable hard drive and say, "These are all financial spreadsheets," or "These are all personal photos," or even, "This is only data on the Acme merger." It is more likely that the device will contain a mix of all those and much, much more. Therefore, the method for determining the type of protection this data requires—the answer to "what are you trying to protect?"—becomes much harder. In such situations, the only thing to do is to provide sufficient security (authentication, access control, or encryption) to protect the most valuable or sensitive piece of information on the device. This simplifies the management of the device and its associated security controls, but it increases the organizational cost and effort required to provide protections across the enterprise. In the absence of clear evidence that specific devices or data need lesser controls (because the data they contain is less sensitive), or that some employees don't store any sensitive data on mobile devices (as unlikely as that may seem), the organization has no choice but to plan for (and spend money on) appropriate security technology to cover all data, employees, and devices, whether or not they need it. This raises the expense of security to the organization and, depending on its size, may send the cost of security beyond the organization's ability to afford it.

In the end, data at rest is an inviting target. Given the general casualness with which most people manage and track their mobile devices, the lack of built-in controls many devices have, and the ever-growing amount of data users store on them, most mobile devices contain at least some valuable personal or corporate information that could be of benefit to an information thief or broker. In addition, because the data is at rest—because it is fixed in place even though it is on a mobile device—there is no need for an attacker to gather and collect it from multiple locations. This makes for a very inviting target, and one that is not difficult to exploit. It becomes a simple matter of time, effort, and resources that determines how long it will take the attacker to access the information.

However, because it's your device—and because you (or your company) have control over the protections used on that device—you do have the ability to provide effective security to make the attacker's job harder. Remember the basic defense-in-depth approach to security and use a combination of physical and logical controls to protect data at rest. Remove data from a mobile device when it is no longer needed, and apply whatever authentication, access controls, and encryption are available and appropriate to cover the sensitivity of the data and the threats that exist to obtain it.

Protecting Data in Motion

Data at rest is not our only concern, however. Remember, the alternative to data at rest is data in motion. While data residing on a mobile device is considered at rest, that data must get on the device in some manner, and the method used to move data to a mobile device falls into the category of data in motion. To give but a few examples of data in motion, consider the following:

- Synchronizing e-mail and calendar information to a smartphone or PDA over a cellular network
- Transferring data files to a mobile device over a WiFi network connection
- Using a Bluetooth network to attach a keyboard or headset to a mobile phone
- Exchanging e-mail or text (SMS) messages using a mobile device
- Downloading digital media content to a mobile device over a wired or wireless network

All of these scenarios use the mobile device as the source or destination point in a communications session, and in each case the device interacts with data in motion to complete its task. The data in motion might be a file; general information that the user can read, write, or store on the device at a later time; or "command and control" information sent to the mobile device (for example, keystrokes from a Bluetooth keyboard or phone-dialing instructions from an in-car hands-free set). Nevertheless, the data in motion can be just as important—and just as exploitable—as the at-rest information stored on the device.

The main difference in the approach to securing data in motion vs. data at rest is one of ownership and control. With data at rest, you typically own (or have the authorization to possess) both the data in question and the environment in which the data resides (the mobile device). That ownership gives you wide latitude with which to configure, operate, and manage the device and its information. By contrast, data in motion often travels through an environment that is primarily outside of your control, which limits your ability to change the environment to suit your particular security needs. You probably don't own the cellular network that your mobile phone uses to communicate. You can't control the Internet links and infrastructure where your data travels. You don't have a say in the TCP/IP or SMS protocols that are used to send your data. You probably don't even have much ability to configure your communications and application services to define the type of security you expect or require. In short, data in motion is often at the mercy of a number of different services and service providers, none of which may have your best interest in mind as your data winds its way through their systems and networks.

Despite this, you still need to ensure that both data and control information are as secure as possible through those networks. The good news is that there are a number of things you can do to inject security into the stream and have a chance of keeping both the data and the device relatively secure. Just as we did for data at rest, let's split the analysis of data in motion into physical and logical components.

Physical Controls

Unfortunately, there's not much but bad news on the physical security side of data in motion. With the exception of the mobile device itself, the physical security of data in motion is almost entirely outside of your control. During the discussion of data at rest, an emphasis was placed on protecting the location where the data resides, namely the mobile device where it rests. With data in motion, the data doesn't "rest" in any one place for very long and may travel hundreds or thousands of miles through multiple network devices between its source and destination. Therefore, every bit of that journey must have adequate physical security protection to ensure that the data is safe all along the communication path. This includes the entire network infrastructure between the source and destination of the journey. Routers, switches, hubs, wireless access points, firewalls, and all the other technology that is essential to moving information from point to point must be secured against intrusion (both physical and logical). Since you don't own most of that infrastructure, you must rely on various service providers along the way to ensure that security, and none but the largest of their customers may have the ability to verify that security in any meaningful manner.

Despite that, if you have physical control over the endpoints of the communications (for example, a smartphone and the server where the e-mail and calendar information is stored), you must do all that you can to ensure the physical security of those devices. This involves taking the appropriate measures for physically securing mobile devices discussed earlier, as well as employing a defense-in-depth approach to securing the data server.

Logical Protections

As much as the physical protections may be out of your control, there are a number of things you can do from a logical-protection standpoint that will provide effective controls for the data as it moves in, out, or through your devices. Some of these protections are similar to those you can use to protect information in a nonmobile environment, while others are unique to the mobile environment. For example, you should ensure that the operating system and all the software used on mobile devices are up to date with available security patches and configuration options, just as you would in a desktop or server environment. Because more malware and protocol attacks are now specifically targeting mobile devices, it is important that these devices remain as up to date as possible.

The Rise of Monocultures

The need to keep mobile devices updated represents a dramatic change of behavior in the mobile environment because mobile users are not accustomed to updating the software on their phones and PDAs. With standard PCs and laptops, users have come to understand that the system and application programs need to be updated on a regular basis. While there is still a large percentage of the user population that does not actually perform the required updates, the need and process for doing so are well understood among system administrators and becoming more so among the general public. In addition, commercial and government enterprises typically have enterprise-wide processes for keeping their systems up to date, and commercial operating systems have capabilities to automate the download and installation of updates and patches should the user (or his organization) elect to enable them.

Until recently, the need for continuous update and configuration modification was virtually unheard of when it came to mobile devices. Most consumers purchase a phone or PDA and *never* update the software on the device. Historically, this has not presented much of a problem, as malware and protocol attacks against mobile devices were mostly theoretical and difficult to execute. In addition, the mobile device market (in particular the mobile phone market) has been extremely fragmented, with no single company gaining decisive dominance of the market. Contrast this with the personal computer market, where Microsoft is far and away the dominant operating system, with Apple and various Linux distributions running a distant second and third place. An attacker wishing to launch a successful attack in that environment has historically aimed that attack at Microsoft-based systems in order to have the biggest impact on the widest possible audience. Over the past several years, as Apple and Linux have gained in popularity, new attacks targeting these specific platforms have likewise been on the rise.

The mobile phone market, however, has had no such dominance. The market has been fragmented by many manufacturers, and the operating systems used on mobile devices have often been custom-built for particular device families. An attacker wishing to have a large impact would need to discover a vulnerability that was common to a number of different platforms, then develop code that could successfully exploit that vulnerability on all those platforms. Though not an impossible scenario to imagine, in reality this has kept the number of mobile-specific attacks to a minimum.

In the past few years, however, the mobile device landscape has changed. There are now several dominant (or potentially dominant) mobile device platforms, such as RIM's BlackBerry family, Windows Mobile, the iPhone OS (a derivative of Mac OSX), Symbian, and (more recently) Android. Manufacturers and application developers are beginning to line up behind these systems in an attempt to streamline development and production costs and satisfy growing consumer demand. As a result, the marketplace is seeing the rise of monocultures in the mobile device market, just as it saw in the PC computing market. Once one or two of these platforms become the dominant players in the marketplace and a critical mass of devices are designed and built around these dominant platforms, the number and severity of platform-specific attacks will rise sharply. Because of this, consumers— who until now have never had to pay attention to updating the software on their mobile devices—will need to begin doing so, and antimalware companies will need to step up their efforts to provide more effective protection on these new platforms. In addition, software developers will need to begin understanding how to develop secure applications for these mobile devices, a skill that is still sorely lacking in the nonmobile application development space.

With all this gloom and doom, however, comes a ray of hope. Because of the experience and the long history of security and antimalware protections that are now available in the nonmobile marketplace, the transition of these capabilities to the mobile device space should not take nearly as long as it did in the general computer industry, nor will it be as painful. The antimalware industry is now mature enough to deal with the newest threats as they come along,* and software developers now growing up in the industry are being taught the importance of secure code development, something their predecessors had to learn for themselves. While there will always be mobile security issues to deal with, the industry appears to be addressing these problems much more quickly and with greater resolve than ever before.

Insecurity in the Links

Keeping up to date with patches and upgrades is not the only protection to be considered to protect data in motion. The transmission of information to and from the mobile device (the very essence of data in motion) needs to be protected as much as possible. As data travels across the network (or, typically, several networks), it passes through many different junction points along the way where the data may be observed, copied, interrupted, or altered. These junction points are the links

---

* Not perfect, mind you. Just mature.

between networks and the various devices organizations use to deploy, maintain, and protect their infrastructures—devices like network routers and switches, firewalls, load balancers, proxy servers, intrusion detection/prevention devices (IDS/IPS), relay systems, and communications servers. At any one of these points, the traffic is visible and highly susceptible to interception. Not all of this interception is necessarily malicious, however.

There are many situations where network traffic needs to be observed and recorded for legitimate purposes. Network operators and administrators routinely monitor network traffic to ensure optimum performance on their networks. Load-balancing devices must analyze network traffic to ensure that the traffic load is efficiently spread across the enterprise's infrastructure. Proxy, firewall, and IDS/IPS systems must analyze network traffic to detect and block harmful or malicious activity. In all these cases, however, the traffic is being analyzed in order to understand the flow, intent, and impact of the data and to react accordingly (by altering the traffic flow, blocking the traffic, or changing the network's operating parameters). In none of these examples is the data captured for nefarious purposes or with the intent of causing harm to the sender or the organization.

Unfortunately, there can be no good without a corresponding evil. If these junction points were all operated by benevolent personnel with no other agenda than the quick, efficient, and economical flow of data from point to point, we would have no further worries. However, that is clearly not the case, nor can we assume this to be true even within one's own organization. All of these junction points present opportunities for an attacker to tap into the network and observe the traffic, either to copy and use the information at a later time or to disrupt and alter the transmission for an immediate evil payoff. Because the junction points may span several networks run by multiple organizations, there are many, many points of control where information can be intercepted—almost all of them outside your direct control or ability to manage—and there is no way to comprehensively ensure that all the junction points along the way are secured or operated in a secure manner. For that reason, the best approach to ensuring protection of data in motion is to secure the transmissions themselves, as this is one of the only ways to guarantee the security of information as it moves from the source point to its destination.

The most common way to do this is through the use of encryption to protect data transmission between the mobile device and the system with which it needs to exchange data. Encryption, however, is not universal, nor is it uniformly applied on all devices or applications. Depending on the particular device you possess and the application on that device that is transmitting or receiving information, encryption may or may not be available. For example, users of the BlackBerry family of products enjoy the use of encryption as e-mail and calendar updates are transmitted back and forth between the BlackBerry device and the e-mail and calendaring systems in the enterprise. This e-mail and scheduling information cannot be decrypted as the data moves over the network. Those same devices, however, have the ability to run other applications, such as instant messaging (IM), Web browsers, external e-mail applications, business applications, and games. The use of encryption in these applications is dependent on whether or not the application itself has encryption designed into its operation. Most IM packages do not use encryption (or only make it available as a selectable option), and Web browsers use it intermittently based on the security requirements of the Web server it is accessing at any given time. Some third-party e-mail systems (like Yahoo! mail) have the ability to use encryption but rely on the end user to enable this feature. In fact, Google's Gmail system had such an option until early 2010, when it switched to the use of encryption by default for all users. Other business and entertainment applications generally do not use encryption to protect data transmissions, but may do so on a selective basis. Therefore, do not assume the presence of encryption for data transmissions from mobile devices.

As a result, organizations may want to consider limiting the applications that have the ability to exchange data with systems in the enterprise. Many organizations allow their users to install applications and programs that transmit data to and from the device without understanding the security controls of those applications or the information-protection mechanisms that may be available. Users, who see these applications as a way of increasing their productivity (both professional and personal), install and run them without giving a second thought to how the application protects their information. Organizations wishing to stem potential information loss or compromise may want to review what applications it allows on mobile devices, with an emphasis on understanding the data these applications transmit and how it is protected.

Multiple Networks Mean Multiple Data Paths

An organization should also look at the various types of system and network connectivity that it allows on mobile devices within its environment. "Dumb" mobile devices (such as flash drives and optical media) generally don't have network connectivity and rely on the actions of the user to move data to and from the device. "Smart" devices (such as PDAs, smartphones, and some media players) usually have one or more network connectivity options, ranging from cellular services and WiFi to Bluetooth and Ethernet. Because data is transmitted to and from the device using these network connections, they should be a point of consideration when establishing mobile device configuration standards. Users will want to have all possible connectivity options available to them, while organizations may want to restrict one or more for security reasons.

For example, suppose an organization's smartphone synchronization service connects to its employees' phones using the cellular phone network. This gives the organization the ability to specify the use of encryption during all such transmissions, thus securing the data that is sent to the devices over the air. However, the same devices also often have WiFi or Bluetooth networking capabilities as well, which require separate connectivity and configuration. Ironically, information that is painstakingly secured when sent from the enterprise server to the device can be immediately retransmitted out of the same device over an insecure WiFi connection found at the local Starbucks. The careful protections established by the organization may not be pervasive on all the device's connectivity options. For this reason, organizations wishing to place tighter control on the mobile devices in their enterprise might want to examine the effects on security and usability of restricting the use of the various connectivity options available to mobile device users.

Organizations must also consider the security of Personal Area Networks (PANs), such as those enabled by the Bluetooth protocol. Bluetooth allows for devices like cell phones, computers, printers, keyboards, and headsets to connect and exchange data over a small geographical area. Bluetooth has been a boon to the mobile device market because it provides the ability to add peripherals and extend functionality for mobile devices without the need for dedicated wires between each device. For example, smartphone users can use a Bluetooth headset connected to their cell phone to speak on the phone without the need to hold the handset (a great aid while doing things like typing or driving), connect a keyboard and mouse to a PDA to overcome the limitations of the small built-in keyboard, or print files to a Bluetooth-enabled printer without being directly wired to the printer.

One of Bluetooth's greatest strengths (and, of course, its greatest security weakness) is the ability to connect Bluetooth devices together with minimal effort. Many Bluetooth devices, by default, allow themselves to be "discoverable," meaning that any Bluetooth device in the area can scan for other discoverable Bluetooth devices and, once found, connect to them without the need for authentication. This enables two Bluetooth users to exchange contact information and ringtones easily, but it also means that an attacker can scan for open and accessible Bluetooth devices in a crowded area. Once connected, the attacker may be able to read e-mail, download phone book information, or copy data from the device without the victim's knowledge or consent. The Bluetooth specification does allow for authentication to be required before two Bluetooth devices can connect, but most devices have a default authentication PIN of "0000" or "1234," and users rarely change this code. Attackers know this, making infiltration of Bluetooth devices a simple matter.

For this reason, Bluetooth capabilities on mobile devices should be closely monitored and possibly restricted, as dictated by the organization's security stance and policies. At a minimum, Bluetooth devices should have their discoverability turned off by default to prevent surreptitious connections to the device without the device owner's knowledge. Turning off discoverability on your Bluetooth-enabled phone will not prevent you from initiating a connection from your phone to another Bluetooth device; it just means that you will have to manually (and intentionally) initiate the connection.

An organization should determine which Bluetooth devices and functions it will and won't allow. For example, it might permit the use of headsets and keyboards but determine that the transfer of data files or contact information may be an unacceptable risk. If so, the organization will need to determine whether the technology exists to restrict certain types of Bluetooth functionality on the devices it manages. If not, it may have to step up its communications and awareness efforts to inform employees of the potential dangers and risks of Bluetooth usage and try to enlist their assistance in reducing threats from Bluetooth connectivity.

Finally, any effort to secure data in motion should not focus exclusively on wireless connectivity. Wired connectivity between data on the company's computers and data on mobile devices is a primary method for the movement of information to devices that do not have wireless networking capability. Many mobile devices come with management software that helps the user administer the device and synchronize data between the device and the user's desktop computer. Unless the organization has restrictions on the applications that can be loaded onto end-user PCs and the devices (such as docking stations) that can be attached to those PCs, there is little that can stop an employee from attaching his smartphone, PDA, or portable music player to his PC, installing the device's synchronization software, and moving data between the two systems at will. Even if the data on the PC is tightly controlled and protected, there is no way to ensure that the protections will survive the transfer from PC to mobile device. For instance, if the data in question was encrypted on a PC using full-disk encryption, that file will not be encrypted once it is moved to the mobile device unless that device also uses full-disk encryption. Although access to the data may be restricted by user-based access-control mechanisms on the PC, those same mechanisms may not exist on the mobile device, allowing anyone with access to the device to view that data.

Establishing PC Restrictions

To counter this problem, many organizations have begun placing restrictions on the devices and software that end users can install on their PCs without corporate approval and support. While some companies have hesitated to initiate this practice (fearing losses in productivity and end-user backlash), many have begun to increase the level of control they place on their workstation environment. The goal is to restrict the applications that can move data to the mobile device in the first place to prevent the unauthorized transfer of sensitive data. We'll take a closer look at workstation-based configuration management in Chapters 7 and 8.

Conclusion

While data at rest is a difficult security problem to deal with, data in motion is an even tougher security nut to crack. Because the data moves rapidly outside of your control, it's exposed to hostile forces throughout its journey. In many cases, particularly with data transmissions across public networks, your data will be intermixed with the data from hundreds or thousands of other transmissions along the same network path, thus getting lost in the mix and becoming slightly less susceptible as a direct target of interception. However, as we discussed in the section on data at rest, obscurity alone is not considered an effective defense against information attacks. Therefore, you should assume that the data will be visible and vulnerable as it passes through every network device, firewall, load balancer, and IPS on the network. The paranoid assumption to make—in fact, the most secure assumption that can be made—is that each of these devices, networks, and junction points exists in a hostile environment, or at least has attackers monitoring those points looking for data to exploit. Therefore, in order to protect data in motion, you need to adopt two basic approaches:

1. Encrypt data in motion wherever possible.
2. Limit the use of applications and devices that cannot support approach 2.

While the ultimate desire would be to have a uniform security effort to cover both data at rest and data in motion, the reality is that such comprehensive controls are not available with current technology and within the context of the average mobile data user's work habits and security consciousness. Few within the typical enterprise would say that they are unconcerned about protecting mobile data or are willing to put the organization's data in jeopardy. However, their actions and insecure behaviors—the use of USB drives on public machines, execution of files and disks from unverified sources, loading of unknown and unverified applications on their smartphones, connecting to open WiFi hotspots, enabling open Bluetooth discoverability on their phones, and the disclosure of sensitive company information through mobile-based instant messaging and peer-to-peer applications—belie their security protestations.

It is precisely for these reasons that organizations are looking to regain control of the "personal" electronics environment in their enterprises. They are continuously evaluating the state of the mobile device security market and the ability for their infrastructures to take advantage of changes in that market. Until that happens, however, both data at rest on mobile devices and data in motion to and from mobile devices will be vulnerable to eavesdropping, disruption, interception, and alteration, even as they continue to enhance the effectiveness and productivity of the workforce.

This chapter began with an adaptation of Newton's first law of motion. Data at rest will stay at rest until an outside force sets it in motion, and data in motion will continue in motion unless an outside force stops it. Both states of data are interrelated, and the movement of data in, through, and from mobile devices is a natural process we all now take for granted. In the same way that Newton's objects were in a continuous flux between motion and rest as they interact with the forces around them, data in the modern enterprise continuously moves between rest and motion in an effort to satisfy our continual need for information access, movement, and management. As data moves between these two states, its availability, susceptibility, and overall risk profile changes based on the current environment, the available security in that environment, and the nature of the "outside forces" seeking to change its state.

There is no way to completely protect all mobile data all the time. To do so would most likely render it unusable and (as a result) valueless. To help keep it useful and retain its value, you need to understand these two states of data. Securing mobile data—whether in motion or at rest—is a process of bringing the appropriate "external forces" to bear so that data in either state maintains the highest level of security available without unduly interfering with the data's motion or path. Managing data at rest and data in motion does not require the intelligence or insight of a legendary physicist. It just requires the knowledge of one's own needs, capabilities, and environment.

Action Plan

The basic premise of this chapter was to understand the characteristics of both data at rest and data in motion, as well as gain an understanding of how data moves between both states. An in-depth treatment of Newton's laws of motion is not necessary to fully appreciate these two aspects of mobile data, but it does help characterize the ways that data moves between motion and resting states.

The following activities may also help characterize your own company's plan for securing mobile data, both at rest and in motion.

1. Evaluate where your most valuable mobile "at rest" data may be located.
   - Laptops and portable computers
   - Smartphones or PDAs
   - Portable media
   - Mobile applications and utilities

2. For each of these locations, determine if there are any physical security protections in place (or that can be added) to protect those "at rest" points.
   - Specialized containers
   - Specialized packaging
   - Specialized couriers or transportation methods

3. Evaluate the logical protection methods that your company would consider applicable and acceptable to protect the mobile data and devices in your environment, both at rest and in motion.
   - Passwords or PINs
   - Biometrics
   - Access controls for devices or individual data sets
   - Encryption
   - Application restrictions
   - Removal of unnecessary data
   - Tighter device configuration controls

Notes

1. I. B. Cohen and A. Whitman, "Isaac Newton, *The Principia*, A New Translation" (Berkeley: University of California Press, 1999).
2. Times Online, "Major MI5 operation against al-Qaeda endangered by security breach," April 9, 2009, http://www.timesonline.co.uk/tol/news/uk/crime/article6061914.ece.
3. Glen Collins, "A Treasure Travels, Inconspicuously," *New York Times*, June 16, 2008, http://www.nytimes.com/2008/06/16/nyregion/16coins.html?_r=2&oref=slogin.

Chapter 5

Mobile Data Security Models

You are faced with the task (or "problem," or "challenge," or "opportunity," depending on how you look at it) of protecting your organization's mobile data and somehow managing the proliferation of that data on the abundance of mobile devices cropping up in your organization like weeds in a flower garden. What's been made clear in previous chapters is that the two aspects of the mobile security issue—the data itself and the device on which that data is transported—are intertwined both in their ability to enhance and accelerate the exchange of information between people and in the security concerns and risks that each present to the organization. Despite this interdependence, however, many companies approach the protection of mobile data and the protection of mobile devices as two independent tasks, each requiring its own policy, technology, and process changes to implement. In such an approach, the belief is that protecting either the data or the device independently will provide sufficient security to enable the protection of the organization's sensitive information without the need to apply additional controls or "over secure" the company's assets. In order to evaluate the effectiveness of such a strategy, let's look at two approaches to mobile security—the device-centric approach and the data-centric approach—to determine how each can (and cannot) independently protect the organization's information from prying eyes.

A Device-Centric Model

The device-centric model of mobile security focuses on mobile devices themselves as the root of mobile security problems. The model is based on the notion that mobile devices are the vehicle for transporting information from place to place. Therefore, in order to secure that information, you must secure the devices themselves against compromise or corruption. Each device in a device-centric model is treated as an individual entity capable of storing and transporting confidential data and can be used as the sole transport mechanism or as a single link in a chain of multiple transport mechanisms. To provide the protection that mobile data needs, each mobile device in the communications chain must be capable of supporting one or more of the following security services:

■ Access control
■ Data-flow restrictions
■ Device management
■ Selective feature restrictions
■ Logging and auditing capabilities

Access Control

The device must support the prevention of access to the device's data store without the proper authentication and authorization. This can come from the knowledge of a basic password (the most common type of mobile device authentication) or through more complex credentials, such as a smartcard, token authenticator, certificate, or directory lookup. Whatever method is used, the device must be able to distinguish not only whether a user is authorized to access a device, but whether that access is restricted in any way. For example, most secured flash drives utilize a single password for access control. If the user knows the password, she will have access to all the information on that drive. Laptops, on the other hand, have a more complex access-control mechanism. When a user logs into Windows (the more recent versions) or Linux on a laptop, she will only have access to those files and directories that have been specifically authorized for her use. This allows multiple users on the same device while reducing the risk that one user's confidential information will be visible to another.

Another form of access control for mobile devices is to restrict the availability of mobile devices within the enterprise and limit the number of people who are permitted to use them. Through a combination of policy and technology restrictions, the organization may be able to limit the mobile devices that can connect to users' workstations in the first place to only those devices that have proven (and manageable) security controls. In addition, the organization can also try to limit the availability of mobile devices to only those employees who have a demonstrated business need for one. While this will not necessarily protect the information on the device itself, it will reduce the number of people who can move sensitive data from the enterprise to mobile devices, somewhat reducing the overall risk of a random employee stealing confidential information by attaching an arbitrary device to the network. This should not be considered a primary control, as authorized people can still do bad things with the data to which they have access, but a true defense-in-depth strategy encourages any additional layers of control that can be employed easily without placing an undue burden on the organization or its employees.

Access control on dual-use devices can be trickier to implement. If the data-storage portion of the device is separated logically or physically from the operational portion of the device, access control is more easily accomplished, as available technology can recognize the two components separately. For instance, it can allow access to a USB keyboard but deny access to the flash drive slot embedded in that keyboard. This will enable the productive use of the device while limiting the connectivity of portable media. For many devices, however, this separation is not as easy to implement. For example, smartphones not only manage a wealth of sensitive data, they may also provide the ability to insert a flash memory card for additional storage. Blocking access to the flash drive only solves half the data-protection problem on such a device, since the unblocked portion may still contain company secrets. This may be a case of "some protection is better than no protection at all," but understanding the limits of the available technology and the limited extent to which information can be protected at the device level is a key factor in a device-centric approach.

Other devices, such as many portable music players, use the data-drive portion of the device for both content storage and random data storage without any meaningful way to distinguish between the two types of data. Blocking access to the drive disables access to all data, both operational and general storage. The organization that is willing to allow such devices in the name of productivity or employee satisfaction must be willing to accept the risk that they may be used to store much more than just music or movies for personal entertainment.

Data-Flow Restrictions

There is now a great deal of useful information distributed via mobile media, so a complete ban on all mobile devices may not be practical for some organizations. For example, software installations often come on CD or DVD, vendors and marketers provide technical documentation and product information on DVD or flash drives, and meeting or conference materials are now often provided to attendees on flash drives for convenience. Prohibiting access to these devices and media presents a legitimate obstacle to an employee who is trying to get work done using the material on that media. As a result, viewing access control as something other than a binary on/off or allow/deny proposition is in order. For example, an organization might be more concerned with information leaking *out* of the organization through a mobile device than it is with malware *entering* the organization through that device. The organization taking such a position makes the assumption that there is sufficient malware control available in the environment to detect and block any malicious code coming from the mobile device. Therefore, it may allow unrestricted access to the device for reading data, but prohibit any data from being written to the device.* This will enable users to reap the benefits of mobile devices and media for activities such as software installation or receiving technical documentation, but protect the organization against the use of those devices to extract the company's own internal technical information out of the organization.

Device Management

As the number and types of mobile devices continue to proliferate, organizations are facing the daunting task of determining which devices to permit onto their networks and how to track those devices to ensure continued efficient and secure operation of the enterprise. A primary consideration for a device-centric security environment is the ability to manage all those mobile devices in a centralized, enterprise-wide manner. Enabling some of the security and data protection mechanisms described in this book can be effective if deployed on an individual basis to each device, but managing that deployment in such a manner will quickly tax the resources of any organization once the number of devices and the complexity of the security controls reach a critical mass. Larger organizations may be able to absorb the effort as a part of their standard end-user support function, but even the largest organizations will struggle to effectively manage the security of mobile devices numbering in the hundreds or thousands without centralizing and streamlining the configuration of those devices.

For this reason, an organization utilizing a device-centric approach should standardize and limit the number of supported devices to a select few types and models. These device models will be the ones that offer the best combination of features and functionality, data protection capabilities, and (most importantly) the ability to track and manage the devices through a centralized device-management system. The organization may need more than one of these systems to manage different types of devices. For example, it may have one system to manage all the smartphones in the company and another to manage and secure mobile PCs. No matter how many there are, several factors will weigh into the selection consideration for such a service:

■ Does the management system support the devices the organization uses (or wants to use)? This includes general device types as well as specific device models.

---

* This may be a false assumption on the organization's part, since even the best antivirus programs don't detect a significant portion of the potential malicious code in the wild. Nevertheless, through a combination of malware detection, configuration control, and effective operating-system access controls, the organization may feel comfortable enough with its malware prevention and detection capabilities to take this stance on mobile device readability.

- Does the system enforce a standard security configuration for those devices? Is that configuration in line with the organization's security policies and standards?
- Does the system prevent the end user from bypassing the security controls on a device?
- Does the system allow for managing exceptions to the standard configuration? Despite the security policy, exceptions may be required for specific business reasons. The system should be able to handle this in a controlled manner.
- Does the system have adequate reporting capabilities to track usage and compliance with the security configuration and policies?
- Does the system allow new devices to be integrated into the "approved" list easily?

As you conduct a search to find the best device management technology, you may find that fulfilling all these requirements is difficult with the tools currently available on the market, so some trade-offs may be necessary to find the best fit for the organization. In addition, implementing a system to enforce device control across the enterprise might be too complex a task for some organizations to undertake. In response, many organizations are adopting a "hybrid" approach to device management.

In such an approach, the organization adopts a finite set of mobile devices it is willing to support within the enterprise. Employees wishing to attach mobile devices to the organization's infrastructure must choose devices that fit within the specifications established by the organization's device-management policies. If an employee does not wish to use one of the supported devices or is unwilling to comply with the security or operational restrictions using a supported device would entail, he is free to use a device of his own choosing. However, that device would not be allowed to connect to the organization's infrastructure, nor would it be allowed to exchange data between the device and the network. For an organization to put such a policy in place, it must have the ability to enforce it through tight controls over its end-user environment to ensure that unauthorized devices do not attach to, or exchange information with, the company network. Many organizations do not yet have the technical maturity or infrastructure control necessary to completely implement such a scheme on an enterprise-wide basis, and many potential device-control technologies do not have the capabilities or enterprise-scale maturity to absolutely enforce such a policy. Nevertheless, as organizational and technology maturity improve, this may be an approach that becomes more appealing for organizations looking to implement a policy that appeals to a broad set of employee needs.

Another option for an organization unable (or unwilling) to invest the resources required to implement appropriate technology on an enterprise scale is to implement them on a much smaller scale. The organization can select a few key or critical areas—for example, the legal department or the Human Resources organization—and implement the appropriate controls only in those selected areas. This allows the organization to create the proper security environment where it is most needed without going through the complexity and expense of deploying an enterprise-wide implementation. Once the benefits of the limited deployment are realized (such as fewer data-loss incidents and better control over data access) and the organization has a better understanding of the effective processes and resources required for managing such a program, it can make a more informed decision on whether it wants to expand the program to other areas of the organization.

Selective Feature Restrictions

Sometimes, it's not an entire device that presents a security concern to the organization; it's a single feature or set of features that affects the security of the entire device. For example:

- Many cell phones come with the ability to capture photos and movies, an activity that may be prohibited by organization policy.
- Many mobile devices incorporate the use of Bluetooth technology that, in certain circumstances, an attacker can use to connect to an unprotected device and extract information stored on that device.
- People who regularly give presentations often use a remote control with a wireless receiver attached to the presentation PC. In some models, that receiver also contains flash storage that can be used to introduce malware on the PC or extract data.

Each of these examples illustrates how certain features of a device can create security problems even if the device itself is accepted and supported by the organization. Rather than block the use of the entire device, an alternative is to selectively block particular features that are deemed too risky or unmanageable for the organization to allow. In the examples above, the camera feature of the phone can be disabled to prevent unauthorized photos or videos without affecting the rest of the phone's functionality. The Bluetooth discoverability feature can be disabled without affecting the user's ability to use headsets or hands-free devices. And the data-storage portion of the remote pointing device can be disabled without affecting the device's ability to properly operate the slide show.

These are all examples of selective device restrictions: blocking or modifying selective services on a device while leaving the remainder of the device operational. This can be an ideal solution for managing troublesome services on otherwise acceptable and useful devices. The ability to selectively block services, however, is highly dependent on the method used to manage the configuration of the mobile devices in the enterprise. If a central management service is used, it might be possible to implement selective restrictions uniformly to all devices throughout the organization. Even if the troublesome services are spread among several technologies (such as the above examples illustrate) served by multiple management systems, each management system can be used to apply control to the devices under its command.

However, if such a central management system is not available, the restrictions will have to be applied manually or left to the discretion of the end users to implement. This latter course of action is, of course, the least desirable, as relying on end users to implement critical security controls rarely leads to a satisfactory outcome.

The types of devices in use within the organization may also play a part in restricting the flow of data. Some devices have limitations on the amount of available storage, which may limit the concern the organization may have for its usefulness as an illicit data-extraction tool. For example, an organization may not be too concerned with restricting the flow of data to floppy disk drives because of their limited storage capacity (1–2 megabytes). While an attacker might be able to compress data enough to fit on such a device, or move one file at a time until he has gathered enough data to suit his purposes, the loss might be too small or the incidence of those devices in the environment too sparse to allocate technical or personnel resources to deal with that specific problem. On the other hand, recordable DVDs and flash drives can hold gigabytes of data, and portable hard drives can hold hundreds of gigabytes, which is certainly enough to move significant amounts of data out of an organization. That amount of potential data loss is likely to reach the level of concern that an organization would be willing to allocate resources to prevent. Because no organization will be able to address all the potential risks and potential devices, the knowledge of what is within bounds from a risk perspective—based on the capabilities and capacities of particular devices—is a good way to start focusing these important resources.

Likewise, the security capabilities of a particular device or its supporting services will play into the data-flow decision as well. The organization may decide that hardware-encrypted flash drives are acceptable because of the data protection they provide. Thus, it can block the use of nonencrypted drives while allowing encrypted drives to operate normally. If a particular brand of smartphone allows the organization to configure security settings such as password use and complexity, storage encryption, timeout locking, and remote deletion of data, it may be willing to permit those devices while, at the same time, restricting the use of other devices that do not possess such capabilities. The determination on what feature sets will place a particular device in the "prohibit" category or the "allow" category are based on a number of factors.

The first factor is the detection and control capabilities of the device-management technology used to enforce device restrictions in the enterprise. The granularity with which a particular management system can detect and block certain devices will have a bearing on whether the organization can implement the desired level of device control. For example, if a blocking product can recognize the existence of a USB drive but can't determine if the drive employs encryption or not, that will hamper the organization's ability to enforce the use of encryption for external storage drivers. Because encryption on mobile devices can be enabled through both hardware and software, the blocking technology should have the ability to recognize when either is available.

Many USB-device-blocking technologies recognize the specific type of device based on a descriptor embedded in each USB device. That descriptor includes a unique device manufacturer number (assigned by the USB Implementers Forum, an industry group created to promote and standardize the use of USB technology) and the model number for that particular device (assigned by the device's manufacturer). Devices that employ hardware-based encryption are easily recognized by such technology because it's a simple matter to allow access to those devices whose USB descriptor indicates a device model that has been approved for company use. In contrast, encrypted storage capability that has been added to a generic USB drive may not be recognized by the blocking technology because there is no way of knowing if the encryption is active or not when the device is queried by the blocking technology. This makes the decision logic for allowing or denying access to a particular device more difficult and may raise the overall cost of security for the organization, as the price for hardware-encrypted devices—the only ones where security is provably enabled—are much higher than for generic devices of the same type.

Logging and Auditing Capabilities

Allowing or prohibiting a particular device or device type may also be based on the ability to monitor and audit the information that gets moved to a device. An organization wishing to control mobile devices is interested in one or both of the following two issues:

■ Preventing the loss of data from the device
■ Knowing what data was on a device that is lost or stolen

Some organizations are only interested in preventing the loss of data. These organizations either restrict the use of mobile devices or place controls over the types of devices that can be used and the mobility of certain data. Once data is on a "protected" device (however the organization defines "protected"), if the device is subsequently lost the organization writes off the loss, believing that the protections will keep the data secure from the attackers. The wisdom of such a position may be debatable, for even the best security can often be defeated by a determined attacker. Nevertheless, if the organization is confident enough in the security protections on the device or the data is not sensitive enough to warrant an elevated level of concern, this is a valid position to take.

Other organizations need to know exactly what information was on a particular device, no matter what security protections are enabled. These organizations may be under strict legal or regulatory reporting requirements in the case of a data-loss incident. Likewise, their incident-response or crisis-management plans may require them to ascertain the contents of a missing device in order to enact the appropriate response processes. In these cases, an organization's mobile device management technology must have some ability to track the information stored on mobile devices. This can be as simple as knowing the names of files that are written to the device to have an estimation of the type of information that the device contained. From the file names, the organization can then track back to the originating systems (the user's PC or the file server from which the data was copied) to determine exactly what data was on the device. Alternatively, the logging might contain a full duplicate of the data that is written to a mobile device. This eliminates the need for the additional tracking step, but it greatly increases the amount of storage space needed to contain the full log of all the data. An organization should carefully evaluate its logging and auditing needs (as well as its available budget) before taking the additional step of logging the full content of all mobile data transfers.

Defining Your Scope

Evaluating the access control, data flow, audit, and device-management capabilities of the various mobile device security products available on the market can be a daunting task, as each product provides a different mix of features, services, and security trade-offs. However, to make the task easier and help focus the effort more precisely, the organization needs to go back to the fundamental security question: What are you trying to protect? Or, put slightly differently, what are you most worried about? To guide you in the evaluation of the technology and products that might be available, the following two issues should be considered:

■ *What is the scope of the device protection effort(s)?* At first, an organization may have a simple goal of "blocking or protecting all mobile devices." This is a worthy goal, but one that will quickly become bogged down under its own weight, as the sheer number of different devices grows too large to manage under a single umbrella. In addition, as we have already seen, different types of devices bring their own particular security issues and methods of protection. The controls necessary and available to protect a smartphone are very different from those used to protect a DVD. Therefore, trying to cover them all under a single program or technology umbrella may be futile. Start by selecting the devices or mobile technologies that present the biggest threat or that your users rely on the most for their work, and then develop protection controls for those devices first. This may involve creating several projects or exploring several different technologies to accomplish your goals, but the result may be more satisfactory than trying to fit all the goals into a single technology or program.

■ *Are you trying to create an enterprise-wide standard?* The goal of many device-protection programs (and the one already suggested in this chapter) is to define a single set of devices that all employees can use for their mobile data needs. This small set of devices would have standard security configurations and rely on a single management process. However, as we have already seen, the plethora of mobile device choices and the wide variety of features and capabilities on each of these devices may make the task of narrowing down the available field difficult. This, however, is critical to the success of a mobile device protection program. The organization must decide if it is able (or willing) to impose restrictions on the types of devices its employees can use.

Organizations vary greatly in the size and relative power of the end-user community. Some, like military organizations and very large commercial enterprises, are heavily driven from the top down, and an edict issued from the highest levels of the organization can be propagated throughout the enterprise with a reasonable assurance that the edict will be followed.* Other organizations are more employee-centric and try to create a collegial and "empowering" environment for their employees, or are so geographically or functionally dispersed that central control of the technology environment runs counter to the corporate culture or its ability to centrally manage such a geographically dispersed environment. These companies find it much more difficult to impose top-down standards or strict policies on the types and configuration of mobile devices.

However, their goal may not be universal protection. Instead, they may be looking to secure a particular threat that they feel is more prevalent in their environment. For example, if the biggest worry an organization has is the proliferation of data on flash drives, they may only need to implement policies and technologies that protect against that particular threat. If, on the other hand, they are more worried about the information their executives have on their smartphones, they will lean toward establishing control over that environment exclusively.

This leads back to the central question of the effort's scope, but becomes an issue unto itself when projecting that scope onto the entire enterprise and its users. As a result, the organization must evaluate the extent to which it is willing to inconvenience its users or impose strict standards on them in the name of information protection based on the defined scope of its efforts. The organization that is seeking only to address particular device threats will have a simpler time imposing restrictions and implementing technology to do so, but at the potential cost of ignoring other devices that may have a bigger impact on their security. The organization that is trying to establish enterprise-wide mobile device control but is unwilling to swing too far in the direction of exerting that control over the objections of its users will consistently find itself chasing new devices, new threats, and new protection technologies.

---

* There are always exceptions, and even the strictest of organizations runs the risk that some of its employees will break the rules.

Defining Acceptable Use Cases

Adopting a device-specific security model will require the organization to first establish the specific use cases that it finds acceptable. The organization needs to determine what uses of mobile devices are permissible given the availability of acceptable security controls. For example, the organization may start by asking some of the following questions:

- Are smartphones acceptable and is the company willing to support the synchronization of calendar and e-mail data?
- Is the use of flash storage on smartphones acceptable?
- Is there a need for recordable CD and DVD drives in the organization? If so, does everyone need one, or can the organization make do with just a few key personnel that have the responsibility to burn disks for everyone in the company?
- Does anyone in the organization need a portable storage device such as an external hard drive, or can backup of user data be handled by a network-attached storage facility?

The answers to these questions (and many more, depending on the needs of the organization) will help determine what use cases and what devices the organization is willing to accept and protect in the environment. What are you trying to protect? That fundamental question (once again) will start you down the path to defining the problems you are trying to solve, the devices that can help you solve those problems, and the security controls that will protect those devices.

Who Gets Access?

Once you have established what devices you are willing to support and have deployed the appropriate policy and technology to help you secure it, you will need to establish the criteria for who gets access to the devices and who does not. This may be as simple as a blanket prohibition on all mobile devices, in which case nobody will have access to the technology and your security problem goes away. However, a more likely scenario is that some population within the organization will need to use one or more mobile devices. After all, why would mobile device security even be an issue if nobody in the company wanted to use mobile technology? So, the process and criteria for including or excluding employees from the permitted group must be established.

How do you establish such criteria? As with all access-control decisions, the overriding factor is based on business need for the technology. A strong desire to explore new technology or the need to keep up with the latest trends may be important to the individual, but it may not benefit the organization or its need to protect sensitive information. Alternatively, some teams within the organization may exist *specifically* to understand new technology and develop ways that technology can be applied to address business problems. For such teams, that need would be a perfectly valid reason to be included in the permitted group.

The determination of who is allowed access to a particular technology may be very straightforward. If a desired device has the required security controls and fits within the policies and standards set by the organization, anyone within the company can use that device. However, that approach only works if the business evaluation shows that everyone in the organization can benefit from its use (or, at least, its use won't harm the organization). Anything less than that—the realization that a particular device or technology must be limited to only a subset of the organization—will involve a great deal of evaluation, justification, and (let's be honest here) internal politics between those who control the mobile technology within an organization and those who wish to have access to it.

Keeping Up with Device Technology

When selecting a device-centric model for mobile security, the organization must contend with the rapid rate with which new devices are introduced into the marketplace, bringing with them a host of new features and functionality. In addition, with the rapid advance of "Web 2.0" technologies and services, the pace with which existing devices are adapting to new ways of functioning and interacting with new and useful applications is enough to make both technology and security managers cringe in fear. To adopt a device-specific approach is to commit the organization to keeping pace with changes in technology and capabilities, and committing to understanding the security implications of those changes as they develop. This does not mean that the organization must adopt every new device that comes along in the market, or immediately adopt every new device that users covet as the "next great thing." The technology currently in use within the organization—particularly devices that have been well designed and whose introduction into the environment has been well planned and executed—can function effectively for a long period of time. It does mean, however, that the organization must be willing to keep an open mind about newer technology and be willing to change its supported device and capability standards when business needs or changes in the environment make it necessary to do so. A commitment to a device-centric approach to mobile security is a commitment to keeping pace with the change of device technology.

When faced with a new technology or a request for adding support for a new mobile device, the organization will have to evaluate how the new device fits within the existing scope and operational parameters that have already been established. Here are some criteria that may be useful to that evaluation:

■ Does the desired technology fit within the organization's definition of permitted devices? If not, does it have the same available security controls as devices that are permitted?

- Does the device have any built-in security controls that complement, strengthen, or negate any organization-imposed controls?
- Can the device be managed centrally by the organization, or does it rely on user awareness and diligence for secure operation?
- Does the device include technology that would violate any of the organization's other policies or standards? For example, smartphones with built-in digital cameras may violate a "no cameras on company premises" policy.
- Does the device incur extraordinary cost to the organization to support? If the adoption of an alternate device means the organization must increase its resource allocation for additional or alternative support, that cost must be weighed against the benefit (perceived and actual) of the new device.

Device-Centric Challenges

There are disadvantages to adopting a device-centric approach to mobile security, and an organization considering this approach should weight these carefully before deciding to take this path. The most obvious is that device-centric mobile security only works well as long as the information you are trying to protect is contained on a protected device. Once the data moves off that device and onto another, those protections can be lost. For example, suppose an organization has implemented a policy whereby all flash drives must use hardware-based encryption before data can be written to them, and the organization has implemented the appropriate technology controls to enforce that restriction. This provides great protection as long as the data stays on the hardware-encrypted drive. If the user subsequently moves that data off the encrypted drive to an unencrypted device (perhaps by using another computer that is not under the organization's control), the organization has lost control of the data, and it's now unprotected in an uncontrolled location. Based on the Inverse Distance Principle, for a device-centric model to be completely effective, the organization must have absolute control over all the devices where its data may reside. This sounds great when you say it fast, but it is next to impossible to achieve in reality.

Remember, the primary benefit of mobile devices is the ability to move data to and from the device with minimal effort. To maintain the proper level of security, the device must be intrinsically tied to the infrastructure where it is managed, and the security controls on the device must recognize when it is (and is not) attached to a protected system to prevent the offloading of any data if the destination is not part of the organization's protected infrastructure. The maturity of the security features on the current crop of mobile devices and the capabilities of enterprise mobile device protection systems do not yet rise to meet this challenge. That is not to say that such end-to-end protection is not possible, just that it can be extremely difficult to achieve in a purely device-centric model. End-to-end protection may be achievable in a data-centric model, which we'll explore later in this chapter.

To compensate for this lack of purely technical means to enforce end-to-end security in a device-centric approach, an organization using a device-centric approach must rely heavily on compensating measures to try to achieve an acceptable level of security for mobile devices. One of the most basic compensating measures is to establish clear and comprehensive policies around the acceptable use of mobile devices as it pertains to the protection of mobile data. While an organization should develop these in any case, they are especially important in a device-centric environment. Employees need to clearly understand what their specific responsibilities are with respect to handling and protecting mobile data and mobile devices, and the organization's policy is the best place to define those responsibilities. We'll discuss mobile data policies in more detail in Chapter 9.

The policy is only the first step. Like speed limits and tax laws, policies are only as good as the people who are willing to abide by them. Members of the organization who are unwilling to abide by the policy, or who don't clearly understand what the policy requires, will violate the policy in order to get their job done. Therefore, the policy needs to be supplemented with good technology controls (to the extent that they are available) and appropriate administrative processes to deploy, track, and maintain the security of the devices that are approved for use. As with all other things related to security, how well the policy is followed (by the people who are subject to the policy) is half the battle.

Given all these negative factors, what would lead an organization to adopt a purely device-centric solution? A device-centric approach makes sense for an organization trying to maintain control over mobile devices without getting too bogged down in the complexity of managing multiple technologies and capabilities and without the ability (or desire) to implement a model that requires managing and protecting specific data in transit. Device-centric approaches work well if you have complete control over the user environment, technology, and information-processing systems within the enterprise. In reality, very few enterprises can exert that level of absolute control over their environment, and certainly not without the complete cooperation of and commitment of their personnel. Therefore, this may only be applicable for smaller environments or smaller groups within a larger organization. However, if an organization is capable of ensuring that only specific approved devices are allowed to attach to its infrastructure, that only approved personnel can access those devices, and that those devices do not leave the confines of the controlled environment, a device-centric approach might be worth examining.

A Data-Centric Model

If the rigorous requirements of the device-centric model are too much for your organization to contemplate, or if you know outright that you need more flexibility in the selection of available mobile device technology than a device-centric model affords, the alternative is to approach mobile security from the standpoint of protecting the mobile data rather than concentrating solely on the security configuration of devices carrying that data. This data-centric model stands in sharp contrast to the device-centric model just discussed. Like the device-centric model, however, it is not a panacea for mobile security problems, and brings its own technical and management issues that must be dealt with.

A data-centric model tries to account for the fluidity of data as it moves from device to device, and recognizes that coordinating the security of those devices can be a challenging task. A data-centric model embraces this data movement and uses it to its advantage. Rather than worrying about the security capabilities a particular device may possess, and worrying again whether those capabilities will be present on the next device in the chain, a data-centric model tries to protect the information itself no matter what device it uses for transport. The data is secured before it is placed on the first mobile device in the chain, and that protection stays with it until it reaches its final destination. By protecting information rather than just devices, it no longer matters where the data resides. If the device itself has additional security protections (such as access controls or built-in encryption), so much the better, as that gives an added layer for a defense-in-depth approach. Even without device protections, the applied data protection moves as the data moves from PC to flash drive to CD to PDA. This approach also works well if the information must be transmitted to another party without the use of a "mobile device," such as an e-mail attachment or an FTP file transfer.

The device-centric model relies on the ability to understand and manage the available protection controls on a variety of different platforms and devices. The matrix of devices and protections can become quite large in an environment where there are more than a few devices available for use. On the other hand, a data-centric model relies primarily on four types of controls to protect data in transit:

- Data-centric access controls
- Blocking certain data types
- Encryption
- Information Rights Management

Data-Centric Access Controls

Some devices, such as optical disks, flash memory, and tapes, have no built-in access control mechanisms because the underlying media specifications do not support them. In such cases, access controls must be imposed on data placed on the device through auxiliary means. This can be accomplished by encrypting the data on that device. The encryption provides the access control by allowing access to the data only to those who have the proper decryption keys. This process is commonly used, for example, in data-center tape backup procedures. There are a couple of different approaches that can be applied here. First, an organization might rely on each system or application to encrypt its sensitive information before it's backed up onto tape. This requires each of those systems to incorporate encryption into its operation, potentially adding development costs for the system and increasing overhead for key management. The result, however, is that all data coming from those systems is encrypted before it ever reaches the backup service, simplifying the process for protecting the media against data loss but at a potentially high overall cost to the organization.

As an alternative, the organization can place the encryption process at the point where the backup media is created, encrypting all data in bulk as it is written to the media and decrypting it as it is read from the media. Because the encryption process is centralized in the backup management system (and not applied at each individual system) this can result in lower implementation costs for the organization and effective access control (via the encryption) on the mobile device (the tape or disk). The drawback is that any application or process that must later read the data from an encrypted disk or tape must be able to decrypt the information. Unless all the groups that may need to read the encrypted media have access to the same encryption technology that was used to create it, this may limit the practicality of such a process to only the media within a single enterprise or among a small, tightly coordinated group of organizations that need to exchange information and can agree on a standardized process and technology.

Encryption is not the only way to provide access control to data, however. The organization can protect the data with a password before it is moved onto a mobile device. This will limit access to the data to only those who know the proper password. Some applications (Word, Excel, and Acrobat, for example) have the ability to password protect files they create. For applications that do not have this feature, separate utilities can be employed to encapsulate and password protect any file on your computer. The amount of protection may be variable, however, as an attacker may be able to guess the password, or the program used to protect the file may have a flawed implementation that allows an attacker to bypass the password protection. Nevertheless, in situations where encryption is not a viable option, password protection is a good alternative for providing access control to your sensitive data.

Blocking Certain Data Types

One of the fundamental principles of a data-centric approach is that information should only move to a mobile device if it is both acceptable to do so by organizational policy and provided with the proper data protections before (or as) it is moved to the device. One of the best ways to enforce this type of restriction is to use the organization's information classification program to identify and label data based on its sensitivity or need for security protection. Data that is given a lower classification (often denoted as "internal" or "sensitive") may get some basic protections, such as password protection or special access controls. Data with a higher classification level (often termed "confidential" or "secret") will require more stringent protections, such as multifactor authentication for access control or encryption to protect the contents. The specific classification levels will be dictated by an organization's individual requirements and policy, and the protections required for each classification level will be based on the organization's own evaluation of the type of protection that should be placed on each level of data. The end result, however, is that the protection controls are matched to the type of data needing protection.

Simply identifying the data and determining the classification it requires is only the first part of the process. In many classification programs, the data is then "labeled" or "tagged" to ensure that anyone who uses that data understands the classification level and will understand the type of protection (based on that level) that is required to secure that data. For physical media, such as paper, tapes, or disks, the label is a visual notification of the classification level of the data. A common classification label may look like this:

MoDevCo Confidential Information
Only for use by authorized company employees

Anyone who receives a paper report or backup media marked with this label will (or should) know immediately how to handle the information and the type of security procedures that are required to protect it. However, if the information is stored digitally, there may be no physical representation of the data's classification. Likewise, a single storage device can contain hundreds or thousands of files, each individually classified and with no guarantee that the classification level is uniform throughout the file set. A system that must process those files will need to know the classification level of each file in order to apply the appropriate security controls. In cases such as this, files can be labeled (or tagged) with "metadata"—information placed in the file that describes certain attributes of that file. For example, Microsoft PowerPoint places metadata tags in all PowerPoint presentation files describing the name of the file, the author, and the dates and times the file was created and last modified. This information can be referenced both by PowerPoint and other programs to evaluate the file for their own needs and determine how to process the data. For data that is generated by a company's internal systems, metadata can be generated to include information about its classification level. A program reading that data can check the classification metadata, then make determinations based on that tag. For example:

■ A file with a low (or no) classification level can be opened for both reading and writing.
■ A file with a higher classification might require a program to open the file in a read-only mode.
■ A file with the highest classification level might require users to authenticate themselves before accessing the file.

Again, how this is all applied is very specific to each organization, and the exact details are not incredibly important here. What *is* important is that the classification metatags can be used in a data-centric mobile security model to determine the proper course of action based on the tags embedded in the file. For example, a file tagged with the lowest classification might be allowed to move to a mobile device, a file with a medium classification might have to be encrypted before it moves to a mobile device, and a file with the highest level of classification might be blocked from being copied to any mobile device.

The technology to enable this blocking must be embedded into whatever systems or applications are used to access mobile (or potentially mobile) data and, unfortunately, are not yet predominant in the commercial marketplace. However, some products have begun to explore the blocking of certain types of data based not only on metadata tags, but also on keywords embedded into the document or the presence of certain patterns of data (such as lists of credit card numbers). The technology to provide this functionality is still early in its maturity cycle. However, as with all technology, it continues to improve in accuracy and performance. Once it becomes both mature and reliable, it will become a powerful tool to use for keeping sensitive information off mobile devices, before it has a chance to become lost.

Encryption

Encryption can be another powerful tool in protecting a data-centric mobile environment. In fact, it is the most data-centric of all the security mechanisms. It is also the most commonly used, and is the first thing that most people think of when they begin to examine ways of protecting mobile data. The idea behind encryption is simple: Wrap the data inside a protective shell (the encryption) while it is present on the mobile device. That shell can only be unwrapped by the person on the other end who has the secret key to decrypt the data. We'll examine encryption in much more detail in Chapter 6, but here we'll examine some of the benefits and drawbacks of using encryption to protect mobile data.

The best attribute of encryption is that it can be independent of the device or transport mechanism used to move data. Once a file is encrypted, it stays encrypted while it moves from device to device. However, this attribute is only the case when a process external to the mobile device is used to encrypt the data. If the data is encrypted through a process embedded on the mobile device itself, the data will lose its encryption protection once it is removed from the device.

Figure 5.1 depicts an example of how this works. In this example, our data is a document of some importance. The document doesn't go through any special processing, but in order to protect it, the owner of the data places it on a mobile device with built-in encryption. As long as the data is on that device, it is protected. When the data is subsequently removed from the device, as shown on the right side of the figure, the data loses the encryption and is returned to its unencrypted form. Hopefully, the device receiving the data on the other end is either not mobile or contains sufficient security protections to adequately protect the information. The important point here is that, in this scenario, the encryption is only protecting the

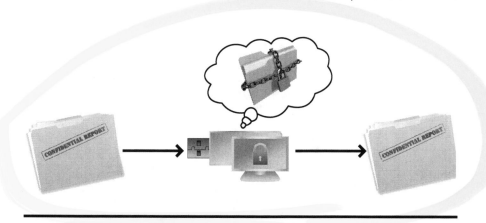

Figure 5.1   Hardware-based mobile data encryption.

contents of the single device and has no effect on the data before it is stored on the device or after it is moved off.

In contrast, Figure 5.2 shows the use of an external process to encrypt the data before it is stored on the mobile device. On the top left side of the diagram, you can see the original document ready for transport. This time, however, we will put it through an encryption process before storing it on any mobile device. This process can be an encryption application on the user's PC, or perhaps specialized encryption software in a backup process that encrypts all data before it is backed up. Regardless of the specifics of the process, the point is that the protection of the data does not rely on encryption built into the mobile device; it is protected by encryption before it becomes mobile. What makes the use of an external process so appealing is that the data can continue to travel from device to device and retain all the protection that the encryption provides, as seen in the flow of the data in the figure. As the data moves from the flash drive to the CD to the tape and on through an e-mail transmission, the bits are still encrypted and protected from prying eyes. Unlike the situation in Figure 5.1, where the encryption was effective only as long as the data resided on a particular device, there is no need to worry about the protections available on each device—or *any* device. As long as the data remains encrypted (and as long as the key to decrypt the data remains a secret), the data will remain protected.

Encryption works both independently and in conjunction with other forms of mobile device and data control, such as access controls and device restrictions. It can be used in conjunction with data-flow restrictions as well, but the results may be mixed, depending on how the restrictions are incorporated. Some data controls rely on the ability to read identifying information inside a file or data set, such as a metatag or data field inside the file. Encrypting the file will prevent those control mechanisms from properly reading (and acting on) that identifying information. If, on the other hand, the data-flow restriction mechanisms rely on information outside the file, such as an independent database of files and their classification level or

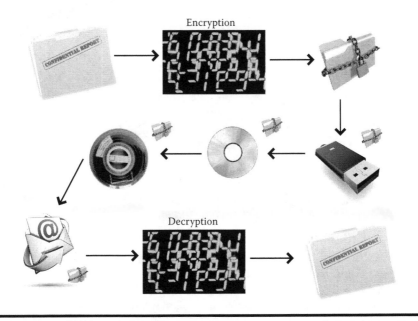

Figure 5.2 External mobile data encryption.

a hash value of the encrypted file, encrypting the data will not diminish the ability to track and control the data.

The use of encryption may have some disadvantages as well. The biggest task an organization will need to face when implementing encryption is the issue of key management. All encryption is based on keys, and each user in an encryption system will have one or more keys he will need to manage in order to successfully encrypt and decrypt data they need to access. In addition, most encryption systems keep the actual encryption keys under wraps within the system and protect them with a password or passphrase that the user must remember. This makes the user's job easier (remembering a password—even a long and complex one—is much simpler than remembering a 56-bit or 128-bit string of binary numbers), but it adds to the complexity of tracking the components needed for successful encryption and decryption. Depending on the organization's approach to key management, the process can be extremely simple or tremendously complex. Key management and the issues an organization must address when trying to implement a key-management system will be discussed in more detail in Chapter 6.

Enabling encryption to protect data on mobile devices also requires that both sides of the transport (the origination and the destination) utilize the same encryption system so the data can be properly decrypted once the final destination is reached. Data originally encrypted with PGP cannot be decrypted with TrueCrypt or any other product. While the underlying encryption algorithm between products may be the same (for example, AES or DES), extracting the protected keys from the encrypting application and manually applying them to decrypt a particular message is beyond the capability of most end users. If the encryption mechanism is completely contained within the mobile device (as is the case with hardware-encrypted flash and hard drives), the originating and destination systems must both be capable of supporting that device in order for the data to be successfully transferred. All this may not be a problem within a single organization, as all users will presumably be using the same encryption systems to secure data in transit.

It may, however, be a much bigger problem when moving data between independent organizations, particularly through e-mail. While there are several standards for e-mail encryption (S/MIME and PGP are the most commonly used), managing keys and passwords across those organizations may present more of an issue. A centralized directory service such as LDAP, Active Directory, or a PGP key server can be established to allow users in those separate organizations to send and receive encrypted e-mail, but this will require those directory services to be publicly available so external users can access them to receive and verify the keys needed for the process. While this brings another level of complexity to the infrastructure, it may be necessary if cross-organizational access is a requirement.

There are commercial e-mail encryption services that can integrate with an organization's e-mail system and automatically encrypt messages as they leave the organization's network. The encrypted messages are stored on the service provider's system, and a notice is sent to the recipient that there is a secured message waiting to be retrieved. The recipient then logs into the commercial service to retrieve and decrypt the message. This type of service makes encryption much simpler for the end user, who no longer needs to remember when and how to encrypt outgoing e-mail. From the recipient's viewpoint, there is the required extra step of logging into the commercial service to retrieve the e-mail, but this seems to be an acceptable trade-off to better secure sensitive information in transit.

Encrypting portable media such as disks or tapes for long-term storage presents another issue: time. Archival backups have long been a part of data-center operations and are used for storing data for disaster recovery purposes and for saving records still required by the organization but not required to be immediately accessible. This data is stored with the idea that it must, at some point, be recovered and used, perhaps years later. With the recent interest in securing all forms of mobile media, many organizations are looking to encrypt backup and archive tapes containing sensitive or private data to prevent a potential data leakage if that media is lost. This is a good idea, but the organization must be sure to account for the continuous advances in technology and functionality. The device that writes data to tape today must still be around and serviceable years from now so that today's tapes can be read at some indeterminate time in the future. As if that weren't tricky enough, any add-on or integrated encryption systems used to encrypt the data on those old tapes or disks must likewise be available and serviceable to perform the decryption when needed. An organization looking to encrypt long-term storage must account for this fact and either plan to keep old equipment around in the event it is needed for recovery or begin a program of "upgrading" its backup and archived data on a periodic basis to transfer that data using newer technology, newer media, and updated encryption systems.

Information Rights Management

One final method of protecting information in a data-centric approach is through the use of an Information Rights Management (IRM) system to control access to particular data or documents. IRM is an umbrella term for a number of different technologies that can be used to limit who has access to data and what they can do once they have obtained access. IRM is often used synonymously with the term Digital Rights Management (DRM). The two technologies are very similar; DRM is commonly used in reference to consumer-oriented protection mechanisms for entertainment content, while IRM is commonly used in reference to business-oriented data. An IRM system works by tracking every file under its control and using a combination of cryptography and access-control technology to place access restrictions on each file. Once a file is protected, the IRM system can provide the following controls:

- Prevent unauthorized access to a document
- Prevent the copying of documents
- Prevent the copy-and-paste operations of information within a document
- Prevent the unauthorized forwarding of a document
- Prevent the alteration of the information within a document
- Track the use and distribution of information

If the organization has a robust information-classification program and has correctly tagged its data and files to properly identify their classification levels, the IRM system can use that classification as part of the restriction and access-control criteria. This can include identification of certain data that can be moved to mobile media. As long as the organization is able to clearly define how access rights should work, and as long as it has the ability to properly identify and tag the classification level of each document or file, an IRM system can be extremely valuable in enforcing the access restrictions that are a part of an effective information-classification program.

In order to be most effective, the IRM system must be pervasive throughout the environment. Every file and electronic document requiring any kind of access control must be included as part of the IRM system. Even if IRM is used for only a subset of the organization's total information (limited, for example, to all legal documents or project planning files), each potential file in that subset must be included under the IRM system's control. In addition, as new files are created, they must be placed under the control of the IRM system before they are made available for distribution. Likewise, documents that are protected by IRM cannot be made available anywhere outside the system. For example, if a company has all its legal contracts under IRM control, placing additional copies of them on a networked file server for access by the legal team not only defeats the purpose of having the IRM system in the first place, but also provides a potential avenue for an unauthorized person to gain access to the data without being authenticated and tracked by the IRM system. Having such an alternative storage location for IRM data may also allow people to shortcut the IRM process by reading and writing information directly to the alternate location. Most people will choose the path of least resistance when trying to accomplish a goal, and given the choice between managing their information through the (potentially cumbersome) IRM system or simply reading and writing directly from a network drive, most will choose the network drive despite the fact that this may be less secure.

The IRM system must be available on all platforms on which the data users work. Almost all IRM systems work on common PC and e-mail platforms, but support for mobile devices is limited. If the IRM system is in place specifically to *prevent* the movement of data from standard desktop environments onto mobile devices, IRM systems can be a big benefit to enforcing those restrictions. If, on the other hand, users require the availability of IRM-protected data on their mobile devices and the IRM platform of choice is not supported on those devices, then the organization faces a difficult choice. It can either deny those mobile users access to the data they require or remove IRM protection from the required data and allow it to be transferred onto the mobile device. To avoid the need to make this type of risk decision, an organization should pay careful attention to the breadth of platforms an IRM system supports to ensure that the devices its users need the most are included in the IRM system.

Companies wishing to implement IRM must face the limitation that IRM-based data must live within its own infrastructure, and that infrastructure generally doesn't scale very well. In other words, if you implement IRM restrictions on a document, all other users of the document must also be part of the IRM infrastructure in order to have access to that file. This can work well if you have a closed environment where you can control the users and enforce the use of IRM on their systems, but it can fall apart quickly if you must share information with users over whom you do not have infrastructural or organizational control. Those users must either agree to cooperate with your IRM system (along with the appropriate software and procedural changes) or risk losing access to IRM-protected content. In addition, most IRM systems begin to get cumbersome as the number of users grows to very large proportions, driving the management and operational cost of the system upward.

Over time, information finds its way into all areas of an enterprise: PCs, laptops, network drives, portable media, etc. IRM systems require the organization to gather, identify, and classify all the organization's information and relocate it to the IRM system. Finding all this data in all the nooks and crannies where it may be stored can be a monumental task, and some data will probably be missed. Limiting the implementation of IRM to a small part of the organization or a small subset of documents and data types will help the situation, but finding every last piece of data will still be a chore. If any nonprotected data is permitted to exist outside the IRM system, Murphy's Law dictates (a) that the data will leak into unauthorized hands and (b) that the data will be the most damaging information possible to the organization. All joking aside, if the organization is serious enough about protecting its information and intellectual property to go through the effort of implementing IRM, it should make an equally serious effort to discover and migrate all data under IRM protection.

Rights management systems—particularly those targeted toward consumers—have also been very susceptible to being defeated or bypassed by clever users who disagree with the economic, social, or political implications surrounding their use. Almost all consumer DRM systems, from the CSS system used to protect commercial DVDs to the FairPlay system implemented in Apple's iTunes, have been defeated by attackers trying to preserve their ability to get digital entertainment content free from DRM restrictions. When considering the implementation of a rights-management system, an organization will have to weigh the potential for a compromise of the system and the likelihood that the user base for the system will exploit any discovered vulnerabilities in the protection mechanisms. For its part, the entertainment industry (in particular, the music business) has all but abandoned large-scale DRM measures and is now looking for ways to benefit financially from non-DRM-protected digital content distribution services.

Finally, the security and effectiveness of the IRM system itself should be a point of concern for the organization. Because it holds the keys to locking and unlocking the company's most sensitive information, the IRM system (and the servers that manage it) should be considered a primary target for an attacker looking to compromise an organization's data. All available security controls and protections should be implemented on those servers. However, an attacker may not need to break into the IRM server to compromise data. If an implementation flaw in the way the IRM system protects the data under its control is found, an attacker can use that flaw to gain unauthorized access to the data. Organizations looking to implement an IRM system should first check to determine if a particular IRM product under consideration has been compromised and if the vendor of the system has corrected the flaw that allowed the compromise. In any case, new flaws and circumvention methods for IRM and DRM systems are being discovered all the time, so do not assume that any IRM system will be completely secure forever. Given this fact, an organization implementing IRM should continue to use the other mobile protections described in this book to provide defense-in-depth protection for the company's sensitive information.

When it comes to managing mobile data, IRM and DRM offer big benefits for organizations that can overcome the technical and logistical problems currently involved in deploying these technologies to large-scale mobile environments. To date, however, the available technology has not been able to completely overcome the diversity of device technology and the lack of a platform-independent standard for implementing and enforcing DRM restrictions on the wide variety of mobile devices currently in use.

Data-Centric Challenges

Given all these points, it is clear to see that a data-centric protection model has some distinct advantages over the device-centric model. For starters, protection in a data-centric model is determined by the owner of the information. The owner decides if the information needs protecting and what form that protection will take. If the organization is able to integrate protection controls with its information classification program, the level of protection can be determined by the classification of the data rather than being left to end-user discretion. If such integration isn't possible, data can still be protected (albeit in a less integrated or enforceable manner) from end to end, regardless of what devices the data is moved to or where those devices travel. If a device is lost along the way, gets stolen, or its data simply gets moved to a device that has no built-in security protections, the data will still be secure from disclosure or compromise. The data may be irretrievably lost (an issue that the organization will need to deal with separately), but it is still secure.

A data-centric approach encapsulates the data inside a secure container and allows that container to be sent into the wild. The security of that container may be based on access controls, encryption, or some digital rights mechanism, but the container is there to protect the data no matter what hostile forces it may encounter. This becomes especially important as data moves further and further from its source (remember the Inverse Distance Principle). By not relying on device-specific controls, such data has a reasonable chance of remaining protected for the lifetime of its journey.

That's not to say that a data-centric approach does not have its drawbacks. The biggest of these is that the data protection mechanism must be resistant to attack and "de-encapsulation." Because there may be no device-specific controls available to protect the data, the encapsulation mechanism may be the only thing standing between the attacker and the sensitive information. As a result, it is critical that the organization select a protection technology that is mature, well tested, and based on publicly available algorithms and methodologies. No matter what protection methods you employ, whether they be access controls, encryption, digital rights management, or any other technology, attackers will try to subvert the control mechanisms. Some will succeed. That's why it's important to employ data controls that have a history of technical and market success. Even if the implementation technology is proprietary, it should be based common standards like Active Directory, PGP, LDAP, AES, DES*, UNIX, or Windows access controls, or any other number of commonly known and commonly understood security

---

* Although DES is a well-known and commonly used standard for data encryption, it is now considered obsolete for encrypting most sensitive data.

mechanisms. These are the ones that have proven over the years to be resistant to attack. While none can claim to be entirely secure or have lasted without the discovery of any security flaws, all are backed by responsive and responsible vendors and user communities that can respond to vulnerabilities and attacks quickly to close any potential security holes.

Given all this information about the pros and cons of a data-centric approach to mobile security, what would lead an organization to adopt this approach? Data-centric mobile security can be very effective if you are unable to dictate or predict the type of device that will store your data. Additionally, if you expect that the data will be transported to devices completely outside of your environment and over which you have no ability to monitor or secure, a data-centric approach may be your best (or only) hope of securing that data. In an environment where mobile devices are self-selected by users or the organization has not (yet) implemented any policies or technology to control the use and security configuration of mobile devices, a data-centric solution allows the organization to account for this variability and to protect the data no matter what device may be in use. A process that encrypts all e-mail leaving the organization protects that e-mail no matter what systems or services the e-mail passes through. A program that encrypts data as it is being written to a mobile device can ensure that the data continues to be protected even if it leaves the confines of that device.

Which Model Do You Choose?

This chapter has presented two very different approaches to mobile security. One approach concentrates on securing the devices and technology that will store and transport data from place to place regardless of what that data may be. The other concentrates on securing the data itself no matter what device or technology is used for storage and transport. As we have seen, both approaches have their advantages. But neither is perfect, and we have seen examples in both cases where that particular approach is impractical, cumbersome, too costly, or just plain impossible. So how is an organization supposed to determine which approach it should take?

There is a classic joke told among lawyers that every legal question can be answered by just two words: "It depends." The joke, of course, is that issues of right and wrong, guilt and innocence, or proper and improper are rarely black-and-white matters. There are always shades of subtlety involved, and the skilled attorney is able to argue multiple sides of a case with the available facts. That's why we have lawyers, judges, and juries: to settle subtle questions that have no clear answer based on the collective wisdom and experience they bring to the matter at hand and the ability of all involved to understand the nuances put before them. The point here is that many important issues have no clear answer and are subject to a great deal of debate as to the correct course of action.

So, with that as background, which approach should your organization take to effectively secure its mobile information and devices? It depends, of course. (You had to see that coming.)

That's not just a cute way of throwing in the towel. It really is the truth. There is no "best" approach to mobile security, just as there is no best approach to any aspect of information security in general. The approach an organization takes will depend on its own security goals and risks, its available resources, its technology infrastructure, and the collective experience and wisdom of its leaders, technicians, and employees. How they perceive their needs for data mobility and mobile security will play just as much a part in determining which way to approach the issue as will strict adherence to one particular security model or another.

Perhaps it's a problem with the idea of a "security model" in the first place. The common belief about a model is that you can put one together and everything else will suddenly emerge based on the ideas and goals expressed in that model. Because the model contains the archetype for everything that is to follow, deviation from the model's specification is discouraged. But that is just not possible with many aspects of security. Because protecting the flow of information is at the heart of all security efforts, and given that information flow is often random, unpredictable, and spontaneous, no model can clearly express the complete blueprint for protecting information or devices in any meaningful manner. So neither model can be thought of as a complete approach to mobile security—not the device-centric model, not the data-centric model, not any model. The best that you can hope to achieve when determining the best approach is a technological "it depends."

As a result, based on all that we've seen in this chapter, the best approach may turn out to be a hybrid of the two models. Due to current limitations in technology, the incompatibility of security features between devices, and the lack of common device-management platforms, a purely device-centric approach will not be able to fully protect all your organization's information. Likewise, because data movement is random and the technology to automatically track and detect data movement and apply appropriate controls is still immature, a purely data-centric path will likewise fall short of expectations. The best path, then, is to combine the best of both approaches.

Start by abandoning the notion that the organization can exert absolute control over the devices used in its environment. Yes, it is true that there are some organizations that can have that type of influence. Military and government institutions come to mind, but even those are experiencing difficulties enforcing significant control over their technical environment. For the rest of the world, a complete lockdown on device management is just not a reality. This admission can be a significant culture shock to some organizations that are under the belief that—with enough diligence, effort, and technology—they can completely lock down every device in their environment.

The second realization that must be made is that data will live beyond the confines of a particular device (or even a particular technology) and, despite everyone's best efforts, will move to places never intended or desired by the information owner. We saw this in the Gadgetron project report example from Chapter 3. In that example, despite the data owner's best intentions—and through no intentional hostile action on the part of the data recipients—the data moved well beyond the owner's original intent and into places of which she was completely unaware.

Once you've gotten past these two attitude adjustments, start by working on the parts of the environment that can be controlled and over which you have knowledge and influence. Specify a set of devices and technologies that the organization can support and for which the security controls are acceptable from both protection and usability standpoints. Put another way, understand your environment, determine the devices that can interact and be managed well in that environment, and determine the security controls and processes that are needed to protect information on those devices. That's the device-centric portion of the plan.

Next, determine the points in the enterprise through which data moves from fixed devices to mobile devices. Examples include desktop, laptop, and mobile computers, portable media devices, smartphones (and the data synchronization processes that go along with them), and e-mail systems. For each of these data-mobility points, determine the available technology that can be used to protect that data as it moves into, through, and past that point. Examples here include passwords and other authentication technology, encryption, and IRM systems. That's the data-centric portion of the plan.

Here's where the two intersect. For the devices that you have defined as "controllable" in the environment and for which you have available (and enforceable) data protections, establish the technical and procedural controls needed to secure those devices and keep them securely managed. This will provide the first layer of mobile defense and create an environment where the majority of devices have effective data-protection controls in place. For all other devices—the ones that could not be secured or for which the organization has determined it will not support—use device-control technology to keep those devices away from your infrastructure as much as possible. These devices should be considered "hostile," and the organization should make every effort to keep sensitive information off them. There are bound to be some "outliers" in the device set. These will be devices that may be considered "hostile" or, at least, do not have effective information-protection controls, but there is no foolproof method of keeping these out of the environment. Nevertheless, every effort should be made to keep the number of "outlier" devices to a minimum.

The second layer of control comes from the data-centric model. Implement the technology you have identified that can be deployed on an organization-wide basis to secure data as it goes mobile. The coverage of this technology will not be complete: There will be gaps in protection where either the technology is insufficient or the burden on employees or their workflow is too great for the organization to support. As with the technology outliers, these data-protection outliers are bound to exist, and the goal is to keep those to a minimum as well.

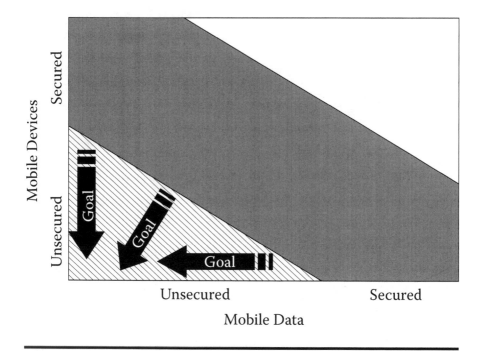

Figure 5.3 Optimum device and data combinations.

This process will protect as much data as possible in any case where the data becomes mobile.

The combination of mostly secured mobile devices and mostly secured mobile data will lead to a situation where most of the mobile information in the enterprise is secured. Figure 5.3 shows a graphic illustration of this point. In the figure, security is charted as four characteristics, with two on each labeled axis: secured and unsecured devices, and secured and unsecured data. The striped area at the bottom left of the figure indicates the placement of unsecured data on unsecured devices, and is the least desirable of all possible situations. The white area on the top right corner of the figure represents the best of both worlds: secured data on a secured device. The goal of the mobile security program is to continually reduce the number of unsecured devices and amount of unprotected data to the minimum possible (thus reducing the size of the striped area). This correspondingly increases the size of the middle area of the figure—the place where data is either secured or placed on a secured device—leading to an overall increase in the amount of mobile security in the environment. The combination of the two characteristics—secured data on a secured device—provides an extra layer of security depth. The point here is that if an organization is able to enforce controls over enough data and enough devices—even with the outliers mixed into the environment—it will have a reasonable chance at effectively protecting the mobile environment.

You have probably observed that this chart is very similar in nature to Figure 1.1 from Chapter 1, and for very good reason. Both charts show the relationship between data and devices when implementing a mobile security program. However, where Figure 1.1 shows the importance of balancing controls on either devices or data, Figure 5.3 shows the effect that increasing the security level of both devices *and* data has on the overall security of the environment.

Conclusion

Models are a wonderful thing. As kids, we build them, study them, and take them apart. As students, we use them to understand how the world works, or how specific parts of the world interact. As adults, we rely on them to give order and structure to the world around us. But as we grow and gain more experience with models, a funny thing happens. We stop looking at models as literal interpretations of the world around us and begin experimenting with them. Whether it is a financial model, a structural model, a scientific model, or a security model, we begin to understand the model for what it is: not an absolute determination of The Way Things Are, but a representation and suggestion for The Way Things Could Be. We learn to use models as a springboard for thoughts and ideas. What if we change this variable? What if we put this piece over there? What if we make this part look like this? What happens? How does this change things?

Mobile security models are no different. There is no practical way to implement a strict data-centric or device-centric model into a modern enterprise. It just won't work, so don't try. But you can use these models as a suggestion for understanding the way things could be. Understand them, play with them, introduce variables and see how they affect the model's outcome. Most of all, find the form of the model that works best in your particular environment. If you ask a security professional which mobile data model to use, his answer is likely to mirror that of the lawyer: "It depends." Once you understand how these security models work, how they don't work, and how to implement the best of each into your environment, your answer won't be, "It depends."

Your answer will be, "Like this."

Action Plan

The selection of a particular approach or model as a guide to securing mobile data is as individual and full of organization-specific criteria as any other security problem. Nevertheless, both the device-centric and the data-centric models have certain characteristics to their approaches that may make one or the other easier to implement (or extend) in your own organization.

The action plan for this chapter summarizes the decision points for each model. Review these decision points and determine the extent to which your organization has addressed each of the issues presented. If the result is a majority of issues falling within either the device-centric or the data-centric models, you may use that approach as the foundation for your own mobile security program, filling in from the other model as needed or desired.

Device-centric criteria: For each of the following questions, determine the extent to which your organization has addressed that area to enact a device-centric approach to mobile security.

1. Do you have a defined set of devices that require protection or advanced security?
2. For each of those devices, are the following services available:
   - Device-based access controls (e.g., passwords, tokens, biometrics, etc.)?
   - User-based access controls (e.g., separate user data spaces, user/group permissions)?
   - Data-based access controls (e.g., file permissions)?
   - Encryption?
3. Are you able to block certain devices from your infrastructure?
4. Are you able to limit the availability of devices within your infrastructure through policy, process controls, or technology?
5. Are you able to restrict the flow of information to, or from, specific devices?
6. Are you able to control or manage the availability of specific features on the mobile devices in your enterprise?
7. Do you have a central device-management service?
   - Are all the mobile devices it's capable of managing under its control?
   - Are all the capabilities of the service being utilized?
8. What logging and auditing capabilities are available on the mobile devices in your infrastructure?

Data-centric criteria: For each of the following questions, determine the extent to which your organization has addressed that area to enact a data-centric approach to mobile security.

1. Do you have an information-classification program in place that can identify your sensitive or confidential information?
2. Do you have the capability to restrict access to information based on its classification?
3. Do you have any access controls in place:
   - Full-disk or partial-disk encryption for computers?
   - Volume- or file-based encryption (for data on mobile devices)?
   - Data-specific access controls (e.g., password protection)?
4. Do you have a Document Management or Information Rights Management service established in the enterprise?
   - Does the IRM service extend to data on mobile devices?

Chapter 6

Encryption

It's impossible to research the security of mobile data without quickly coming across the suggestion that encryption will solve all your mobile security problems. Encrypting all mobile data, says the popular literature, protects it from end to end and provides absolute assurance that your data is safe from prying eyes. Encryption vendors will tell you there is no need to look at any other control or protection mechanism if you properly and effectively utilize encryption on every mobile device. The U.S. National Institute for Standards and Technology (NIST) says, "The primary security controls for restricting access to sensitive information stored on end user devices are encryption and authentication."[1] Multiple state breach-notification laws even specify encryption as an acceptable means of protecting sensitive private information. It would seem that an organization wishing to protect its mobile information need only enable encryption technology on all those devices. Period, end of discussion.

Is it really that simple?

If it is, why spend so much time and effort worrying about various kinds of mobile devices and data protection? Why bother with access controls and device blocking and all the other forms of available mobile security? You would think that a security mechanism that has received such popular acclaim and endorsement from multiple sources would be a sure-fire cure for mobile data and device security problems. If so, then why is encryption not yet universally adopted as an industry standard feature on mobile devices, and why haven't more organizations begun encrypting all their sensitive information on mobile devices (or *all* devices, for that matter)? That answer is not so simple, and it's the subject of this chapter.

To begin with, let's get some quick definitions out of the way. The term *encryption* is commonly used to refer to a number of processes that all serve a single purpose: to scramble information in such a way that it becomes unreadable to those who do not know how to unscramble it. There are some basic terms that are used to describe these processes:

> **Encryption**: The use of a cryptographic process to transform information into a form that cannot be understood by unauthorized people
> **Decryption**: The use of a cryptographic process to transform encrypted information into readable form
> **Key**: The information used to enable the encryption and decryption processes

Uses for Encryption

The primary purpose of encryption is to protect information that needs to be kept secret from would-be attackers. In fact, cryptographer Ron Rivest has famously stated that cryptography is about "communication in the presence of adversaries."[2] Throughout history, people have needed a way to communicate in secret—for both honorable and nefarious purposes—without fear that their communication will be discovered. Along any communications path, there may be people that wish to eavesdrop on the communication. The use of encryption protects against such eavesdropping by creating a secured container or channel through which information can pass and allows the message to go from sender to receiver undisturbed. When applied to mobile data security, this is precisely the type of problem that has been discussed throughout this book: the need to move information securely from point to point using potentially hostile communications paths and devices. Encrypted information can move securely from Point A to Point B regardless of the security (or lack of it) at intermediate points or devices along the way to its destination.

The Importance of Standards

Over the years, many encryption systems have fallen prey to sophisticated attacks that allowed attackers to break the encryption and discover the secret information being protected. In addition, as time goes on, attack techniques get more sophisticated and computer processing capabilities get better, allowing attackers new opportunities and capabilities to break encryption systems. That's why it is critically important to select an encryption algorithm that has withstood the test of time and is recognized within the industry (or by government decree) as able to withstand a wide variety of attacks and subversion techniques. Proprietary encryption systems that have not been made publicly available for review and testing by the cryptographic community, or have not had a history of commercial and government use, are poor choices to protect your most valuable secrets.

That is not to say that selecting a particular algorithm like AES, RSA, or 3DES automatically guarantees the security of the encryption or the secrecy of your data. How those algorithms are implemented in a particular product is just as important as the algorithm itself, and a poor implementation can render the encryption useless. Imagine building the world's strongest safe, complete with 12-inch steel walls, motion and heat detectors, and a locking mechanism requiring three forms of biometric identification before entry, yet building the safe's door from balsa wood and painting it gray to match the walls to make it harder to see. A quick glance at the safe might make some would-be thieves think it is impenetrable, but rudimentary examination by any moderately skilled thief would reveal the safe's flaw immediately.

Likewise, some encryption products have used a state-of-the-art algorithm but made common implementation mistakes, such as not erasing the keys from memory when not in use or storing them unprotected on the computer's disk. These are the cryptographic equivalent of the balsa wood door; they get the job done but provide opportunities for an attacker to quickly get past the encryption. While many of the algorithms embedded in today's mobile encryption products are considered strong enough to withstand a cryptographic attack, the products themselves are new and untested and raise the question of whether their implementation contains any as-yet-undiscovered flaws that would allow an attacker to defeat the encryption system. That's why it's important to thoroughly research any mobile security products under consideration. Knowing the history and longevity of the product, whether it has undergone independent analysis and testing, and whether there have been any published flaws or vulnerabilities in the product (and the vendor's response to those flaws) are crucial to ensuring that you are getting a product that will properly protect your mobile data.

Symmetric Encryption

There are two fundamental types of cryptographic algorithms that are commonly used: symmetric (or secret key) and asymmetric (or public key). The simplest is the symmetric algorithm. This is the easiest to understand and is the one most people think of when they imagine how cryptography works. In a symmetric encryption system, there is a single key that is used for both the encryption and decryption processes. Figure 6.1 shows a symmetric encryption process. In this example, the single encryption/decryption key for the message is "xyzzy."* Alice wants to send Bob a file, so she runs it through a symmetric encryption algorithm and supplies the appropriate key. The output of the process is an encrypted file, which she then

---

* In practice, cryptographic keys are large strings of binary numbers protected by a user-memorable password. For simplicity, these examples will use simple alphabetic strings as keys. In actual use, these would make for very poor cryptographic keys and poor passwords.

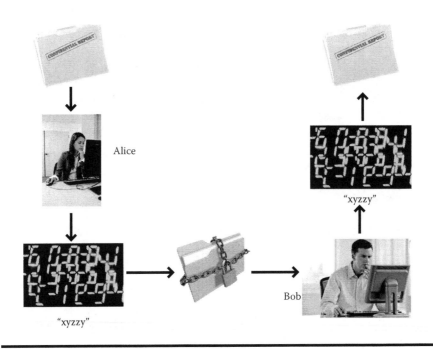

Figure 6.1 Symmetric encryption process.

sends to Bob. Bob runs the file through the decryption algorithm using the same key ("xyzzy"), revealing the original unencrypted file. Symmetric algorithms are great for securing both large and small messages because they are very fast (in terms of computational complexity) and they are simple to understand and operate.

As good as symmetric algorithms are, however, they only provide one security feature: confidentiality. A message encoded with a symmetric algorithm will be secure from prying eyes, but because there is only one key involved in the process, anyone who knows (or discovers) that key will be able to encrypt and decrypt messages. Second, symmetric algorithms provide no proof of the identity of a message's originator. Bob knows that Alice *could have* encrypted the message, but he has no way of proving that Alice *did, in fact,* encrypt the message. This is an authenticity problem. Unknown to either Alice or Bob, Carl may have stolen Alice's key and created a special message from "Alice" to Bob to send him false information.

Symmetric systems also suffer from a lack of integrity protection. There is no way of knowing if the message Bob received is one that Alice originally sent. For example, rather than creating an entirely new false message, Carl may just intercept one of Alice's messages and alter the contents. Instead of a message from Alice reading, "Don't trust Carl. I think he's a spy!" the altered message might say, "I've checked Carl out. He's a great guy!" Carl can then reencrypt this altered message using the single shared key and send it along to Bob, who will be none the wiser that Carl is sending him bad information. The symmetric encryption system provides no way to ensure the integrity of the message Bob eventually receives. Bob might ask Alice to verify the information she sent in her message through some other means (like a telephone call), but in many cases that might be impractical (Bob might not have Alice's phone number) or undesirable (the message was encrypted using the supposed "secret" key, so Bob may have no reason to doubt Alice's message). Finally, if Bob does discover that the information is bad, he might wrongfully accuse Alice of originating the false data. Because there is no way to distinguish all the holders of a particular symmetric key (and nobody knows that Carl has been intercepting their messages), there is no way for Alice to disprove that she originated the bad message. Thus, symmetric systems suffer from a lack of nonrepudiation capabilities: the ability for the receiver of a message to prove the identity of the message's originator or, conversely, the inability for a message originator to deny her origination and ownership of the message.

The lack of authenticity, integrity, and nonrepudiation features of symmetric encryption systems may not be big a concern for an originator (depending on what type of data they need to encrypt), so their absence may not pose a problem. However, one problem that is common to all users of symmetric encryption systems is one of key distribution. Getting the encryption keys to the proper people and keeping those keys secret is a major issue with symmetric cryptography. If the number of people who need access to a particular message or series of messages grows beyond a few, the complexities in securing that key grow considerably, as do the logistics involved in securely delivering the keys to all the authorized parties. This problem also occurs in real life. The more people who know a secret, the less likely it is to remain a secret for very long. Every organization wrestles with this problem.

Despite their limitations, however, symmetric encryption systems are widely used for a variety of purposes in every corner of the world. The most commonly used symmetric systems today are the Data Encryption Standard (DES), Triple-DES (3DES), The Rivest Ciphers (RC4, RC5, and RC6), the International Data Encryption Algorithm (IDEA), and the current Federal Information Processing Standard (FIPS) algorithm, the Advanced Encryption Standard (AES).[3]*

Asymmetric Encryption

Unlike symmetric cryptography, with its single key shared among all participants, asymmetric cryptography uses two mathematically related keys for each user. One of the keys is the user's private key and is never shared with anyone. The other is the user's public key and can be shared with anyone or stored in a public directory. Because of the use of the public key, asymmetric cryptography is often called

---

* Readers should note that DES, RC4, and RC5 are now considered obsolete and should not be used for new applications. In addition, IDEA requires a license for commercial use.

"public key cryptography." The relationship between the two keys is such that any action performed with either key *can only be reversed with the other key* in the pair. In other words, any action done with the public key can only be undone with the private key, and vice versa. The use of any other key, or the incorrect key in the pair, will not work.

Figure 6.2 shows how basic encryption and decryption work with an asymmetric algorithm. In this figure, Alice takes her message and encrypts it using Bob's public key. Once Bob receives the message, he decrypts it with his private key. This solves the biggest problem of symmetric cryptography: key distribution. Bob never has to distribute his private key to anyone, and he can freely distribute his public key to anyone. He can post it on a public key server, his personal Web site, or his Facebook page without any recrimination. The key-distribution problem is solved. If the key pair is generated for Bob by his company, the private part of the key pair will need to be transmitted to him securely, but secure transmission of a private key to a single person is much easier to manage than distributing a shared key among multiple recipients. The most commonly used asymmetric algorithms are Rivest, Shamir, and Adleman (RSA) and Elliptic Curve Cryptography (ECC).

Asymmetric cryptography shares the same confidentiality properties with symmetric cryptography, but it adds authenticity, integrity, and nonrepudiation as enhanced features. Because of the mathematical relationship between the public and private key, in addition to the use of hashing functions (also known as a one-

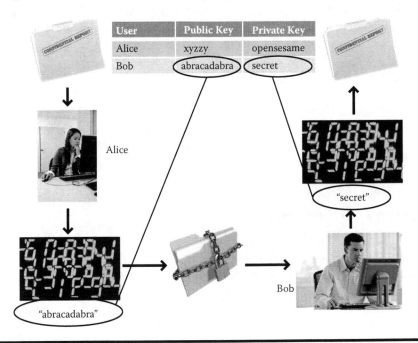

Figure 6.2   Asymmetric encryption process.

way cipher: an algorithm that creates a unique "fingerprint" of a piece of data), the sender of a message can be provably verified (authenticity), and any tampering with the message in transit can be detected (integrity). In addition, the properties of asymmetric encryption prevent an originator from denying that she is the originator of a particular message that she did, in fact, send (nonrepudiation).*

As a result, asymmetric cryptography adds different beneficial features to the mix, and it also eliminates most of the key-distribution problems that symmetric algorithms suffer from. But these features come at a cost. The first is that asymmetric algorithms process data much more slowly than their symmetric counterparts, so they are rarely used for encrypting very large messages or continuous data streams (such as a network transmission or a phone conversation). To solve this problem, many applications combine the two types of algorithms. They need to use a symmetric algorithm to encrypt a lot of data, so they generate a symmetric key (often called a session key) for that purpose. They then use an asymmetric algorithm to encrypt and send that symmetric key to all the participants in the communication. The asymmetric process is much slower, but it is only needed briefly at the beginning of the communication to distribute the symmetric session key. Once each participant in the communication has securely received the symmetric session key, that key (along with a symmetric encryption algorithm) is used to encrypt the rest of the communication.

Asymmetric systems don't suffer from the key-distribution problem, but they have a corresponding key-management problem. There are two keys for every user in an asymmetric system, and those users need some way of letting others know their public key. This requires users to send their public keys to everyone they know or for an organization to establish a publicly available key server for people to access the public keys belonging to people with whom they need to communicate. Rather than leaving the creation of keys to the user, some organizations generate the key pairs on their users' behalf so that they (the organization) can store and recover keys if the user loses them or leaves the organization. We'll discuss this point further in just a bit.

It's important to understand the basic operation of each type of algorithm and where it's appropriate to use each type. This will be important to apply as you begin exploring the use of encryption for mobile data and mobile devices. Most bulk-encryption systems (such as full disk encryption or mobile device encryption products) use symmetric algorithms as the primary encryption method because they're fast and compact. However, they may add asymmetric capabilities to manage the distribution of keys, provide for data-recovery services, or manage authentication and access-control functions. Understanding how each of these two types of encryption work will help you evaluate the various products and,

---

* Exactly how asymmetric systems provide these services is well beyond the scope of this book. The reader is advised to seek out any number of good references on the subject of encryption systems and algorithms for further information.

more importantly, the claims the product vendors will make when trying to influence your purchasing decisions.

When to Use Encryption

Knowing how encryption works and knowing when to use it (or not to use it, in some cases) are two separate things. Despite all the hype, media attention, and legislative pressure, there are instances where encryption can provide real benefits to an organization and, more important, instances where it does not. In a 2005 report, Gartner Research identified three specific use cases where encryption can provide a large benefit to an organization. Those three cases are:

1. When data moves
2. When existing access controls aren't sufficient to protect the data
3. When it's mandated by an authoritative body[4]

Despite the age of the report, all three rules are still important to the discussion of encryption for mobile data and devices. Let's look at how each one affects an organization's decision of whether or not to use encryption for its mobile data.

> *Use encryption when data moves.* This would seem like a natural lead-in for the use of encryption for mobile data. The move can be either virtual (over a network) or physical (on a mobile device), but data on the move—what was previously labeled data in motion—puts that data at a heightened risk of loss or interception. Encrypting this data adds a layer of protection that compensates for the loss of the safety of a stationary location.
>
> *Use encryption when existing access controls aren't sufficient to protect the data.* Previous discussions addressed the use of access control to protect mobile data on mobile devices. Encryption can help compensate for the lack of effective controls on many mobile devices by adding access control (in the form of knowledge of the decryption key) where it doesn't already exist. For example, many off-the-shelf flash drives do not have built-in password features or other access-control mechanisms. The use of encryption can address this problem by forcing the use of a password or passphrase to unlock the encryption for a particular set of data. Devices that do provide built-in access controls may not provide the ability for multiple users to store information securely on the same device in such a way that each user's data is protected from view or modification by the others. If multiple users use the same device, each user can use her own individual encryption keys and passwords to encrypt her data, keeping it secure from other users. Using encryption to protect data on CDs and DVDs is also a smart move if the media will be carried or transported out of the control of the organization. For commercial use, general-purpose encryption

products are readily available that provide strong encryption for data files that need to be protected on mobile devices.

Use encryption when it's mandated by an authoritative body. The growing concern of the public that their personal data is being mishandled both by corporations and the government has led to a corresponding growth in government legislation and industry regulation that requires data on mobile devices to be encrypted. Many companies are now also demanding that the sensitive information they provide to their suppliers and service providers be encrypted on mobile devices, and are rewriting their service contracts to require this. In many situations (some of which have been highlighted in previous chapters), it is not feasible or effective to put encryption on a particular mobile device, and alternative controls may be available that compensate for the lack of encryption. Nevertheless, encryption is currently the hot buzzword in mobile protection, and many are latching onto its use regardless of its practicality or efficacy.

Using these three factors as a guide, it is clear that encryption has a place in mobile data protection, and few people would argue against that. At a technical level, with no other considerations in play, encryption (when properly designed and implemented) is probably the best all-around method for protecting information in any form, and especially so for mobile data. However, we can rarely single out just the technical criteria for any business decision, because technology is rarely the sole factor affecting such decisions. Although encryption may be the best technical solution, there are a number of mitigating factors that make themselves apparent as soon as you begin taking a closer look at implementing mobile data encryption within an enterprise's infrastructure.

Infrastructure and Workflow Compatibility

The biggest consideration, and the one that causes most organizations to take a second look at alternative forms of data protection, is that encryption technology is often incompatible with the organization's infrastructure, architecture, or existing technology. Many organizations have invested heavily in automated business systems, data processing capabilities, and commercial off-the-shelf applications that help improve their information use and management capabilities. Some of these applications can be years (perhaps decades) old. Introducing encryption into these systems and applications may be an expensive proposition, if it's possible at all. In addition, encrypting data introduces processing overhead, which older hardware may not be able to support. Even if encryption is being implemented solely for the purpose of protecting mobile data, this may impact the source of that data and the way data is managed and stored on nonmobile systems.

Upgrading the technology infrastructure within an organization solely to support encryption is a difficult decision to make for any enterprise. As a result, these limitations reduce the ability to introduce encryption at the system or application level, leaving only the individual workstation and the mobile device as the insertion points where encryption can be introduced. As discussed previously, the technology available for these devices may not natively support encryption, and devices that do can be difficult to integrate into an existing infrastructure. That is not to say that implementing encryption is impossible. In fact, the opposite is true, and the technology for doing so is constantly improving. Organizations with older technology or infrastructure, however, may find it more difficult to implement than organizations with newer technology or those with the ability to upgrade their infrastructure.

Once the decision has been made to implement mobile encryption and the technology impediments have been overcome, you will quickly find that the process of encrypting mobile data is not nearly as automated or transparent to the end user as the product vendors would have you believe. Some encryption systems and devices work very well without user intervention. For example, most workstation-based full-disk encryption systems are extremely transparent to the end user and function well with little or no user intervention. The most that users of these systems will see of the encryption process is the possible addition of a boot-time password, hardly an unacceptable intervention into the user's time or workflow.

Other encryption systems are much more intrusive into the user's workflow. E-mail encryption systems often fit this category. Unless the organization has established the technology to automatically encrypt all e-mail coming from its e-mail system (or selectively encrypt e-mail from particular users or to particular recipients), users must make a security decision each time they send an e-mail. They must ask themselves whether the information in the e-mail is sensitive or confidential. Is the recipient expecting that this information will be encrypted? Is the data covered under some law or regulation that would require its encryption? Will the recipient be able to retrieve and decrypt an encrypted e-mail? Should I even bother with this encryption stuff? Will anyone really notice if I skip it altogether?

A similar thought process occurs when users are required to encrypt information on flash drives or optical media. With the majority of flash drives, the user must go through extra steps to encrypt the data on the drive. Either the user must start an encryption application and encrypt the data first, or the user must create an encrypted data container on the drive before reading or writing data. This may require additional passwords or software execution on the users' part, and the same thought process they went through with e-mail encryption will begin running through their heads here, culminating with that all-important question, "Will anyone really notice if I skip it altogether?" This is not the question you want users to be asking themselves, as the answer they typically arrive at will invariably be "probably not." That is, of course, until one of those drives is lost or one of those e-mails is misdirected and sensitive company or customer data is lost or compromised. Thus, integration of encryption into the organization's existing technology and the ability to be as transparent as possible is an important consideration when it comes to implementing encryption within an enterprise. The less an end user has to think about the encryption, the more effective it will be and the less likely that the user will try to bypass or ignore it.

Encryption Impediments

Sharing data between users within a single organization is much easier than sharing encrypted data with outsiders, as the organization can define the acceptable hardware and software standards that all employees will use to ensure encryption compatibility across the organization. However, exchange of encrypted data with outsiders is a normal business requirement. If the two organizations use different encryption products, the underlying encryption algorithm may be the same between them (for example, both may be using AES or RSA to encrypt the data), but the interface and key-management systems for the two will be different. A document encrypted with PGP is not readily decrypted by someone using TrueCrypt. Getting all your business partners to agree on a single encryption standard may be possible, depending on the business relationship and security needs, but as the number of partners grows, it will become more difficult to get agreement or cooperation on a common encryption standard.

It's also important to understand that enforcing end-to-end encryption of mobile data across an entire communications path is extremely difficult. We already saw how this can be the case in the Gadgetron example from Chapter 3. In that example, the data moved rapidly from person to person and from device to device. Even if the original data had been encrypted, each of the recipients of the data would have needed to decrypt it to work with it. As a result, it is unlikely that the data would have remained encrypted throughout its journey, especially if one of the participants had sent the information outside the organization. There are too many links and too many opportunities for the data to be moved to an unprotected device, or for one of the users to forget to maintain either the data or device encryption as it moved from point to point. Remember the Inverse Distance Principle: the more complex a communication path becomes, or the more users that are involved in that path, the less likely it is that any protection mechanism will be maintained throughout that path.

Finally, there is one last situation for which encryption, no matter how automated or pervasive, will fail to protect data. To illustrate this problem, it's beneficial to look at an example that the entertainment industry is currently wrestling with. Over the past decade, the industry has enabled a progressive series of technologies that seek to protect its digital content, trying to limit the devices on which content can be viewed and restricting the ways that content can be moved from device to device, all in an effort to protect its intellectual property—movies, music, and television programs—from illicit copying and distribution. As long as the content remains in digital form (and as long as the protection mechanisms in use have not been cracked by hackers or digital pirates), this system can work well.

You may be quickly tempted to point to the widespread piracy of digital music and movies as evidence to the contrary. However, digital music from compact disks (the primary source of digital tracks) is not copy protected, thus no subversion of a content-protection scheme is involved. CSS (the content-protection mechanism for commercial DVDs) was quickly cracked due to a poor implementation of its cryptographic functionality, not from failure of the cryptography itself. There are content-management systems that are in use and *do* work, including Apple's FairPlay and video devices that adhere to the HDMI specification. Digital-content management systems can work when they are implemented well and are not overly burdensome to end users.

Unfortunately, entertainment content can't always stay in digital form because, somewhere along the chain, the media must be converted to an analog format to be displayed or heard by humans on a device like a TV set or music player. Once the content is converted to analog format, it is easily copied and transformed to other nonprotected media for distribution. This "analog hole" has been a sore spot for the entertainment industry, which has spent much of the past decade trying to close that hole.*

Digital data suffers from a similar problem. Neither application programs nor humans can work with encrypted data. At some point, the data must be decrypted in order for it to be useful and available to applications. Users must be able to read it, work with it, or process it within application programs that need to use it in their own format. At that point—the point where it's transformed into unencrypted data, even for a moment—it's vulnerable to copying, theft, or alteration. This problem can be addressed somewhat within an application, which can be modified to decrypt the data just at the moment it is needed and encrypt it again once it is done with its task, but organizations may not have the ability to modify their applications and, in any event, the "hole" is still there, if even for a smaller window of time. As information moves from user to user and device to device, there are bound to be one or more of these "analog holes" along the way: places where the data needs to be decrypted, even if only briefly. An organization trying to provide complete end-to-end encryption of its mobile data must understand that these holes exist, work to minimize the ones it knows about, and accept (or create compensating controls for) the ones it is unable to close.

Mobile Data Encryption Methods

Despite all the mitigating factors, encryption still remains one of the best ways to protect data, whether that data is at rest or in motion, on a fixed or portable device.

---

* In 2009, the U.S. television industry converted all its over-the-air signals to digital format. This was done primarily to free up broadcast airwave bandwidth for enhanced content and services, but it was also enacted in part to allow for the enforcement of digital content restrictions on broadcast entertainment.

However, not all encryption is the same, so understanding what you need to encrypt and the options available for encryption will help determine the best approach to addressing your encryption needs. To assist in selecting the best approach, let's examine the various encryption options available.

Full-Disk Encryption

As its name suggests, full-disk encryption (or whole-disk encryption) encrypts the entire contents of a computer's hard drive, making it unreadable if the computer is stolen or its hard drive is removed. Full-disk encryption is a very effective way of protecting an entire system, particularly if that system is portable or transported outside the safety of a secured environment. Full-disk encryption works by encrypting all the sectors of the computer's hard drive and integrating with the operating system to transparently decrypt and reencrypt those sectors as data is read and written during the normal course of the computer's activity.

Because the entire drive is encrypted, the computer must have some way of decrypting the operating-system portion of the drive in order to boot the machine. There are various ways of handling this, the most common being the use of a preboot password that the user enters when the machine first starts up. The password is then used to unlock the keys for decrypting the rest of the drive so the operating system can boot. Other alternatives to a user-entered password include the use of a smartcard, biometric scanners, or dongles that attach to the computer, all of which can hold the appropriate credential and decryption-key information. These methods, however, may require the use of additional equipment or devices attached to the computer, which will increase the cost and support requirements of the system. Some manufacturers are beginning to ship laptops with built-in smartcard readers and fingerprint scanners, but these are still not standard equipment on most models today.

Full-disk encryption works well because an attacker is unable to glean any information from the encrypted drive. The operating system, directories, data files, and application software are all protected, and without the key to decrypt the drive, no part of the drive can be read or analyzed to gain any intelligence or confidential information. This reduces the cost of a lost portable computer down to the cost of the lost hardware, an acceptable loss for many organizations. Although most laptops are stolen simply for the ability to resell the hardware, any confidential information on that computer will be accessible to the thief or to the eventual buyer of the system. If they are able to view that data and have the knowledge (and desire) to exploit any confidential information they may find, the organization that lost that data could face serious financial and reputational consequences. Full-disk encryption reduces that concern for an organization.

That last point is important: Full-disk encryption *reduces* the threat of information loss, but it does not completely *eliminate* it. Once the appropriate credentials have been entered and the decryption keys retrieved, the computer will automatically decrypt any information that is read from the encrypted drive. If an attacker can gain access to the running system (either physically or by obtaining a connection over a network), he might be able to extract decrypted data. In addition, most full-disk encryption systems are susceptible to attack techniques that exploit the properties of computer memory chips to retain their data for a certain period of time, thus allowing the decryption keys to be retrieved before that memory is lost. This exploit, however, requires an attacker to have physical access to the system while it is still running. Thus, mobile system security is susceptible to the same primary vulnerability as many other aspects of information security: If an attacker has physical access to your system, he has the ability to launch almost any attack. Full-disk encryption systems will not prevent such a real-time physical threat. It does, however, provide excellent protection against off-line data theft or the loss of a mobile device with sensitive data.

Full-disk encryption can also have an impact on the performance of the system where it is loaded. Every disk sector that is read or written must pass through the encryption engine, which uses system processor and memory resources to execute. In the past, this load has been significant in some cases, especially on older systems. As computers (and mobile computers in particular) get faster and more powerful, the drag imposed on the system from encryption is becoming reduced to the point where most users will not notice a change in system performance. Nevertheless, an organization wishing to implement full-disk encryption software on its portable computers would be wise to run full performance and usability testing on the most common equipment in its environment to ensure its compatibility and performance acceptability before committing to a particular encryption technology or product.

One of the biggest drawbacks to the use of full-disk encryption is that it is not universally available on all mobile platforms, so the problem of protecting data transported between mobile devices is still an issue even if full-disk encryption is in use on some of them. The current crop of full-disk encryption products are targeted primarily at the PC and workstation market and are not available on other types of devices. While some devices (certain models of smartphones and flash drives, for example) already have built-in device encryption, moving mobile data from device to device still requires the user to determine the encryption capabilities of each device before moving any sensitive information.

File- and Directory-Based Encryption

For the organization that doesn't want to implement full-disk encryption but still needs encryption to protect its sensitive information, a more targeted solution may be in order. The use of file-based or directory-based encryption is a good alternative to satisfy this requirement. A file/directory-based system encrypts just a portion of a user's disk, specifically the files and/or directories where sensitive information is located. Organizations that implement file/directory-based encryption generally choose to encrypt user and application data files while leaving the operating system and supporting files unencrypted. The operating system is rarely considered propri-etary or sensitive to a particular company and is easily replaced and reloaded if it is lost or corrupted. However, data files are the organization's intellectual property and thus worthy of a higher level of protection through encryption.

In a file-based product, the user selects the specific files to be encrypted and runs the encryption software against those files. In a directory-based system, the user (or the administrator, in a centrally managed system) selects specific directories on the computer that need to be encrypted. Once that designation is enabled, any files stored in those directories (and all subdirectories) are automatically encrypted as they are written to the directory. As long as the file stays in that directory, it will remain encrypted. However, if a file is moved out of the designated directory (including copying it to another system), it will be decrypted before moving to its new location.

File/directory-based systems provide the organization with the ability to pro-tect particular information on a user's PC without incurring the processing over-head associated with full-disk encryption for data that is not considered sensitive. Implementation and product features of file/directory encryption systems vary from product to product, but most offer several of the following features: [5]

- Designing specific files and folders for encryption by users and/or administrators
- Automatically encrypting the contents of designated folders
- Identification of certain file types that require encryption (for example, .DOC, .XLS, and .PDF files)
- Identification of specific system users whose data files must be encrypted

Given these capabilities, it is easy to see how file/directory encryption is a popu-lar approach to protecting mobile data. There are, of course, some trade-offs when using this approach. To begin with, the user must know what directories on his computer are encrypted and make sure all sensitive information is placed in those directories. For example, some organizations designate the "My Documents" folder on Windows computers as an encrypted directory, as this is the most common place on Windows systems for users to store their important documents. Unfortunately, if a user stores information outside the My Documents folder, those files will not be encrypted. Therefore, diligence on the part of the end user to maintain sensitive documents in designated directory locations is a requirement for such an encryp-tion system, and some users may not be diligent about following this practice.

Another disadvantage of file/directory-based encryption is that it still leaves part of the computer exposed to potential data loss. Because only a portion of the computer is encrypted (namely, the user's designated data directories), information may still exist in the nonencrypted files and directories that contain potentially valuable information. Although these areas may not contain sensitive company information, they may contain configuration data, system access information, and other intelligence about the system and the way it interacts with the company's infrastructure that may be potentially useful to an attacker or someone looking to further infiltrate an organization using information found on that system. Additionally, many applications generate temporary working files and directories during their operations. That temporary data is often not included in the list of files and directories designated for encryption. The data stored in those temporary files is then available for inspection by someone perusing the drive for data. Finally, temporary files are often not deleted after their use, and even applications that delete their temporary files do not do so securely, leaving the information on the drive for forensic inspection by a knowledgeable attacker with physical access to the device.

Virtual Disk and Volume Encryption

Virtual-disk encryption systems work by creating an encrypted container on a target drive. The container is a standard data file and is seen as such by the operating system, just another file among thousands on a user's system. However, the encryption program that created the container can open the file (when provided with the correct user authentication, of course), decrypt its contents, and mount the file as a new drive or file system on the computer. At that point, the user can read and write data to the new drive and (as was the case with the directory-based encryption) all files on that new drive will be encrypted. Once the user is done working with the files on the virtual drive, she can close that drive and the operating system will once again see only the original container file, with no visibility into the secured contents of that container. Virtual-disk encryption is essentially a form of full-disk encryption, but on a smaller scale. To the user, data is written to and from a normal operating system drive, but behind the scenes the data is being written to the file container.

Related to virtual-disk encryption, and closely related to full-disk encryption as well, is volume encryption. Volume encryption takes an entire physical drive (or volume) and creates an encrypted container from that volume. When the user opens the encryption application and supplies the proper authentication credentials, the application will mount the encrypted volume as another disk drive or file system on the computer, much in the same way that virtual-disk encryption mounts a container file as a separate drive. The user then reads and writes data to that new drive, and that data is stored on the encrypted volume. Volume encryption is similar in function to full-disk encryption, since the full drive in both technologies is protected by encryption. However, volume encryption does not need to manage the preboot authentication process, as the encrypted volume does not contain any of the operating system boot code needed to start the system. Volume-encrypted drives can also be easily moved to different computers, as long as the new computer supports the same encryption program that was used to encrypt the drive. Full-disk encrypted volumes (with their operating system boot code) are not nearly as portable.

Virtual-disk and volume-based encryption are a great solution for mobile devices that support file-based operation. An organization can purchase common flash drives or flash memory from commercial sources at considerably lower cost than specialized hardware-encrypted models. It can then create encrypted containers or enable full-volume encryption on those devices, providing the equivalent encryption protection (through software) at a lower cost to the organization. Of course, any positive security benefit is always tempered by a corresponding challenge to its implementation. With both virtual-disk and volume encryption, that challenge comes from the end users of such systems. Virtual and volume encryption systems require more work and effort on the part of the user to load the encryption software, mount the virtual container or volume, supply the proper password, then remember to store all their files on that encrypted drive. Some of this process can be scripted to simplify the steps for the end user, but it is still much less transparent to the end user than full-disk or directory-based encryption systems.

Hardware-Encrypted Storage Drives

Previous chapters explored the use of hardware-based encryption in flash drives and other portable media. Recent developments in hard-drive technology have now made built-in hardware encryption available on standard hard disks for use in standard computers. Although more expensive than their nonencrypted counterparts, encrypted hard drives bring all the benefits of full-disk encryption without the need to use resources from the host computer. The drive contains all the cryptographic hardware, software, and key-management logic it needs, freeing the operating system from the need to manage those functions. The password to unlock the decryption key is provided at system boot time, and from then on the drive appears to the operating system as a normal hard disk with the ability to read and write data like any normal drive.

When evaluating whether to go with hardware-based or software-based encryption systems, the organization needs to balance out the advantages and disadvantages of each method. On the positive side, hardware-based solutions generally run much faster than software solutions, because the dedicated and specialized hardware in these devices can manage the encryption and decryption processes much faster than software-based components running as part of the general operating system. In addition, most hardware-based encryption products provide good tamper resistance against an attacker disassembling the device to discover the encryption keys.

Software-based encryption systems have an advantage over their hardware-based counterparts in that they don't require the added expense of hardware procurement, installation, and ongoing support. However, when you factor in the cost of software licensing, maintenance, support, and key management, the cost difference between hardware and software solutions may not be as great as originally thought. Software solutions can be much easier to deploy, as automated software distribution is already part of many organizations' operating environments. Because most solutions can be installed on existing equipment, they usually don't require a hardware upgrade or a support technician to physically visit every system in the environment. A disadvantage to software-based systems is that they can have a performance effect on some computers, especially older models with slower hardware. However, for most users the difference will not be noticeable, especially if they have a more recent system.

Table 6.1 shows a summary of the various file and disk encryption options. As you can see, although there is no clear choice, there are enough options available that most organizations should be able to find a solution that fits their operational needs.

Tape Encryption

Encryption is not just restricted to hard disks and flash memory. It can also help secure the numerous data tapes that organizations generate for data storage and backup purposes. An option to reduce the exposure a company may have to a lost-tape incident is to encrypt any data that gets moved to tape. Encrypting the data ensures that the data will remain confidential, even if an attacker intentionally steals the tape and has the appropriate equipment with which to read and process the data it contains. Such encryption can be accomplished in one of two ways. The methods for doing this were discussed briefly in the data-centric security model discussion in Chapter 5. The data can be encrypted as it is stored on the organization's systems or databases, then backed up to tape in the same manner as any other file or data set in the environment. The advantage to this method is that the tape units do not need any special facility to manage the encryption process and key storage. However, this method requires that the systems and applications need to be able to manage encrypted data, or an additional step must be added to the backup process to encrypt data before it is sent for archiving. This may increase the time it takes to back up a system, may potentially increase storage costs due to the additional disk space needed for temporary storage of the encrypted data on its way to the tape drives, and adds complexity to the backup and restoration process as the additional encryption and decryption steps are added.

Alternatively, some organizations augment their tape drives with technology that encrypts the data while it is in the backup process and decrypts it during restoration. This method does not require any changes to normal systems processing, nor does it require much change to the organization's backup procedures, but it does add cost for the hardware needed to encrypt and decrypt the data going to and from the tape, and those units are expensive. In addition, it forces the organization to consider the longevity of the hardware and software used during the backup process. Because this method bundles the encryption and backup process all together, the equipment capable of rereading and decrypting the information will need to be kept available and in working order for as long as the organization

Table 6.1   Encryption Benefits and Challenges

Item	Benefits	Challenges
Full-disk encryption	Protects entire system Reduces threat of information loss Attacker can't get any information from system for data or analysis Reduces cost of lost system to hardware value	May require additional equipment if smartcard or biometric scanner is used to unlock system Most systems susceptible to cold boot attack Can affect system performance Not universally available on all mobile platforms
File/directory-based encryption	Apply encryption only to sensitive files or directories and leave the rest of drive unaffected Flexibility with the type and amount of files that get encrypted	User must ensure that sensitive data is stored in encrypted areas of drive Part of the drive is still exposed; can lead to information leakage
Virtual-disk and volume encryption	Virtual disk and volume may be portable to other systems Good for mobile devices that support file-based operations	Requires more work from end user to properly mount, use, and unmount virtual disk or volume
Hardware-encrypted drives	Generally runs faster because cryptographic processing is performed in dedicated hardware Can provide good tamper resistance against attack	May be more expensive than software-based solutions

may need to restore or process those encrypted backup tapes. Depending on the organization and its data-retention requirements, this life cycle could be 5 to 10 years in the future. This has the potential to complicate the ongoing maintenance costs of the tape processing and restoration operation. If the retention life cycle is short enough (for example, 1–2 years) this technology migration may happen as a natural course of events as the organization continues to enhance and replace the technology it uses for backups.

The third option is to select a backup system that automatically encrypts data as it is read from the disk and before it is sent to tape for storage. This method has the advantage of eliminating the need for specialized encryption capabilities in either the business applications or the tape units, thus avoiding the increased cost for either of those facilities. However, not all backup systems have this capability, so an organization should select its backup system carefully if this is a key requirement. In addition, because not all backup systems use compatible processes, the backup system used to create the backup is usually required for reading the backup tape again at a later date. The organization must plan for this and have the same backup system available for as long as the media it created needs to be accessible.

A final option, and one that is being explored by more and more organizations, is to eliminate tape transport altogether and use network-based transport to move data to an off-site backup storage location. Using this method, the primary and backup sites are connected by a high-speed network, and backup data is transmitted over the network from the primary site to the backup site. This eliminates tape packaging, delivery trucks, tracking systems, and the need to explain how a tape can go missing between two locations. Once the data gets to the backup site, it may still be transferred to tape for economic long-term storage purposes, but it remains in (presumably) controlled conditions and under the watchful eye of the organization at all times. Without the perils of traveling between the two locations "in the wild," many of the risk factors pertaining to the use of backup tapes (as well as the need to encrypt those tapes) are eliminated or greatly reduced.

Key Management

The need for effective key management and a method for ensuring that encryption and decryption keys are properly and securely stored has, hopefully by now, become clear. Proper key management is essential for ensuring that authorized users and the organization's authorities have proper access to those keys. However, organizations establishing encryption capabilities too often leave the issue of key management unaddressed until the very end of the encryption project, at which point they become overwhelmed by the number of potential approaches and technical possibilities involved in establishing a proper key-management system.

The organization must first understand what key management really is and (more important) what it is not. A key-management system is really no more than a database of all users' encryption keys along with the policies and processes for managing the full life cycle of events for those keys. This includes their creation and distribution to users, storage and maintenance (potentially far into the future), procedures regarding key expiration and reissue (for users whose keys have expired or been compromised), and (perhaps most important) the determination of the proper authentication and access rights for users to have access to keys stored in the system. In short, the key-management system is the lifeblood of managed encryption in an enterprise, for without it users are left on their own to determine proper key creation, use, and management. Every organization will implement key management slightly differently based on its own particular needs, but evaluating those needs is particularly important when trying to apply key-management principles and techniques in a mobile device environment, where multiple technologies and device interfaces make a uniform approach to key management extremely difficult.

The process of key-life-cycle management, including the software, hardware, processes, policies, and standards surrounding key management, are often (and incorrectly) referred to as a public-key infrastructure, or PKI. The term *PKI* is used to describe the process for managing the public-key portion of an asymmetric encryption-key pair and the validated certificates (authenticated verification of the validity of a particular public key matched with the identity of the key's owner), but the term is also sometimes used to describe any general process used to manage all encryption keys. The main difference between a true PKI and a general key-management service is that PKI deals only with public keys and certificates. A general key-management system also manages and tracks users' private keys in addition to their public keys. PKIs are extremely important if the organization wants to take full advantage of the security benefits encryption can bring to the enterprise, such as confidentiality, integrity, authenticity, and nonrepudiation. However, a full key-management system is necessary if the organization needs to add full data recovery and investigative capabilities into its encryption program.

The first consideration any organization must make is to determine whether or not it wants to establish a key-management system in the first place. Key management is not easily or quickly established, but it is necessary if the enterprise wants (or needs) to track key distribution and usage for all its users. For some organizations, this may not be necessary. An organization may need to ensure that sensitive data is protected in a mobile (or even a stationary) environment, but that's the extent to which it is willing to go in the process. It may establish and standardize on a particular technology to enable encryption on the various platforms it will support, but may leave it to the users to create and maintain their own keys. This approach will suit an organization that is able to establish its own requirements for key management. However, it is not an approach that would suit organizations whose requirements may be dictated, at least in part, by legal or regulatory guidance requiring encrypted data to be recoverable for investigative, audit, or legal-discovery purposes. These organizations would require a more detailed tracking of keys (both current and historical) for all its users (both current and historical). The keys may be necessary to recover data from the device of an employee who is no longer with the organization, or whose device may be part of an internal or criminal investigation. It may also be necessary to recover the key of an employee who has lost or forgotten his key and needs a copy to access his data.

As a result, the organization must also determine the extent to which it wants to keep a user's historical keys—keys that were previously assigned to the user but may no longer be valid, either through expiration or because they were lost or compromised. Keeping historical keys can assist the recovery or investigative efforts if the encrypted data is older than the lifetime of the current key, but it will greatly complicate the efforts to establish the key-management system, as key lifetimes and replacements have to be more closely tracked in the system. In addition, any request for past key recovery must not only identify the user and device for which the key is required, but it must also specify the time frame as well.

Once the organization has determined its true need for a key-management system and resolved the issue of key retention, it must then determine the technologies and platforms for which it is able (or willing) to provide key-management systems. Many popular encryption systems can work with established commercial PKI products and technologies. These systems can integrate keys and certificates into commonly used operating systems and applications. However, newer mobile devices may have their own encryption and technology standards and, often, their own operating system. Thus, they may not fully integrate with established key-management systems, or they may have their own key-management processes that need to link to an existing company-managed system. The degree to which existing key-management systems can integrate with new devices and platforms (or the lack of support for such integration) may determine the organization's ability to fully manage the key life cycle on mobile devices under its control. If an organization must create its own programming to link existing key-management systems with newer mobile devices and technology (or worse yet, rely on the users themselves to properly transfer key information into or out of their devices), that will add cost, complexity, and error to an already complex process.

Of the many ways that organizations can approach key management—from the most basic (leaving users on their own) to the most complex (establishing a full-blown key-management system and/or PKI)—one thing remains constant. All encryption processes are based on keys, and the security and integrity of those keys is the single most important factor in successfully establishing an encryption program to protect a company's secret information. The organization's encryption keys are—quite literally—the keys to the kingdom, and their protection and proper management is essential to keeping that kingdom as secure as possible. Establishing the need for a key-management program, then implementing the policy and technical processes needed to maintain that program and keep those keys secure, is one of the most important steps any organization can take to ensuring its kingdom's encrypted secrets remain as secure as possible.

Data Protection vs. Data Recovery

One of the selling points of a full key-management service is the ability to recover data if the encryption keys are lost or the user is unavailable to provide access to the private keys used to encrypt a particular data set or device. However, before entering into the complex (and often frustrating) world of full key management, the organization needs to examine its goals for both encryption and key management.

Often, that examination hinges on whether the organization merely wants to protect its data or whether it will need to recover encrypted data in the future.

Data protection is the fundamental point of all encryption processes. Keeping the data secure from attackers, or (more specifically for our purposes) keeping mobile data secure as it traverses mobile devices, is the reason many organizations turn to encryption in the first place. However, many organizations just need to ensure that their data is safe from prying eyes. If that data is lost or stolen, knowing that it won't be discovered or disclosed to someone who does not have the authorization to possess it satisfies the organization's information-protection goals. This doesn't mean that the organization is falling short of its security obligations or that it doesn't take the security of its information seriously. It just means that its business case and justification for using encryption stop at the point where the data is protected. The ability to recover data from an encrypted drive or device is nice to have, but the added expense and complexity required are not worth the extra cost they would entail. For these organizations, deploying the appropriate encryption technology and instructing employees on its proper use is all that they require.

Selecting data protection as the sole reason for implementing encryption, thus forgoing a full-blown key-management system, means that the organization will not be able to take advantage of some of the advanced features such a system can provide. If the encryption keys are lost or the employee is not available to provide access to the keys, the organization is stuck. There is no way to recover the encrypted information without the required decryption keys. However, if the data is easily re-creatable—for example, the results of a data search or a file that already exists on a user's PC or a network server—this may not be a big concern. If the encrypted data is something that was specifically created on the mobile device and no additional backup is available, this protection-only approach means the organization must be willing to accept its loss.

A protection-only approach is not appropriate if the organization needs be able to recover the data on an encrypted device. In this case, it must turn to the use of a data-recovery approach. A data-recovery approach requires that the organization invest the time, effort, and money to build a full key-management system and actively manage the deployment of the encryption technology on all the mobile devices in its infrastructure. An organization with full data recovery as a goal must establish the technical and procedural means to recover encrypted data from protected devices. However, this does not necessarily mean that key-recovery and key-management processes must be implemented on all mobile platforms in the enterprise, as such technology might not exist or be creatable within the organization's existing infrastructure. It does mean that the organization needs to develop standards for ensuring that encrypted data is accessible via other means if the encrypted file or disk is lost or if the decryption keys are not available.

For example, the organization may need to establish better backup procedures for its users' computers. This will allow access to data that can be moved to mobile devices without the need to install key-recovery capabilities on each device. The organization may also implement technology (currently available and discussed previously) to track the data that is moved to (or created on) mobile devices so that it may know what information was on the lost device and be able to recover the data without access to the device or its encryption keys. No matter what supplemental or compensating technology an organization may implement, however, a data-recovery approach will take considerably more investment and effort to implement on an enterprise-wide basis than a protection-only approach.

Conclusion

Encryption is not a new technology. In fact, the first crude encryption techniques were established thousands of years ago, and the beginnings of what we now know of as modern cryptography were established in the 19th century. What is new is the heightened need for encryption to protect the proliferation of sensitive data that traverses the networks and devices where that data is stored. What is also new—and what strikes fear in the hearts of information owners and security managers alike—is the rapid proliferation of mobile devices and the rapid movement of mobile data to places outside the ability of any organization to manage or control. To amplify that fear, the lack of mature encryption capabilities on new mobile devices—the same encryption capabilities that are considered mature on more established platforms such as PCs and data networks—means that a great deal of sensitive and private information is moving around cyberspace unprotected and uncontrolled.

The good news, however, is that the technology, and the marketplace that delivers that technology, is rapidly evolving. It is only a matter of time before the confusion of products, services, and processes in place today evolves into the mature technology of tomorrow. Until then, organizations will need to tread carefully when considering and implementing encryption in their mobile environments. The technology is certainly available, if only in the form of disjoint products and cobbled-together linkages between systems and devices. But if an organization is serious about encrypting its mobile information and mobile devices, it needs to take a serious look at the available technology. There will be gaps. There will be situations where the technology does not quite meet the needs of the business, and there will be situations where the business and its employees' workflow will need to adjust to the capabilities of available encryption technology. Nevertheless, those gaps should be small enough to begin an implementation that will address the majority of the organization's needs, with the understanding that the technology (and the way it interacts with the environment) will improve over time.

Encryption is a great tool for protecting sensitive information when it is used properly and managed well. However, an organization needs to understand encryption's place in the security ecosystem. Encryption is a tool, like so many other tools in the security manager's tool belt. Used properly, it can provide a valuable service to the organization. However, it is not the only tool available to an organization for protecting sensitive information. Other tools, like access control, authentication, and data partitioning, also provide security for important data on mobile devices. Because encryption is not yet universally available on all devices, these other data-protection approaches should also be part of the organization's tool belt.

Unlike in times past, encryption is now commonly available to the public; more and more systems are incorporating encryption to protect data; and there is a growing call from the public, legislators, and the media for encryption of all private data. However, encryption is still far from a universal or ubiquitous utility. Despite huge advances in functionality and ease of use for encryption systems, the use of encryption to protect data in the modern mobile world is still far from an automatic process. Different devices use different, independent, and often incompatible encryption systems; key management is often left to the user; and seamless insertion of encryption into the processing and transportation scheme is still a hit-or-miss proposition. In short, there is still a great deal of manual intervention required for effective use of encryption, especially as it pertains to mobile data and mobile devices. Organizations today must look to encryption to satisfy their need to protect sensitive and private information, but they may need to create their own processes and technology for linking together the various products they choose to deploy.

Action Plan

Encryption has become one of the most recommended means of protecting mobile data on mobile devices. There is a great deal of confusion as to how to properly select an encryption tool, how it is best implemented, and how to ensure that the right data is encrypted at the right time. Consider the following factors when attempting to address your company's encryption needs.

1. What aspects of encryption are most important to your organization?
   - Confidentiality
   - Integrity
   - Authenticity
   - Non-repudiation
2. Does your organization already have encryption systems in place?
   - Full-disk
   - File/directory encryption
   - Virtual disk or volume encryption
   - E-mail or network encryption
   - Hardware-based encrypted devices
3. Are the encryption products already in use capable of protecting data on mobile devices?

4. Are encryption services available on the most important or critical devices in your enterprise (as identified in previous chapters)?
   - Where are the gaps?
   - Are these gaps critical to your mobile data protection program?
5. How do you want to manage keys in the enterprise?
   - End-user generated and managed
   - End-user generated, centralized management
   - Centralized generation, end-user management
   - Centralized generation and management
6. If you are considering centralized key-generation management, do you already have a working key-management system and/or PKI in place?
7. Which aspect of data management is most important to you?
   - Data protection
   - Data recovery
8. Do you need to exchange encrypted information outside your organization or infrastructure?

Notes

1. Karen Scarfone et al., Guide to Storage Encryption Technologies for End User Devices, Special Publication 800-111, National Institute of Standards and Technology, November 2007.
2. Ronald L. Rivest, "Cryptography," in *Handbook of Theoretical Computer Science*, ed. J. Van Leeuwen (New York: Elsevier, 1990), vol. 1, chap. 13, 717–755.
3. National Institute of Standards and Technology, Guide to Storage Encryption Technologies for End User Devices, Federal Information Processing Standard (FIPS) 197, November 2001.
4. Rich Mogull, Use the Three Laws of Encryption to Properly Protect Data, Gartner Research, August 24, 2005.
5. This feature list is based on a similar list from NIST SP 800-111, Guide to Storage Encryption Technologies for End User Devices. This is an excellent resource for information about mobile device encryption.

Chapter 7

Defense-in-Depth: Mobile Security Controls

Throughout this book, we've talked about different types of controls. In fact, this book is primarily about the use of good security controls in mobile environments and how those controls can be implemented to provide the protection needed for your mobile data and devices. However, the term *control* has not yet been clearly defined, and there are some controls that have not yet been covered in detail that should be included as part of your mobile security program. This chapter will cover controls in all their glory: the good, the bad, and the ugly.

Controls are really at the heart of all information security processes, and are especially important when it comes to mobile security. As demonstrated time and time again, mobile data without the proper controls in place is merely data waiting to be lost or exploited. Let's start where we usually begin a new subject: with a basic definition. Like many terms used in information security, the term *control* has a very specific definition. ISACA (the Information Systems Audit and Control Association), provides the following definition for controls:

> **Controls:** The policies, procedures, practices and organizational structures designed to provide reasonable assurance that the business objectives will be achieved and undesired events will be prevented or detected.[1]

In this book, controls have referred to technical measures enacted either to enforce or prevent particular aspects of mobile security, but a control can have many forms, as the ISACA definition indicates. A control is not just a particular technology, policy, or process; it's the combination of all of these to create the environment wherein the desired security behavior is achieved. In addition, controls must recognize the role that people play in the establishment and maintenance of good security. To summarize, a control is something you do—or something you put in place—to ensure that a desired outcome happens.

Countermeasures as Controls

In Chapter 2, you were introduced to the basic formula for risk evaluation:

$$\text{Risk} = (\text{Threat} \times \text{Vulnerability} \times \text{Value}) - \text{Countermeasures}$$

That chapter included a thorough discussion of the various aspects of risk, threat, vulnerability, and value. It's now time to conclude that discussion with the last part of the formula: countermeasures.

If you recall, countermeasures are the policies, processes, and technologies that you enact to counterbalance the threat and vulnerability components of the risk equation, and which have a direct effect on the overall level of risk for any given area or activity. As an example, imagine you are in charge of security for your company's Web-based e-commerce system. You believe your biggest risk to be hackers trying to break into your system over the Internet. For that particular risk, you may not be able to reduce the threat, because you can't easily eliminate hackers on the Internet. You may not be able to directly reduce your vulnerabilities, as your Web server may be running an old version of software with many known security flaws, but upgrading the system would require major infrastructure investments. Finally, the value is significant, as this system is your company's primary source of income. As a result, the overall risk is high, but your ability to directly reduce the specific elements of that risk is limited.

That's where countermeasures come in. Countermeasures work in risk situations where threat, vulnerability, or value cannot be changed directly, but the overall risk still needs to be improved. For our Web server example, an effective countermeasure would be to install a good network-based or application-based firewall between the Web server and the Internet to identify potentially malicious network traffic and block it, if necessary, to protect the system and the company's revenue stream. Although the risks and vulnerabilities are still there (the hackers haven't gone away, and your server is still running old software), the risk of an attack has been reduced through the introduction of the firewall. Keep in mind, however, that countermeasures should not be considered the only ways to reduce risk. If you are able to directly reduce the level of threat or vulnerability within a given activity, those methods should be addressed first. The use of additional countermeasures will serve as a defense-in-depth tactic to enhance the security of the activity.*

Controls, therefore, are really a form of countermeasure, designed to lower overall risk for any particular process, system, or technology. Some controls are straightforward. For example, blocking all USB devices on personal computers is a control many organizations consider. This does not mean that such a control is *desirable* (it may, as we have seen, have a large impact on the organization's employees and how they move information), just that it is relatively straight-forward to implement and enforce. Other controls are much more complicated. Classifying all the organization's information to ensure proper protection and handling of sensitive information can hardly be considered straightforward or easy, but it can be a very effective control for safeguarding an organization's con-fidential data.

Despite their many forms and implementations, all controls can fit into one of the following four categories:

- Directive and administrative controls
- Deterrent controls
- Preventive controls
- Detective controls

The chart in Figure 7.1 shows all four categories of controls and the various meth-ods and technologies that can be used to establish mobile data protection for each type of control.

The figure shows the control categories as a layered model, in much the same way that defense-in-depth provides layers of protection between an attacker and a potential target. Some controls are applicable to only one control category, while others span two or more categories. This follows the defense-in-depth approach, where some defenses address a particular risk or threat, while others can be used to address a broader spectrum of security problems.

The next few sections will discuss each of the four control categories in more detail.

---

* There is some debate in the security community about the classification of countermeasures as a separate entity in the risk equation. Some security professionals see the implementation of countermeasures as a way of directly reducing vulnerability. Others see it as a separate activity that can reduce the level of threat, reduce vulnerability, or mask the target's suscepti-bility to that vulnerability (the approach taken in this example). Regardless of which side of the debate you choose, the result is the same: Countermeasures are an effective way to reduce overall risk.

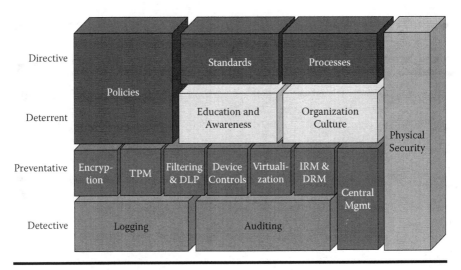

Figure 7.1 **Mobile security controls.**

Directive and Administrative Controls

Directive controls—sometimes referred to as administrative controls—provide guidance to personnel as to expected behavior toward a particular area of security (in our case, mobile security). Directive controls provide employees with the guidelines they must follow if they are to be permitted access to mobile information, devices, or systems. Directive controls are not just applicable to an organization's employees, however. Contractors, guests, vendors, and anyone else that will have access to the organization's information and systems must be made aware of the controls and agree to abide by them.

Policies

The most common example of directive controls is the organization's security policies and standards. These documents (and the procedures that support them) provide the basis for information security throughout the organization and provide personnel with the model that must be adhered to as they perform their work. Directive controls are generally implemented in the form of documented statements of organizational policy, and should not be considered optional or modifiable by organization personnel. Directive controls are the guiding tenets within the organization and should be as strongly followed as any technical or procedural control.

Many organizations compile their directive controls into a single acceptable use policy (AUP). The AUP provides a concise listing of the proper rules and behaviors that all personnel must follow in order to gain and maintain access to information and systems within the organization. It is considered a best practice for all employees to agree to the policy and sign the AUP before being granted access to any organizational resource. If the employee is unable (or unwilling) to abide by the terms of the AUP, no access should be granted. Some organizations require their employees to sign the AUP annually, either as part of regular security awareness training or as part of the annual performance review process. Specific controls pertaining to mobile devices or data may be included in the AUP. However, it is more likely that the AUP will mention the general use of technology for accessing company information and proper protection of company data. Specific direction pertaining to mobile devices or mobile data will usually be established in a separate policy statement and incorporated by reference into the AUP.

A great deal of thought must go into the development of an organization's mobile data security policy, as its requirements can have a large impact on the organization's ability to securely implement mobile devices within the enterprise. Because of the importance of properly crafting such a policy, the creation of a mobile security policy will be covered in detail in Chapter 9.

Administrative Changes

Once you have a solid policy in place to enforce the appropriate behavior, you can begin to enact changes to the way you manage systems and information to better protect both. This is the "administrative" part of directive controls. If the risk you face is enabled through a poorly implemented process or poorly defined procedures, you can launch an effective countermeasure by changing your process to close the threat's loophole. For example, suppose you are concerned with the movement of sensitive information onto flash drives. After some research, you determine that your biggest vulnerability to this threat is the use of unsecured flash drives easily purchased by employees from their local retail store. An administrative countermeasure might be to require all drive purchases to be made through the company's official purchasing group. The purchasing group can then enact administrative procedures to ensure that all purchased flash drives have built-in hardware-based encryption to protect any information stored on the device. The use of such administrative and procedural countermeasures allows you to combat particular threats through changes in the way the organization functions, rather than simply changing policy and hoping everyone will follow the new rules.

Administrative countermeasures can also address holes in an organization's current processes that allow malicious insiders to move confidential data outside the organization on portable media. For example, suppose your current procedures allow your data-center employees to copy any tape in the data center without requiring any additional authorization. This could allow a malicious administrator to copy backup tapes of consumer data and ship the copy to an accomplice outside the company. By changing the process to require management authorization for any tape-copying activity, and then requiring the approving manager to document information related to the copy (including a description of the contents of the duplicated tape), you can counteract the threat of the malicious administrator by forcing another party to understand and approve the administrator's actions (a process called dual control or segregation of duties). While this doesn't rule out the possibility of the administrator and manager colluding together to steal the information, it does provide an effective countermeasure to a potential "nefarious administrator" threat.

Deterrent Controls

Deterrent controls seek to prevent unauthorized activity not by creating an impenetrable barrier between the valuable asset and the potential attacker, but rather by making the attacker believe that the effort required to circumvent the control is far greater than the potential reward if the attacker is successful, or that the negative implications of a failed attack (getting caught) outweigh the benefits of success. For example, if the security policy states that any employee found to be using an unauthorized mobile device will be immediately fired, the threat of employment termination might be enough of a deterrent to keep employees from using anything but authorized mobile devices. Deterrent controls reduce exposure to risk by specifying the consequences for ignoring or bypassing the control, and those consequences act as the deterrent.

The effect deterrent controls have on a potential attacker will vary with both the type of control and the motivation of the attacker. For example, a well-meaning employee whose outbound e-mail is blocked because it contains unencrypted sensitive information will most likely heed the directive warning and resend the message using encryption. The disgruntled or malicious employee trying to extract the same information from the organization will bypass the e-mail channel (the point where the control is enforced) and instead find a communications channel whose restrictions are not so tightly controlled, such as IM, an FTP transfer, or burning the data to a CD. In a similar vein, blocking wireless e-mail and calendar synchronization from all devices except those that have the proper enforceable security controls will deter well-meaning employees from utilizing nonstandard PDAs and smartphones, but it will only force the scofflaws in the organization to seek alternative means to synchronize their devices, such as using the stand-alone desktop-client software that comes with many smartphones. As the sophistication and determination of the attacker rise, so do the sophistication and cost of an effective deterrent to prevent an attack. As a result, the effectiveness of deterrent controls is based less on the ability to implement airtight technical restrictions than on the ability to convince an attacker that bypassing the control isn't worth the effort.

Policies

Policies were discussed in the previous section as an effective preventive control, but they can also be considered a deterrent control. However, their effect in this capacity is only as good as the organization's willingness to enforce the policies. The organization that strictly enforces policies, with appropriate and *visible* consequences for policy violation, will see the deterrent value of those policies having a positive effect on the behavior of its employees and the security of its information. On the other hand, the organization that does not enforce its policies, or whose enforcement is random and arbitrary, will see no deterrent effect from its mobile security policies and, in fact, may see a rise in mobile security incidents. This is because employees will feel that nobody is watching, the likelihood of getting caught is minimal, and the consequences if caught are likely negligible. This can lead to widespread misuse of mobile devices and inadequate security to protect the mobile data on those devices. Deterrent controls are often considered optional by those subject to the controls because they are based so much on employee acceptance and adherence. Employees may not be free to ignore them, but they often do anyway. The attackers (both external attackers and malevolent insiders) will rarely let deterrent controls keep them from performing their evil deeds.

If your threat comes from inside the organization (in the form of damaging employee action, improper use of resources, or inappropriate employee behavior), policy changes can act as deterrent controls to reduce the bad behavior or reinforce the good behavior. Unfortunately, policy changes may have little effect if the threat comes from outside the organization, because an organization has no direct influence or control over nonemployees. Finally, deterrent controls alone, including policies, will rarely cure a security problem or completely counteract the threat of intentionally malicious behavior, so their benefit as a sole countermeasure is limited. Nevertheless, they are a good first step in addressing internal threats and provide a solid foundation for the implementation of other procedural or technical controls.

Education and Awareness

A commonly used deterrent control is the creation of a strong education and awareness program to inform employees of the issues and acceptable practices surrounding the use of mobile technologies in the organization. Because the implementation of mobile technology is driven primarily by end-user needs, educating them on the risks of its use and the precautions they should take can be a highly effective means of preventing mobile data incidents. Users often display a cavalier attitude toward their mobile data and engage in behaviors that put that data at unnecessary risk. This is particularly true when the use of mobile data is perceived as a "mission critical" service and users place expedience and ease of use above information protection and organization security.

An awareness program directed at mobile device users can be a specialized program of its own, but it is most often included as part of the general awareness and education efforts the organization already has in place. The theme of the awareness messages should align with the organization's general security-awareness themes, which are typically:

- Abide by policies and standards
- Protect the company and its information
- Protect customer information
- Comply with the law
- Report any suspicious events or activity

To address specific mobile data issues, the awareness program should explore the topics covered in this book with an emphasis on how the employee can specifically and personally contribute to the mobile data security effort. For example, some of the more important messages should be:

- *Mobile data risks*: Inform employees of the general risks they face when mobilizing their data or incorporating mobile devices into their work. Teach them about the ways their mobile information can be compromised, and give them examples of everyday behaviors that can lead to an unwanted data loss. More important, give them specific and actionable steps they can take to protect their mobile data. These include compliance with the technical measures the organization has provided for their use or the adoption of behavioral or operational changes that don't require any additional technology support.
- *Common mobile data mistakes:* To highlight the general mobile data risk message just described, employees should also be told about the specific ways that users put mobile data at risk. Provide examples of unacceptable behavior that the user can understand and avoid in the future. Review such topics as the failure to use device controls like passwords and screen locks, leaving (or losing) mobile devices in public places, storing sensitive information on devices without proper protection, and using nonstandard or unauthorized mobile devices to store company information. If there have been recent mobile data security incidents within the company, highlighting these can be a great way to get the point across to employees. By describing the mobile actions and behaviors that the organization deems harmful, the employee can begin to understand the expectations for proper mobile behavior.
- *Sensitive information management*: Employees generally want to do the right thing and will follow the security policy and guidance as long as they understand the premise and purpose of the security controls and the controls do not unduly interfere with their ability to get their work done. To reinforce their desire to do the right thing, the awareness messaging should give employees clear guidance on how to protect different types of mobile information they may encounter. Whether it's documents on laptops, synchronized e-mail, flash drives, or optical media, give the employees clear and proper instructions on how to protect these different types of mobile data. If a technical

control exists, explain how and when that control should be used. If no technical control is available, suggest alternative ways to protect the data, even if that advice is to refrain from mobilizing that data. Again, this won't prevent the determined employee or information thief from stealing confidential data, but it will give the people who want to do the right thing a clear method for conforming to the security requirements.

- *The use of encryption*: The awareness program should introduce employees to encryption technology and explain how it can be used to protect sensitive information. If the organization has implemented specific encryption services on its mobile platforms, these messages can explain how to use the technology. Most important, the messages should instruct employees on when encryption is required and how to properly encrypt different types of information (for example, e-mails, disk files, flash drives, etc.).

- *Mobile device standards*: The program should inform the employees what mobile devices are permitted and approved for company use, and how those devices can be procured and properly configured. The standards should be clear and easy to follow. If the standards are difficult to understand or too difficult to implement in practice, users will ignore them, use their own nonstandard devices, and continue to place the organization's mobile data at risk.

- *Malware control*: Malware has long been a problem for personal computers in the past, and a great deal of awareness material has been sent to employees detailing the risks of malware and ways to prevent and detect it. As new technology and devices become prominent in the workplace, malware of the future will adapt to those platforms and find new ways to infiltrate the organization. Make employees aware of new malware threats for the mobile platforms found within the organization, and explain to them the extent to which the organization's existing antimalware capabilities will (or won't) protect them. For those cases where the malware controls are not available, provide suggestions on how the user can avoid a malware infection (for example, turning off Bluetooth discovery or not clicking on mobile e-mail links).

Finally, it is important that the awareness effort be bidirectional. Simply delivering security commandments to employees in the hope that they will heed the message will result in disappointment from both the security team and the employees. The awareness efforts should incorporate a "feedback loop": a mechanism to enable employees to provide commentary and suggestions for how to improve the security of mobile devices and protect mobile data.

For example, the company can provide a Web site or e-mail address where employees can discuss their experiences with the security policies, explaining how they have helped or hindered their work efforts in the past. Such a discussion might reveal widespread dissatisfaction with a particular policy (or supporting control) that should be addressed. This form of feedback can also give valuable insight into the ways employees deal with security issues on a daily basis and can be an effective avenue for soliciting commentary and suggestions on future policy changes. Remember, the end users are the ones closest to the technology and are intimately familiar with how it works and how to use it to address pressing business needs. They will also be the ones who must deal with the consequences of the security controls the organization establishes. Therefore, it only makes sense to enlist their cooperation and incorporate their suggestions for improvement into the communications cycle. It gives them a sense of contribution to know that their voices are heard and provides the security and technical teams with instant feedback on how the security controls are really affecting the business, as opposed to how those teams *think* they are affecting the business.

Organizational Culture

Every individual organization has its own unique and specific culture, and that culture is a fundamental part of everything the organization and its employees do to further the goals of the organization. The effect of this culture also impacts the way the organization approaches and secures its mobile information. For example, an organization that highly values data security will place that value at the core of its policies, procedures, and technology. It will have an information-classification program that is rigidly followed and built into all its systems and applications. It will continuously reinforce the need to protect information in its awareness and education program, and it may even have strict disciplinary consequences for employees who fail to live up to expectations for safeguarding company information. In such a culture, you can expect that most employees will take security seriously and do what they can to ensure that their mobile data is secured at all times. In this environment, the organization's culture acts as a deterrent control to assist in the protection of mobile data by guiding employees' behaviors and attitudes toward security and creating a form of peer pressure to ensure that everyone in the organization is living up to the cultural expectation of security.

Some organizations may place other cultural values more highly than security, such as customer service, increased profitability and market share, employee loyalty, and workforce harmony. While these companies will not ignore security, they will not emphasize it within the company as much as these other values. As a result, getting employees to take mobile data security seriously may be much more difficult in these types of organizations, and the deterrent effect of the company's security culture may be negligible.

In order to ensure that your organization has the greatest opportunity to protect its mobile information, it is important to begin fostering a culture of security awareness and attention within the organization. This certainly starts with the organization's security policies and awareness campaign, but it needs to go much deeper than that. Senior management must endorse the need for security and publicly demonstrate their support for securing the enterprise. Management needs to enforce security policies and procedures with the company's staff, including appropriate disciplinary consequences for violating security policies. In short, the security of the organization (including its mobile data) must become part of the regular discussion among the company's employees. It should not be the only topic of discussion, but it should become part of the cultural landscape and attitude of the company and its personnel. By doing so, the deterrent value of the company's culture will have a much greater effect on the security of its mobile information.

Preventive Controls

Preventive controls keep a user from performing some activity or function. They ensure that the policy, process, and behavioral countermeasures you have put in place are followed by your target population and can be tracked, monitored, and measured for effectiveness. Directive and deterrent controls have a voluntary quality about them. They both work on the theory that it is easier to obey the control rather than to risk the consequences of bypassing that control. In other words, the power for action resides with the user (or the attacker). They have the ability to decide whether or not they agree with the control and whether or not they want to abide by it. They can decide not to follow the security policy, ignore the awareness campaign, or disregard the new procedure. There may be consequences for ignoring these controls, but those consequences are negligible in the employee's opinion. If the controls are particularly bothersome to employees, they may even go out of their way to get around them. Thus, their effectiveness as a countermeasure is limited to those who either voluntarily agree to abide by the controls or who decide that it is not worth their time or effort to find a way around them.

In contrast, preventive controls place the power of action with the system or the organization: Obeying the controls is not optional. The only way to bypass preventive controls is to find a flaw in their implementation or find some alternative means of accessing the desired resource or information. Preventive controls integrate themselves into the infrastructure you are trying to protect, and prevent activities before they happen. For example, by implementing a technical control to ensure that only hardware-encrypted flash drives are allowed to function on company PCs, you can prevent employees from moving sensitive data to nonencrypted drives.

There are many examples of preventive security controls in common use. Firewalls are preventive controls because they examine and block (or allow) network traffic based on predefined rules. Authentication methods are preventive controls because they prevent all except authorized users into a system. Door locks are a preventive control because a person can't go through the door without the appropriate key. However, there is often a fine line between deterrent and preventive controls, and the distinction is not always clear. Few preventive controls are 100% effective all the time, and what may be considered a preventive control for most people would be merely a deterrent control to a sophisticated or accomplished attacker. This brings into clear focus the idea that all mobile data security—indeed, all security measures—must take into account the sophistication level of the potential attacker. Once that is understood, the appropriate sophistication of the mobile security controls can be established.

The most effective preventive mobile data controls are implemented as technical controls within the environment. This allows them to be integrated closely with the devices that carry mobile data and helps prevent their tampering or removal by end users (both malicious and merely well-meaning-but-misguided ones). This technical integration also helps to enforce the nonoptional nature of the preventive controls. Some of the more common preventive controls available include:

- Encryption
- Trusted platform modules
- Content filtering and data loss prevention
- Desktop virtualization
- Device-specific controls

Encryption

We have already covered encryption at length in Chapter 6. However, its role as an effective preventive control cannot be understated. Implementing encryption on mobile devices when it is both technically possible and operationally feasible is one of the best ways to protect mobile data. Unfortunately, as we have seen, it is not always possible to encrypt all mobile data or enable its use on all mobile devices. As a result, other forms of preventive controls must be considered as well.

Trusted Platform Modules

Although not specifically a preventive technology itself, a Trusted Platform Module (or TPM) is an enabling technology designed to aid in encryption and authentication processes and can be used to enhance and enforce the effectiveness of those preventive measures. TPM is both a technology specification and the commonly used name for specific implementations of that specification (such as in the phrase, "a TPM chip"). The TPM specification is managed by the Trusted Computing Group[2] and was designed to provide several security services.

The first is as an aid in cryptographic key generation. The description of cryptography in Chapter 6 should have driven home the point that the generation and security of encryption keys is a vital factor in the overall security of the encryption process. A TPM helps provide this security by enabling secure generation of cryptographic keys. A built-in pseudo-random number generator inside the TPM generates input used in key generation and allows very strong keys to be created on the system where the TPM is embedded. In addition, the TPM can limit the use of the generated keys to ensure that they are used only by trusted applications and system components. This adds to the overall secrecy and effectiveness of the encryption system. In fact, any application that uses encryption can be aided by the use of a TPM, including full-disk encryption, password-protection services, software licensing, and access control.

A TPM also has the capability to generate a "fingerprint"* of the system where it is located. That fingerprint can then be used to identify the specific configuration of the system at a given point in time. If another fingerprint is taken at a later time, it should match the original, indicating that the hardware and software configuration of that system has not changed. If any measured aspect of the system has changed (such as an operating system upgrade, application installation, or the addition or removal of a hard drive), the new fingerprint will not match the original. This is important if you need to be certain that the system has not been altered, tampered with, or otherwise reconfigured, possibly indicating the presence of malware or the system's infiltration by an attacker. If the system has been legitimately changed due to routine maintenance or upgrade, that change should be documented and a new fingerprint taken for future comparison. The need to trust the configuration of a system over time directly relates to the ability to secure the information on that system. Logically, if you trust a system enough to protect sensitive data on it at one point in time and the system has not been altered since that point, it should still be trusted. If, however, the fingerprint indicates that a change has occurred, the system can no longer be considered trusted until the reason for that change can be discerned and the system recertified (or re-fingerprinted).

TPMs have been included as standard equipment in many PC models since 2006. However, their use and implementation has been limited primarily to disk encryption and hardware self-test features. In addition, their deployment has been almost exclusively on personal computer systems. Although they are theoretically capable of operating in almost any device, their presence in non-PC devices is negligible. A TPM embedded inside a mobile phone, a PDA, or even a flash drive could greatly enhance the authentication and data-protection capabilities of those devices, thus increasing their acceptance as a secured means of transporting data. However, TPM technology is still getting acclimated to commercial use in PC platforms. It is assumed that, as the devices become more widely deployed, as their usefulness becomes more apparent, and as their form factor and price drop as a result of advances in manufacturing technology, the presence of TPM technology in non-PC equipment will increase.

Content Filtering and Data Loss Prevention

The implementation of technology to prevent the movement of sensitive information to systems or network areas where it does not belong (including mobile devices) has

---

* Technically, a secured hash value.

been gaining more visibility in corporate environments. This technology is generally known as content filtering in its simplest form or Data Loss Prevention (DLP) for more elaborate implementations. A simple content-filtering system identifies specific types of information to look for, such as all Word .DOC files or spreadsheets containing numbers in the pattern nnn-nn-nnnn (the format for a U.S. Social Security number). When it sees data that matches the defined pattern, it can either send an alarm to an administrator indicating it's found a match or be more aggressive and block the movement of that data to the device or network where it was headed. The specific action a system takes will depend on how aggressive the organization wants to be in its attempt to identify and stop movement of sensitive data.

We have seen, however, that data is difficult to confine to a particular device or technology. Data seems to move in many different directions, enabled by well-meaning (but often misguided) end users trying to get their work done. We have seen examples of this throughout the book, and examined the ways that mobile data traveling on different devices and through different motion paths acquires varying characteristics and degrees of risk. Identifying that data is difficult, and tracking it through all those motion paths is complicated. Training a content-filtering system to specifically identify credit card numbers moving to flash drives and blocking all such transfers may solve one specific problem, but it does not address the organization's general data-mobility risk or track the flow and eventual loss of sensitive data through all the various motion paths and devices through which it may travel.

For that reason, many organizations are now looking at more elaborate DLP systems to cover a wider range of data types, devices, and motion paths. DLP solutions work by placing data monitors (often referred to as sensors) at various points around an enterprise's infrastructure. They may be located at key network convergence points (such as the main firewall, ISP connection, or business-partner network link) or on specific systems within the environment (such as database servers, FTP servers, or e-mail systems). Network-based sensors are specifically trained to examine all data that passes by them, looking for keywords and complex data patterns that indicate the presence of sensitive or confidential information. Host-based sensors can inspect the files on systems where they are installed and identify those that have sensitive information (based on the organization's definition of "sensitive"). The combination of the two can provide end-to-end (data source to data exit point) tracking of mobile data.

The thing that puts DLP in a class above normal content filtering is that the DLP system can be tuned with a great degree of complexity and granularity. For example, the sensors can look for any e-mail message that contains more than five instances of valid credit card numbers, indicating a potential problem in the handling of sensitive data in the organization. Alternatively, it can look for all FTP transfers to a specific organization, such as a competitor or media outlet. This can indicate the leakage of sensitive inside information by a disgruntled employee. The possibilities are limited only by the imagination of the organization and the capabilities of the particular products used.

When a DLP service identifies data movement that matches something on its watch list, it can take a number of actions. It can alert an administrator or security officer that potentially sensitive data has been transmitted out of the organization; it can block the transfer pending approval from an authorized person; or it can redirect the transmission to a more appropriate and secure venue. For example, if the DLP system catches the transfer of sensitive data to a flash drive, it can block that transfer. If it finds that the data is being sent through the organization's e-mail system, it can redirect that e-mail to an encryption service before delivery to its destination.

The biggest benefit of DLP solutions is that, when properly deployed and managed, they have the capability to cover a much larger range of devices and data-transfer points than simple content-filtering systems. Modern DLP services can scan and report on data movement throughout an organization's network, or they can monitor data transmitted outside through e-mail, instant-messaging protocols, peer-to-peer networks, file-transfer services, and a wide variety of mobile devices. They enable a good middle-ground solution between the unmonitored flow of data and a complete restriction of all mobile data movement.

However, DLP may not be the perfect answer to an organization's mobile data monitoring problems. As a technology, DLP is still in its early stages of maturity. The products currently on the market have some very impressive features and represent a true breakthrough in the ability to see exactly what information is leaving an organization's network, providing the ability to prevent its loss. However, as with many immature technologies, a great deal of growth, tuning, and customer experience will be required before it can be said that DLP is a must-have security control for any organization. DLP solutions (like firewalls and intrusion detection systems) also require active participation by organization personnel to be of any benefit to the organization. A properly configured DLP system will identify many potential security problem, especially when it is first established. There is little value in monitoring and reporting on potential security events if the organization is unable or unwilling to allocate the appropriate personnel and establish the proper response procedures to react to any events found by the DLP service. An organization that is truly concerned with mobile data security and protecting sensitive information as it moves between its internal network and mobile devices should research DLP solutions to determine if they might fill a gap in the organization's preventive mobile defenses.

Desktop Virtualization

A big problem organizations face when dealing with mobile data security is that people often need access to their information when they are away from their primary computer. They can bring their laptop and carry *all* their data with them, but that only serves to exacerbate the mobile data protection problem. What if they could access their data from the organization's network, work on and manipulate the data they needed, and store it back on the network without ever copying the data to a mobile device? That's the approach taken by a technology called desktop virtualization or "thin client." Desktop virtualization allows a user to connect to the organization's data network and work on a virtual version of her computer. The virtual workstation is actually located on a central server that manages hundreds or thousands of such virtual machines. The user connecting to such a server will see her own screen layout, applications, utilities, and personalized desktop. She can access the system and manipulate data just as if she were sitting at her office desk. However, she is not directly manipulating her own computer. What she is seeing is a representation of her computer system presented over the network.

The primary benefit of virtualization is that it allows users to access and work on their data without the need to remove that data from the secured corporate environment. Users can run applications and otherwise exchange information with corporate systems from any location where they can get secure Internet access. From an information-protection perspective, desktop virtualization allows the organization to maintain tighter control of its confidential information, protecting it with all the firewalls, intrusion detection, antimalware, and DLP systems it deems necessary. What desktop virtualization prevents is the transfer of that data to a remote system or mobile device. While some users may see that as a detriment ("Hey, I need to download that file for my 9:00 a.m. meeting tomorrow!"), it can represent a reasonable compromise between the total prohibition of data transfer off the network and the free distribution of data to any mobile device that connects to the corporate infrastructure.

Virtualization can be a win for information protection and mobile data access. However, it is not a solution that fits all situations. If the primary purpose of the user's remote connectivity is simply to access data and resources on the company's information network, virtualization is a way to provide that in a more secure manner than allowing users to carry that data with them. If, however, the mobility of network data is the user's specific purpose, virtualization will not be able to satisfy that need. For example, the purpose of synchronizing data with a smartphone is specifically to be able to carry around that information with you at all times. Forcing you to connect to the company's network and access your virtual PC every time you need to check your calendar or send an e-mail defeats the purpose of the smartphone's technology.

In fact, such restrictions may force users to circumvent existing policy or company practice in order to fit their needs. A virtualization service that allows access to a user's files without permitting the direct transfer of those files to a remote system may force that user to attach those files to an e-mail message and send it (probably unencrypted) to their home Gmail account, thus potentially putting the data at a higher risk. This is yet another example of how the security needs of the organization and the operational needs of its users must be balanced whenever new technology or processes are introduced that will have an impact on the way end users interact with their data.

Virtualization may also force the organization to rethink the way it delivers desktop and application services to its employees. Virtualization services can be implemented strictly for remote-access purposes while leaving the internal desktop environment unchanged. However, taking this approach may only be realizing half the benefit that virtualization can bring, and those benefits include operational, financial, and (of course) security gains. Moving to a fully virtual environment for end-user service delivery can allow the organization to switch its desktop architecture to a "thin client" approach: essentially a desktop terminal with limited local storage capacity and processing capabilities. The end user no longer needs a powerful desktop system because the interface is only needed to access data and applications on the network. This reduces the expense for refreshing end-user PCs and laptops (with their typical 2- to 3-year refresh cycle). But, more importantly from a security standpoint, it removes the data from the end-user environment (where it's most vulnerable) and moves it to a more secured and monitored location on the network. This allows the organization to actively manage the data's mobility, allowing it only when it is able to be controlled and protected and not relying on the diligence or attentiveness of the end user to manage its mobile security.

There is one big drawback to the implementation of a virtualized desktop environment. If a user can not connect to a network to access the central virtualization service, she can not access any of her data. Because all her data and applications reside on the company's systems, lack of access will prevent any ability to get work done. This precludes access to information in places where networks are not available, such as during airplane flights or inside a large office building without Wi-Fi or cellular reception. While this might be an acceptable loss of productivity to the organization, it will almost certainly have a negative effect on the employees who require this type of continuous access to their work.

Centralized Device Management

Centralized device management has been discussed in previous chapters as an effective method of enforcing the organization's security policies and ensuring that the mobile devices in the enterprise have a common security configuration. If the organization is able to establish management systems to support its mobile devices (or, more likely, establish several such systems to cover specific devices or technologies), it can establish preventive controls for those devices and ensure that they continue to meet expectations for securing the information they carry. The point of establishing a security control is to ensure that the policy or standard the control supports is uniformly applied and enforced throughout the organization. Central configuration and management systems ensure not only that the policies and standards are in place, but also that users cannot easily bypass or ignore them if they do not agree with the control.

Detective Controls

The primary goal of an information security program is to protect the systems, networks, and information the organization deems valuable and to do everything reasonable to prevent bad things from happening to those resources. The primary way of addressing that goal is through the establishment of appropriate before-the-fact controls, such as those described in the sections on directive, deterrent, and preventive controls. However, it should be clear by now that—as effective as they may be—those types of controls do not fit every situation or adapt themselves to every mobile technology your users may require. In addition, sophisticated attackers may be able to circumvent or defeat the directive, deterrent, and preventive controls the organization has put in place. As a result, they cannot be relied on as an absolute defense against information theft or system compromise.

Subsequently, when the inevitable mobile data incident happens, the organization needs mechanisms to detect such an occurrence. Detective controls are after-the-fact responses that provide notification to appropriate personnel if the before-the-fact controls are not able to thwart an attack or data leak. Detective controls warn when something has happened, and are the earliest point in the post-incident time line when remedial action can be taken. If your detective controls provide a quick enough warning, you can invoke the appropriate incident response before much damage has occurred. For example, if an organization has established services to allow synchronization of e-mail and calendar information to users' smartphones and one of those devices is subsequently lost or stolen, the organization can use the log information from that service to determine if the data transferred to the device contained any sensitive or confidential information. If such data is found, the appropriate incident response process can be initiated.

As another example, your disaster recovery plan may require you to send backup tapes of customer information off-site for safekeeping. A lost tape could both hinder your recovery capability and create an information-breach problem. Your analysis of the problem has determined that encrypting the tapes (a preferred technical preventive control) is too costly to implement, so you need to turn to detective controls to fill the gap. You implement a process change (itself a preventive control) to label and inventory all tapes just before they are loaded on the delivery truck and to check that inventory carefully as soon as it arrives at its destination. If, upon arrival, a tape is missing from the batch, you can immediately begin the search for the lost tape. While this change does not prevent a tape from being lost or protect the information on the tape, it does allow you to detect immediately that something is wrong and take appropriate steps to correct the problem.

The Importance of Logs

Most detective controls share one common characteristic: They require some form of activity log, audit trail, or historical record to be effective. By definition, detective controls are responding to events that have already happened: the file has moved to the mobile device, the data has been sent to the smartphone, or the tape has been lost. Because the controls are not preventive and are unable to act on events before they become problems, the organization must have some way of reconstructing the events that have already transpired to determine the appropriate next steps. Those events need to be reconstructed from activity logs maintained by various network equipment (such as firewalls or DLP systems), system processes (such as operating system logs), or applications (such as transaction or data access logs). This, of course, requires that these systems actually create and maintain such logs, and many (sadly) do not. It is up to system administrators, application teams, or security personnel to establish the need for such logging activity and specify the required information that must be logged. Once those requirements have been established, the organization must ensure that as many mobile data transfer points and devices as possible create those logs and that the system administrators review them on a regular basis for suspicious activity.

This last point is particularly important. Security incidents often do not reveal themselves until well after they have occurred. An organization may not be aware that sensitive information was moved to a flash drive until the device's owner reports that the drive has been stolen. The transfer may have taken place days, weeks, or months prior to the event, so the ability to review historical logging information will be a key factor in the organization's ability to respond effectively. Of course, as more log information is generated, it must be stored, managed, and analyzed. It's not uncommon for an active network firewall or DLP system to generate hundreds of megabytes (or more) of log information daily. That quickly adds up to a huge quantity of storage space that the organization must allocate for log maintenance, and the cost of maintaining such a system will begin to mount. In addition, creating and storing all that log information is of no use if the organization does not establish a process for reviewing the logs on a regular basis to search for suspicious incidents or data anomalies. As the amount of log data grows, the ability for one person (or a team of people) to manually review those logs becomes nearly impossible. For this reason, the use of automated log review tools or a Security Information and Event Manager (SIEM—a specialized event-log correlation and analysis tool) may prove useful to keep up with the amount of data that will need to be sorted, organized, and analyzed.

While most detective controls operate by analyzing historical events from existing event-log data, some preventive controls can also act in a detective capacity if the situation warrants. For example, firewall systems are usually regarded as preventive controls, yet they can be configured to notify administrators of suspicious network or application activity rather than simply blocking it. Network-based and host-based intrusion-prevention tools are designed to block activity that they deem suspicious, but they can also allow the activity and notify an administrator or create a log entry as an alternative action. These and other similar controls have both prevention and detection modes. The prevention mode is available to block certain events from happening, but that approach may not fit all situations. As an alternative, the detection mode can allow the event to occur and simply report its occurrence to a central administrator or management system. This allows the data to flow (satisfying business or user requirements) but still enable follow-up action by an incident response team if necessary. The use of a specific control as a preventive or detective control is often a matter of the situation and circumstance under which it is used.

Auditing as a Detective Control

Finally, there is one time-honored detective control that can be extremely useful for identifying system problems or uncovering missed security events: the audit. While most people would rather avoid audits altogether, the use of technical, process, or transaction audits can be an extremely useful way to determine if the current controls are adequate and effective for preventing and detecting mobile security events or data loss. A technical or process audit will review the current controls in place and determine their adequacy based on industry standards or the organization's own internal requirements. If a gap is identified between the controls that *are* in place and the controls that *should be* in place, the audit will make recommendations for adjustments or enhancements to ensure that the deterrent, preventive, and detective controls are providing the proper amount of mobile security protection for the organization. A transaction audit serves a similar purpose, but with a slightly different approach. A transaction audit will review the various event and transaction logs to determine if any unidentified suspicious activity has occurred. A transaction audit can be an excellent tool for verifying the effectiveness of any existing log-review or analysis processes.

An audit is not often used as a primary detective control. It's usually performed well after any malicious behavior has occurred or data has been lost; thus its effectiveness for rapid incident response is limited. However, as a secondary detective control—one that is available to detect any previously missed events and validate the effectiveness of the process itself—it can be a valuable tool in the organization's overall mobile data security program.

Physical Security

Although the emphasis of most information security is on the creation and enforcement of electronic controls to protect an organization's information and systems, the organization's physical security controls play just as important a role as any technical control. The need for good physical security controls has been discussed at various points throughout this book, but the importance of ensuring the physical safety and integrity of an organization's assets (including its people) plays a fundamental role in the overall security of the organization and its data. In fact, physical security is so fundamental to good information security that its use as a control can be applied to all of the control types we have discussed—directive, deterrent, preventive, and detective.

Physical security acts as a directive control because the policies, standards, and processes involved in establishing good physical security are just as important as those aspects of the information-security programs. Like their electronically oriented counterparts, the directive controls required as part of an organization's physical security program help ensure that the organizations physical infrastructure—its buildings, facilities, equipment, and people—are safe from harm or malicious action. Likewise, the physical security of mobile devices contributes greatly to the security of the information on that device, and any policies related to the physical protection of those devices will help to enhance their overall security. An organization may create specific policies for physically protecting mobile devices, or it may include them as part of the general policies regarding physical protection of electronic information assets.

Physical security also has a deterrent aspect to it. The visible security features within an organization can deter potential attackers from trying to infiltrate a company's facilities to perform evil deeds. Gates, security guards, locked doors, and secure-area access controls all help deter attackers from trying to enter sensitive or restricted areas. The more visible the security infrastructure around a company, the more of a potential deterrent value that infrastructure may have. When it comes to mobile devices, visible displays of security can also deter potential thieves from stealing your device or your data. Securing your laptop with a locking cable can be an effective deterrent, as is securing your mobile phone inside your pocket when not in use or securing your mobile device inside a locked container. All of these acts can deter attackers from stealing your devices and your data.

Finally, like their electronic counterparts, the organization's physical security controls should have the intended prevention and detection aspects to maintain good physical security. Controls such as locked entry doors, biometric access controls, motion-sensor alarms, and the like all serve specific purposes as physical controls, much in the same way that encryption, DLP services, antimalware services, and other mobile device controls serve specific purposes as logical controls in the mobile security space. Although physical and electronic controls are often developed and deployed separately, it is more advantageous for an organization to jointly develop both types of controls together. This helps ensure that the organization's entire security program can protect against the full spectrum of threats and that all types of controls—directive, deterrent, preventive, and detective—are used as defense-in-depth to ensure the best possible protection for the organization.

Conclusion

If you've ever attended a security conference, chances are you've heard at least one of the speakers use the "car brakes" analogy to describe how information security works. The car brakes analogy starts with the speaker asking the audience, "What is the purpose of brakes on an automobile?" A brave audience member typically responds by saying, "The brakes on a car slow it down and bring it to a halt when necessary." Others in the audience will nod their heads in agreement. At that point, the speaker will tell them that they are wrong, bringing puzzled looks from many audience members.

Automobiles, the speaker will then explain, are capable of driving at very high speeds under certain conditions, such as bright daylight, a straight and level road, and the absence of pedestrians or other obstacles that might get in the car's way. Given the right situation (and a skilled driver), cars can achieve and maintain quite a fast pace. Think of Germany's Autobahn, for example. Unfortunately, road conditions are not always that controlled or pristine. Drivers share the road with other cars, as well as pedestrians, sharp curves, steep hills, and a variety of random and unpredictable conditions, such as weather, pedestrians, and intoxicated drivers. None of these are very conducive to fast driving (although some reckless drivers do it anyway). Therefore, the brakes on a car are there to control the car's speed. They allow the driver to go as fast as he can (or as fast as reasonably possible given current conditions) and to regulate the car's speed when more caution is warranted. When the conditions are again safe, the driver can release the control (i.e., the brakes) and resume a higher rate of speed.

Mobile security controls are used in much the same way. Today's users want their data faster and in more places than ever before. The technology to allow that is available, but the methods for doing so often leave the data at risk, as we have seen time and time again. Just as the brakes control the car and allow its speed to match road and safety conditions, the various mobile data controls described in this chapter (as well as those to come in Chapter 8) allow that data to move quickly when it can be secured, but slow it down when the environment is riskier or its safety and security are in doubt.

Of course, there is the small problem of brake malfunction. Like any other mechanical component in a complex machine, brakes can fail, resulting in the inability to properly manage the car's speed. If they fail at very low speed, there might be some damage to the vehicle or some bruises for the driver, but the overall impact of the failure is correspondingly small. If the brakes fail at high speed, the result can be catastrophic for the driver, the car, and any passengers or bystanders in the vicinity. Mobile data controls can similarly fail. The directive and deterrent controls can fail through user apathy or maliciousness, and preventive and detective controls can fail through malfunctioning technology or administrative oversight. In any of these cases, the result is a potential data-loss incident. As with a car's brakes, all mobile data controls should be inspected regularly to ensure that they continue to operate properly, provide the expected protection, and do not need replacement with newer (perhaps more advanced) controls to cover newer and more sophisticated mobile data technology and mobile data threats.

The brakes analogy stands up pretty well, and is a good place to wrap up the discussion of mobile security control types. Many people see them as a way of stopping business and preventing the free and efficient delivery of information and services to the people who need them the most: the organization's employees. When used properly and selectively, however, these controls actually provide a lot of latitude for compromise between the traditional "lock it all down" security mentality and the "cool gadgets at all costs" consumer and business user mentality so common today. The different types of controls—directive, deterrent, preventive, and detective—all serve a purpose and have specific ways in which they can control, monitor, and react to mobile data security issues and incidents. Understanding how each of them works, and knowing where (and where not) to apply them, can mean the difference between knowing and actively managing the mobile data activity that is occurring throughout your infrastructure or being blind to both the activity and the risks that are happening every day. Like the brakes on a car, mobile data controls allow that data to move more easily, more swiftly, and *with more control* than is prudently possible without their presence.

Action Plan

This chapter was full of information concerning the various types of controls that are available to protect data on mobile devices, as well as the benefits and challenges to implementing those controls within your environment. Table 7.1 provides a summary of each of the general controls discussed in this chapter as a guide to use when considering the controls that might be applicable in your environment.

Table 7.1   General Controls Summary

General Control	Benefits	Challenges
Policies (including standards and processes)	Provide clear guidance on acceptable employee behavior	Policies can be ignored
	Can enforce security controls through process oversight and dual controls	Ineffective or unenforceable policy can confuse and annoy employees. Without technical reinforcement, standards and processes can be ignored or subverted
Awareness and education	Inform employees of current threats	Awareness information can be ignored
	Demonstrate correct use of process and technology	Difficult to reach all employees in large organizations

(Continued)

Table 7.1 General Controls Summary (Continued)

General Control	Benefits	Challenges
	Enlist employees' aid in protecting company information	
Organizational culture	A culture that values security can reinforce proper mobile security behaviors	Other values may be more culturally significant than security
Encryption	Provides excellent protection against data leakage or loss	Not available on all devices in the organization
	Provides access control when underlying technology does not	Often requires user intervention to operate. Key distribution and management issues
Trusted platform modules (TPM)	Aids encryption, authentication, and system-verification processes	Only available on PC platforms. Not utilized by most applications
Content filtering	Can identify and block data from migrating onto mobile devices based on simple keywords or patterns	Cannot handle more sophisticated patterns of data searches. Difficult to deploy across entire enterprise
Data loss prevention	More sophisticated data analysis and blocking tool	Current technology still maturing
	Can scan and analyze data at host, device, and network level	Can be expensive to deploy
	Can monitor multiple infrastructure egress points	
Desktop virtualization	Can provide remote users with access to data and applications without risk of data loss through mobile transfer	Lack of data-transfer capabilities may not suit all users' needs. May require architecture changes in infrastructure to support

Table 7.1   General Controls Summary (Continued)

General Control	Benefits	Challenges
Central device management	Can ensure common configuration and operation of mobile devices	May not be available for all mobile platforms. Can be expensive to deploy and operate
Activity and event logging	Provides historical record of user, application, system, and network activity	Enterprise-wide logging standards need to be established and enforced
	Can be valuable for incident response process	Storage requirements for log data can outgrow organization capacity
	Will be required for audit purposes	Reviewing and analyzing log data will require automated tools (e.g., SEIM)
Auditing	Can review current operation against industry standards and organization policies	Clear security control objectives need to be established to audit against
	Can make recommendations for improvement	May not detect a data-loss problem until well after it has occurred

Notes

1. ISACA, *CISM Glossary*, www.isaca.org/ContentManagement/ContentDisplay. cfm?ContentID=46894.
2. For more information on TMP specification and implementations, see The Trusted Computing Group's Web site at http://www.trustedcomputinggroup.org/.

Chapter 8

Defense-in-Depth: Specific Technology Controls

The Chapter 7 discussion of the different categories of security controls (directive, deterrent, preventive, and detective) was an important step in approaching mobile security. As that discussion showed, each type of control serves a specific purpose and addresses a different point in the incident life cycle of mobile data (and all data, for that matter). Directive and deterrent controls address the protection of data early in the incident life cycle by prescribing specific actions, processes, or behaviors that protect the information before a potential attack or theft. Preventive controls address data protection in the middle of the life cycle as data is being created, processed, stored, and managed by the people and systems within an organization. They create a barrier between the data and the attacker before any unauthorized access or data loss can occur. Finally, detective controls work at the end of the incident cycle, and seek to provide warning and notification that an incident has occurred and allow the organization's incident-management process to recover the data or prevent further loss.

The organization of security controls into these four layers provides an efficient means for thinking about their application and determining which type of control best fits into a given situation. As you have already seen—and will see again when you begin determining the best controls to implement in your own environment—some controls can span multiple layers or be used in more than one situation. Although we've already covered a number of important and effective controls in previous chapters, there are still some controls that have not yet been addressed or that warrant additional coverage. In this chapter, we will examine how an organization might use specific defense-in-depth controls to provide countermeasures to some of the threats and vulnerabilities often seen in the mobile data environment. This information will round out the discussion of potential controls for protecting mobile data and provide a more complete assessment of all the tools you have available to create defense-in-depth for your mobile environment.

Portable Computer Controls

Portable computers are both ubiquitous and essential in most working environments and possess most of the risks that we've seen in the various classes of mobile devices. There are effective technologies that can protect mobile computers from prying eyes, but more important, there are some critical user behaviors that can provide even greater protection for both the device and its contents.

Antimalware Services

A current and updated antimalware system is an essential technology for all portable computers. This includes traditional antivirus systems as well as newer protections for spyware, adware, botnets, and other types of malicious code. Because portable computers are often connecting to unknown (hence, untrusted) networks in airports, hotels, conference facilities, and coffee shops, the likelihood of coming in contact with a network where attackers are scanning for unprotected systems or a Web site spreading malware increases dramatically. In addition to having antimalware services active on portable computers, it's essential to implement a process for ensuring that the database of detectable malware (often called the signature file or DAT file) is kept current through a regular download of updated signature data. This will ensure that the antimalware system has the appropriate signatures to enable quick detection of new malware.* This update should be performed as frequently as necessary to ensure that the organization has the latest signatures, and it should be automated, if possible, to ensure that the new data is downloaded without the need for user intervention.

Antimalware services for other types of mobile devices, such as smartphones, are only now beginning to emerge, and it will be a long time before such services become as robust and effective on those platforms as they currently are on PC

---

* No antimalware service is 100% effective, and even the best programs miss a large percentage of malware in the wild. However, failing to provide this protection on portable computers is tantamount to negligence in the eyes of any security professional, and (potentially) in the eyes of some courts.

platforms. Nevertheless, as new malware and attacks specifically targeting mobile platforms are developed, the need for antimalware systems on all types of mobile devices will continue to increase. If your organization already has a corporate standard for antimalware services, it would be beneficial to discuss this trend with your antimalware vendor to determine whether they are planning on expanding their product offerings to include mobile device protection.

Workstation-Based Firewalls

All portable computers should have an active firewall running on the machine to help ensure that hostile traffic from unknown networks does not make its way onto the system. However, a firewall is not only beneficial when taking your computer out into the wild. It can also protect your system from malware and attacks while on your organization's internal network. Most operating systems have built-in firewall capabilities, and there are also a number of third-party products with additional features that can be used in place of the built-in firewall. It's important to understand the features and capabilities of the firewall software you use to ensure that you are receiving the best possible protection. For example, the Windows built-in firewall only blocks network traffic coming in to the computer by default. This is good, but it does nothing to detect network traffic originating from malicious software that has already infected the system. That malicious code, whether it is a password sniffer, botnet code, or data extractor, may try to spread from the infected machine to other systems on the network. In addition, the malware may try to make a network connection from the infected system back to a "home base" computer over the Internet to receive commands or deposit the data it has found.

A firewall that does not analyze or block suspicious outgoing traffic will miss an important opportunity to detect and stop that traffic before it has a chance to spread or leak sensitive information. A firewall with outbound traffic protection should be considered for all portable systems. The Windows Vista and Version 7 firewalls have the ability to block outbound connections, but the user must specifically configure that functionality. This means that most users will be unaware of this capability and fail to properly protect themselves.

Standard Configurations

An organization with a large number of portable computers should establish a standard security configuration for those systems. That standard should include setting the proper parameters, options, and defaults to ensure that the systems operate in as secure a manner as possible based on the organization's security policy and business needs. The standard should also include the proper antimalware and firewall controls as well as any other security software or settings that will protect the users as they wander into hostile territory. Establishing a uniform system configuration helps ensure that the enterprise as a whole is uniformly protected from mobile system threats and that any problems or anomalies that do arise are spotted quickly to ensure timely remediation. In addition, a process for regular system updates and patches must be established to ensure that newly discovered security vulnerabilities are addressed in a timely manner and that all systems maintain a current state of security protection.

Standard configurations should not be limited only to portable computers, however. All of the portable devices in the organization should be reviewed to determine if a standard configuration is warranted. In particular, smartphones and personal digital assistants (PDAs) are likely candidates for configuration standardization. Chapter 5 discussed the need for centralized device management within an enterprise, but before any such management can take place, the devices to be managed must have a common (or nearly common) configuration. Otherwise, the management system will not be able to apply security controls uniformly in the environment. Therefore, establishing such a configuration is the first essential step in the centralized management process.

Once the standard configuration (or, more likely, separate configurations for each type of device) is established, the organization must establish two follow-up activities. The first is to review each device currently in the environment to determine if it is compliant with the standard configuration. If it is not, it will have to be modified or upgraded to bring it as close as possible to the new standard. Some systems may not be able to conform to the standard or may require such extensive upgrades that bringing it up to the standard is not cost-effective. The organization will then need to determine whether to allow the device to continue to operate in a nonstandard configuration or to upgrade it to a compliant level of functionality.

The second activity is to ensure that all new devices deployed into the environment meet the new standard configuration before they are placed into service. This is the best way to ensure that all systems in the enterprise meet (or exceed) the mobile security requirements. Even if older systems are not able to be brought up to the new standard, over time these systems will be replaced by newer ones, and the entire environment will eventually consist only of configuration-compliant systems.

VPN and Multifactor Authentication

Organizations that permit mobile workers to connect to their internal networks through the use of Virtual Private Networking (VPN) should require the use of multifactor authentication—combining something you know (like a complex password or PIN) with something you physically possess (such as an electronic token, smartcard, or key card) or some physical characteristic (such as a fingerprint or voice recognition)—rather than simple passwords for such access. If an attacker is able to get access to the portable computer and install a keystroke sniffer or some other password-stealing code, any ID and password information the user enters on that system will be captured by the attacker and subsequently used to gain unauthorized access to the company's networks or systems. This includes access to any applications that the user logs into while the password sniffer is active on his system. Though not foolproof, the use of multifactor authentication for remote access can significantly reduce the likelihood that an attacker will get through the organization's primary authentication defenses.

Network Access Control

When an organization decides to allow its portable systems to connect to uncontrolled networks, or if it allows systems that it does not own and manage (such as employees' home computers or laptops belonging to on-site consultants) to attach to its internal network, it runs the risk that a malware infection on the portable system will affect the security of the entire organization. Once that infected system connects to the organization's network, there is a high risk that the malware will spread to the rest of the company's network. To counteract that threat, many organizations have begun to research and deploy Network Access Control services, or NAC. NAC allows an organization to detect when computers or other devices have attached to its network. Once the device is detected, all access by that device is blocked until the NAC service can determine the device's configuration and (potentially) its level of security threat. Some of the more common tests that NAC can perform include:

■ Determining if the device has prior authorization to connect to the network
■ Checking for up-to-date operating-system patches
■ Determining if the device has active antimalware and firewall services installed and operating
■ Checking for up-to-date antimalware signature files

If the device passes these checks, it will be allowed to access the rest of the network. If one or more of the requirements are not met, the NAC system can block that device or redirect it to a restricted, limited-access segment of the network where the user can obtain and install the necessary software, services, or approvals required for full access. Many organizations are looking to NAC systems as a way of allowing their users the freedom to exploit the potential of mobile computing without incurring additional risk or security problems once those systems connect back to the company's infrastructure.

NAC does not work for all devices, however. It is designed primarily for use by servers, PCs, and some smartphone and PDA devices. As such, it will not work well for detecting (for example) flash drives or optical media that are attached to a running system. For those devices, the organization may need to establish a more targeted device-control solution that will be able to detect (and potentially block) such devices as they are connected.

Disabling Automatic Program Execution

In some cases, operating-system features designed to make life easier for users actually lower the overall security of the system. There are many instances of this in consumer-oriented systems, but the most commonly used is the Autorun capability built into Microsoft's Windows operating system. The premise of Autorun is simple; allow portable media (for example, a CD-ROM or flash drive) to provide instructions to the host computer on how to execute default programs when the media is inserted into the system. The Autorun feature hides the complexity of locating and executing the appropriate program from the end user by instructing the operating system where the startup program is located along with any other instructions or activities that need to be performed to launch the application. It is a feature originally designed to make life easier for end users.

Unfortunately, this feature also makes life easier for malware authors and distributors. The same feature that automatically launches a new application's installation program can just as easily be used to install and launch a malicious program contained on the CD or flash drive. Malware authors are constantly looking for new and more efficient ways to quietly spread their "product." What better way than to let the operating system do the work for them! The malicious program alters the Autorun configuration files on the media to launch the malicious program rather than the original benevolent program. Such Autorun-based malware first became popular in 2007, and its use has grown steadily since then.

To prevent the spread of this threat, the best countermeasure is to disable Autorun-type functionality on all systems in your organization. This will prevent the automatic loading and execution of malicious code without users' knowledge. While this will have a small impact on your users (who will need to go back to the "seek and execute" method of program launching), it will have a large and beneficial impact on your malware defenses by removing a dangerous infection vector for malware. In fact, the recognition that Autorun systems are more harmful than beneficial has come from both Apple (which removed its Autorun feature from its operating system with the release of OS X) and Microsoft (which disabled Autorun by default for all nonoptical media in Windows 7).

Removing Unnecessary Data

As with many other aspects of security, technical solutions cover only part of the total potential controls for portable computers. The other critical protection component must come from the behavior and work habits of the computer's user. How that user protects the portable computer and the information it contains is just as important as the technical controls installed on the system. One of the most basic—yet often overlooked—information protection controls is to simply not carry sensitive information on a device if it is not needed. Too often, mobile workers carry most of their professional and personal data on their computer without giving a thought to the amount of valuable information that could be lost (perhaps irretrievably) if the device were lost. While the convenience of having their information at their fingertips is an overwhelming incentive for some to resist paring down the data carried on a portable computer, doing so denies an attacker the most valuable commodity he seeks. A regular routine for removing old or unneeded information from portable computers should be a part of every user's work habits.

Physical Protection

Finally, the physical protection users give their portable computers can go a long way toward securing the information they contain. Unlike flash drives or optical media, however, portable computers are larger and much more visible when left on the seat of a car or on a chair in a waiting area. As a result, they are much more inviting targets to an attacker, either for the computer itself (and its potential resale value) or for the information it may contain. Securing the computer when walking away from an area—even for a moment—is important, and keeping it out of sight when storing it can go a long way toward ensuring its safety. A laptop locking cable should be issued to every portable computer user and should be considered standard equipment for mobile computing. More importantly, instruct employees on how to use the cable (it's not always as obvious as you may think) and make its use mandatory for all portable systems. Employees are often told to place their valuable belongings in their trunk if they need to leave them unattended in a car, but even putting the computer or briefcase in the trunk may not keep it safe if done so in a crowded parking lot in view of a car thief or an opportunistic burglar. Advise employees to put their valuables in the trunk *before* they reach their destination. Doing so will not draw attention to the act of placing packages or laptop cases in the trunk when they reach their destination. Understanding not just the value of the computer, but also when and how a theft might occur is critical for protecting both the computer and the data. Encouraging the organization's personnel to modify their behavior to maintain their awareness in such situations will be one of the most effective security protections that an organization can take.

The organization should also issue a privacy screen to all portable computer users for working on their computer in public areas, such as an airport lounge, a hotel lobby, or in areas where those in close proximity will be able to easily see the computer screen, such as in an airplane seat. A privacy screen is a thin plastic sheet that fits over the computer screen and prevents anyone sitting next to you from seeing your work as your files, e-mail, and other information appear on your screen. If you regularly work on sensitive or private information in public areas, a privacy screen is a must-have security accessory.

Portable Storage Devices

Portable storage devices have gained a very bad security reputation, and many regard these devices as the root of all mobile security evil. However, as we have seen numerous times, these devices do provide a valuable function to information workers, and there are some very effective means for securing the organization against (or, perhaps, in spite of) the use of these devices. The most extreme step an organization can take is to prohibit all such devices from its infrastructure, backed by the appropriate policy and technical measures to enforce the ban. This can be accomplished on an enterprise-wide basis or limited to a single site or business group. While this may seem like a drastic step to take, given the many positive benefits these devices can bring to an organization, there are situations where such measures may be justified.

For example, a government agency working with classified information needs to ensure that no sensitive information leaves the environment without proper authorization and protection. Organizations that have access to private consumer financial or health information need to ensure that none of that data leaks out of the environment, as such an incident would bring heavy fines, legal implications, and negative publicity. Finally, organizations that research new products with a high market value (such as pharmaceuticals or advanced technology) might want to prevent information about their latest research and products from leaking out of their laboratories. In these cases, the ease of unintentional mobility that portable storage devices offer may lead the organization to determine that the risks of data loss far outweigh the benefits of allowing these devices into the environment.

If banning portable storage devices is the goal of the organization, doing so solely through policy will have, at best, a limited effectiveness among an organization's employees. When faced with the conflicting forces of ease and convenience of data mobility vs. the mandates of a questionable (to them) policy decision, many will choose ease and convenience, especially if they feel that disregarding the policy will have no lasting effect on their job. To ensure greater compliance, the organization must implement the appropriate technical and process controls to enforce the prohibition.

There are a number of available technologies for achieving these goals, starting with physically disabling the device ports on all computers (for example, by filling them with epoxy to prevent devices from attaching to these ports*) all the way to the deployment of sophisticated device and port-control services on all machines in the infrastructure (which we have discussed in previous chapters). In return, the organization gains the ability to selectively enforce varying levels of device control. It can, for example, enforce restrictions on all portable storage devices on its R&D and customer support networks while allowing limited use in the sales and

---

* Although seemingly an extreme measure, this has proven successful in many situations. Before taking this route, however, make sure that the epoxy or filler you use is not electrically conductive, as that might cause a short in the electronics of the device.

marketing areas. This allows the organization to apply the controls in areas where it believes it has the biggest risks. An organization that wants to permit the use of portable storage devices but wants to minimize potential losses or security incidents can specify that only devices that have (for example) built-in hardware encryption are allowed to attach to company systems. The settings can be as restrictive or permissive as the organization's security stance and policy will allow.

Dual-Use Devices

Controls to protect against the security threats inherent in dual-use devices are often difficult to implement specifically because of the dual nature of the devices. On the one hand, the organization may want to encourage (or at least tolerate) the use of these devices because employees can demonstrate a clear business need or personal benefit to the use of the nonstorage portion of the device. This increases productivity and employee morale, and for some occupations, these devices may be a job requirement. Imagine the difficult time a real estate agent might have if he were not allowed to upload the digital pictures of his new home listing to the computerized listing service. How effective would a news reporter be if she were unable to use a digital recorder for interviews or story notes? Prohibiting the use of such devices in these situations would prevent these workers from effectively doing the jobs for which they were hired. On the other hand, the devices do pose a real threat to the organization wishing to keep a tight lid on its sensitive information and intellectual property. Because the devices are so easy to use, hold large amounts of data, and are easily concealed, stealing data using one of these devices becomes a relatively simple matter.

In many ways, the available technology controls for dual-use devices are similar to those applicable to securing general portable storage devices, including port blocking, encryption, file transfer logs, and audits. However, implementing these controls for dual-use devices is trickier because a security control for one part of the device might affect the operation of the other part. If the functional portion and storage portion of the device are separate, blocking access to the storage portion should not affect functional operation of the device. On the other hand, if the device uses the same storage space for system files and general data storage, applying device-blocking controls or encryption to the device will affect both the storage and the system functionality, potentially causing it to fail. This may be the organization's goal, but if not, the organization needs to perform careful testing before deploying such a technology.

Smartphones and PDAs

The state of the current smartphone security market is still immature. To be fair, there are products on the market that can help organizations or individuals lock down and protect selected features of their smartphones or PDAs. There are also some devices whose basic design incorporates features that promote secure communications and information protection for the device. However, security controls are not universally implemented on all devices, and the technology to enforce security on consumer-oriented devices is limited. Most smartphones (indeed, most mobile phones in general) allow the user to implement a password or PIN to lock the device. However, this feature is largely ignored by the general public because password entry on devices with a small keyboard is inconvenient to most users. Second, very few smartphones provide the ability to encrypt data stored on the device, and third-party technology to add this capability is limited to only a few of the most popular devices. Finally, complex access controls (with the exception of the locking password) are almost nonexistent on consumer-targeted devices of any kind, especially smartphones.

On devices targeted at the corporate market, the situation is somewhat better. Organizations looking to manage the security of their employees' smartphones have several options and products available to them. These management systems allow the enterprise to manage security controls such as passwords (including password presence, length, and complexity), the ability to lock out users for incorrect password entry, selective availability of services (such as e-mail synchronization and Bluetooth discoverability), access to flash-based storage on the device, encryption of data, or the erasure of information from a device if it is reported lost or stolen. These are all good tools to have and can lead to good control over the mobile workforce and their data. However, each of the available tools to manage this type of control is limited in scope as to the devices it will manage. For example, RIM's BlackBerry Enterprise Server only manages devices manufactured by RIM itself and provisioned through various mobile carriers. Other products, like Good's Mobile Messaging service, support a much wider variety of devices, but the list is not universal.

When planning to implement such a capability within the enterprise, an organization may be faced with implementing multiple smartphone control services to cover the many devices that are present among its employees. Alternatively, the organization can standardize on one single device or a small set of acceptable devices that it is willing to support for connectivity to the organization's infrastructure. This will reduce the complexity and technology requirements to the organization, but will limit the device (and potential feature) choice to the end users. Most organizations will find this to be an acceptable compromise, though it may leave those users who always want the latest and greatest technologies feeling unsatisfied.

Optical Media

As we have seen, there are no built-in security protections for optical media (such as CDs and DVDs). As such, any desired security controls must be applied directly to the data stored on these devices, such as password protected file wrappers or encryption. These controls have already been covered in detail elsewhere in this book. A bigger problem, however, stems from the need to completely erase data from an optical disk once it is no longer needed. Data on magnetic media (like tapes or disk drives) can be overwritten multiple times to render it unrecoverable, or the media can be degaussed by placing it in the presence of a large electromagnet for an extended period of time. However, optical media can not be erased in a similar manner. To completely protect data on CDs and DVDs, the media must be completely destroyed after it is no longer needed. In fact, NIST specifies that optical media "must be destroyed by pulverizing, crosscut shredding or burning" to protect the data it contains.[1]

Most common office shredders are not designed to destroy optical media, so even the well-intentioned worker understanding the sensitivity of the information in his possession may have difficulty destroying it properly. Many organizations have begun to recognize this problem and have installed media-capable shredders and special media waste bins in office areas to capture all types of media for bulk destruction, which it then sends to a central destruction area or contracts with an external service provider for final destruction. This effort requires a change in user behavior and attitudes, a slow process in any organization. Until users overcome the perception of optical media as a "throwaway" commodity, this will continue to be a problem.

E-mail

The ability to secure e-mail transmissions depends (as does most security) on the security stance of the organization and its willingness to impose restrictions on its users. This effect is more pronounced with e-mail than for other communications technologies because of e-mail's place as a fundamental and essential communications medium. To protect e-mail on mobile devices, you must consider the potential implementation of several technologies and restrictions. The first approach is to simply encrypt all e-mail transmissions. This will ensure that all information that travels through your e-mail system will be fully encrypted and protected along its journey. Using this method, both the e-mail body and any attachments will be encrypted, and the organization does not need to worry if users pay attention to the sensitivity of the information in their e-mail messages or if they are properly protecting that information. If it gets put in an e-mail message, it gets encrypted.

However, this solution has some drawbacks. The biggest one, and the one that stops most organizations from going forward with this type of plan, is that whoever receives the encrypted messages must be able to decrypt them. This requires the receiving organization to use a compatible encryption technology and possess the proper decryption keys to decipher the incoming messages. The technology is certainly available to do this, but trying to implement such a scheme on a large scale presents many logistical obstacles. For example, simply selecting the appropriate encryption technology for all participating organizations to use can be a difficult decision. Should you go with PGP? How about S/MIME? What about proprietary e-mail systems? If you have the size and influence of a huge multinational corporation or a government agency, you can dictate the type of encryption your e-mail partners will need to use. Otherwise, once the number of partners with whom you need to exchange secured e-mail increases beyond a handful, getting agreement from all those partners on which encryption standard to use will be difficult.

This also assumes that all your e-mail is directed at a limited set of partners. In reality, most organizations send e-mail to a wide range of both regular and ad hoc recipients. Implementing a blanket encryption scheme in this type of environment means that everyone receiving e-mail from your organization must be able to decrypt your messages. This presents an even greater logistical issue than determining the appropriate encryption technology for a select but small set of recipients. The fact that there is currently no single universal standard for e-mail encryption on the Internet, as well as the fact that only a relatively small number of organizations and individuals use encryption in their e-mail today, testifies to the logistical difficulty of such a proposition.

In addition, because our primary concern here is with mobile devices, there are many devices that do not yet support any type of encryption for e-mail exchange. Most devices only support e-mail exchange through standard protocols such as the Post Office Protocol (POP), Simple Mail Transport Protocol (SMTP), and the Internet Message Access Protocol (IMAP), so these devices will not be able to process encrypted messages in any case. Some devices allow the use of SSL encryption for accessing Web-based e-mail services, but even that is not universal on all devices. This may be seen as an additional security control preventing the distribution of e-mail to insecure devices, but it is sure to cause an issue with your user population, who will see the implementation of e-mail encryption as an obstacle to their ability to work effectively with mobile devices.

Nevertheless, there is truly a need to encrypt e-mail containing sensitive information, and there is a growing demand in industry for interoperable encryption solutions for commercial use. In the meantime, organizations establishing encrypted e-mail systems have generally taken one of several approaches.

The first is to identify the partners with whom you exchange the most (or most sensitive) e-mail and configure your mail server to encrypt all e-mail to and from those specific partners. By doing so, you can establish the security you need for your most sensitive data while not imposing any restrictions on partners who don't require (or need) such a high level of protection for their e-mail exchanges. The second method is to deploy a keyword-based encryption system. In this process, all outgoing e-mail is scanned for the presence of particular keywords or data patterns, such as Social Security numbers, credit card numbers, or words like *classified* or *secret*. If the scanning detects one of these patterns in the message, it will redirect the e-mail to an encryption process located either within the organization's e-mail system or hosted at a third party. If the e-mail is encrypted within the originating organization's system, the recipients must be able to decrypt the message on their end, as previously described. If, however, the message is sent to a third-party service, the service will store the encrypted message, and the recipient will need to log into that service to retrieve the message. This requires the recipient to take additional steps to retrieve the message, but if the information is important or sensitive enough, there should not be much resistance to its use.

The drawback to keyword scanning is that it is an imperfect method of detecting data that requires encryption. Depending on the sophistication of the detection mechanism, it may not be able to pick up subtleties in data usage, such as identifying Social Security numbers with or without dashes, or payment card numbers with or without spaces. Keyword or content-driven encryption systems tend to have a high number of false positives (e-mail that gets encrypted when it shouldn't) and false negatives (e-mail that doesn't get encrypted when it should). However, newer e-mail scanning methods based on the use of DLP technology have been making progress in trying to detect such keywords and patterns in e-mail as well as for general network-wide data protection.

These two options enforce the organization's encryption policies without the users' need to determine what does or does not get encrypted, eliminating a large potential gap in the organization's encryption controls. Some organizations, however, do not want to make such enterprise-wide policy decisions and prefer a more user-centric approach to e-mail encryption. In such an approach, users are given direct access to the encryption system, either through some type of "Encrypt this" option in their e-mail client or by embedding keywords in the message address or subject field to trigger the encryption process. This per-message encryption method frees the organization from the need to impose encryption rules on its entire user and partner base, which might be desirable if encryption requirements are light or only affect a minority of the employees or partners. However, shifting responsibility to the end users for determining when information needs to be encrypted is placing a good amount of faith in their ability to identify and act appropriately in such situations. Since end users are often not the best judges of appropriate security, the organization that enacts this process can expect that a significant amount of sensitive e-mail will not get encrypted. As a countermeasure to this risk, the organization should place a heavy emphasis on education and training for its employees on how to use the encryption service and how to recognize the types of information that must be encrypted. Regular follow-up audits should then be performed to ensure that employees understand and follow the encryption requirements.

Encryption is not the only method of e-mail protection available, however. The distribution of e-mail attachments is often cited as a concern by security managers who want to limit the spread of sensitive information and feel that attachments often contain more valuable (and damaging) information than do the e-mail bodies themselves. Recalling the Acme takeover e-mail example from Chapter 3, the e-mail body in that example only mentions that there is a pending deal with Acme and the offer price is $13.75 per share. While this is clearly confidential information, the attachment included in the message probably contained much more sensitive information about the deal than the short facts mentioned in the message body, such as specific financial analyses, information about staff reductions and location closures, future product directions, and a host of other information that could be very damaging to both companies if it were to leak to the wrong people. A way to combat this specific problem is to limit the downloading of attachments to certain types of devices.

This is the same type of restriction that is often implemented when companies want to make their internal e-mail system available from employee-owned personal PCs or from an Internet cafe without the need for a VPN connection to the corporate network. While there are many security risks with permitting this type of access, the risk can be reduced by allowing Internet-based clients to attach to a Web-based e-mail interface (with appropriately strong authentication, of course) rather than directly to the internal e-mail system. This allows e-mail to be sent and received but provides the ability to restrict the download of attachments from any received messages to non-company systems. This is a prudent measure to ensure that the confidential information contained in attachments is not left on the public system for others to see and copy.

This same type of restriction might also be effective for e-mail connectivity from mobile device e-mail clients. Unless the connection is coming from a device that's known to have good security and e-mail controls, the connection may be permitted, but the user may not be able to view or download any attachments. This level of content restriction may not be available on all e-mail systems or mobile device management services, so some customization may be necessary to provide this type of control. The inability to view attachments from remote and mobile-based clients will (most likely) not be greeted warmly by your e-mail users, who will (again) see this as an encroachment on their ability to perform their work in an effective and expedient manner. The organization's overall security stance and policy must be called into play here, as this may require negotiation between the information-security group and the user community to develop a solution that's mutually acceptable to all involved.

In the end, because e-mail is such a fundamental part of the way we work, placing any sort of restrictions on its use will be met with resistance, difficulty, and technical challenges. While necessary for the security of the organization and the protection of the sensitive information often distributed using e-mail, the potential to interrupt the users' information flow is high when implementing security practices that impose controls or restrictions on message content. Therefore, any attempt to introduce such new controls must be done in concert with the user community to ensure that they understand the need for the control, how the control will be applied and used, and the expectations as to how the users are required to interact with the control.

Instant Messaging (IM) and Text Messaging

Protecting the organization from the security perils of instant messaging and texting is difficult, given the current state and use of the technology. Some organizations have banned the use of IM altogether or, at least, its use to converse with people outside the organization. While this may seem prudent given the many risks IM brings to the organization, doing so is much easier said than done. Most IM clients are "firewall friendly" or "port agile," euphemisms meaning that they will find a way out through corporate firewalls even if the organization seeks to block them. In addition to blocking the network ports for IM services, the organization can try to block access to the Internet domains where the various IM services reside. Unfortunately, trying to block (for example) Yahoo! Messenger could mean blocking access to the entire yahoo.com domain from within the organization, with the resulting side-effect of blocking other potentially useful services from that site. This is a trade-off that users may feel unduly imposes on their access to essential information. Another option is to enable intrusion-detection devices or to install a DLP system to detect and (potentially) block IM traffic crossing the organization's network. These services are much more sophisticated at analyzing IM traffic (even the port-agile clients) and can log, monitor, or block that traffic much better than standard firewall blocking will be able to accomplish.

Banning the use of texting is much more difficult to accomplish, given the fact that text messages travel directly through a cellular carrier's network and not through the organization's network, thereby preventing the organization's ability to detect and block text message traffic. For organizations that provision all mobile phone and data services for their employees, phone accounts can be provisioned without enabling text-messaging services, or the phones themselves can be provisioned without these features enabled, but this is only a stopgap measure. If the configuration of these devices is not managed centrally, employees can always reenable these services on their phones, or use their personal phones (many of which have unlimited texting capabilities) to send and receive text messages, and the organization will have no ability to stop or control this.

No matter what stance an organization takes with respect to IM and texting, a key component of the security program must be continuous user awareness and education on how to use these technologies responsibly and securely. Like e-mail, IM and texting are now a regular part of the business landscape, and to ban their use is difficult to do without establishing Draconian policies backed up by extraordinary technology restrictions. In some cases, organizations may find this justifiable in the face of the threats these technologies pose to the organization, to its employees, or to its other interests. For the majority of businesses, however, banning these technologies is not a step they are willing to take. To make these technologies safer to use, the organization must train its employees in both their proper and improper use.

Conclusion

Chapters 7 and 8 have introduced a variety of controls that an organization can use to address the mobile data and mobile device security issues it faces. The abundance of available controls is reminiscent of the classic good news/bad news scenario. The good news is that there are many controls that can be used to reduce the risk to mobile data and lessen the security problems with mobile devices in your enterprise. From encryption and access controls to data-loss prevention and user education, the various combinations of directive, deterrent, preventive, and detective controls available to an organization can be both overwhelming and confusing. However, they *are* available, and the organization that uses them with the proper approach and in the right combination can begin to effectively reduce the risk of these mobile technologies.

Now for the bad news. Although there are a number of options available to reduce that risk, none of them is pervasive or universally accepted enough to cover the entire spectrum of data movement, device options, and transportation paths available in modern network enterprises. Encryption is an excellent tool, but it is not supported on all device platforms, and it is not transparent enough to avoid user mishandling. Antimalware systems can catch a variety of threats, but often lag behind the latest attack techniques. Device-management systems can give the organization a method for uniformly applying security configuration and operation standards for mobile devices, but the devices they support may not be the ones the organization is most concerned with. Data loss prevention systems possess a good combination of traffic analysis and information flow restrictions, but the technology is still maturing and can be expensive to deploy across an enterprise.

In short, there is no silver bullet for securing mobile technology. Each control presented here has its own benefits and challenges, and an organization wishing to improve its mobile data and device security will need to determine the combination of controls and technologies that best fits its evaluation of the risks it faces and the extent to which it is willing to apply resources to address those risks. Of course, there is no such thing as perfect security. Each of these controls will address a portion of the mobile risk spectrum, but none will cover it all, and none will guarantee the complete elimination of mobile risk.

Given that, you must determine the greatest risks to your own organization and begin researching the controls that will help to reduce those particular risks in the most effective and efficient way. Starting with the controls presented here, find the combination that addresses your organization's needs best, and determine those that will provide the proper amount of protection, not substantially interfere with the users' ability to move information when necessary, and protect that information while it is moving. That's how defense-in-depth works, and the combination of controls and the way they interrelate can provide the depth and coverage to address the mobile security risks in your organization. That combination is obtainable, but it is different for each organization. It will most certainly involve a compromise (or a series of compromises) between security, cost, convenience, and available technology. However, finding the right balance for your organization will be the key for establishing an effective mobile security program.

Action Plan

Where Chapter 7 contained information on general security controls that can address general mobile security risks, this chapter was concerned with addressing specific mobile controls and identifying the policies and processes that can assist your organization in addressing its specific mobile security risks. Table 8.1 provides a summary of each of the technology controls discussed in this chapter. Use it as a guide for determining which controls to apply within your organization to secure the specific devices and mobile technologies that present the most risk.

Table 8.1 Technology Controls Summary

Technology	Control	Benefits	Challenges
Portable computers	Antimalware services	Prevents and detects malware infection on system	Not 100% effective; newer malware may go undetected. Requires continuous updating of malware definitions. Requires automation and enterprise enforcement. Not available on many mobile devices.
	Workstation-based firewalls	Provides ingress and egress blocking of malicious traffic	May interfere with nonstandard application traffic. Can be subverted/misconfigured by end users with administrative access to system.
	Standard configurations	Helps ensure uniform application of security settings and configuration	May require reconfiguration or upgrade of existing devices to meet new uniform standard.

(Continued)

Table 8.1 Technology Controls Summary (Continued)

Technology	Control	Benefits	Challenges
		Simplifies management of devices across the enterprise	Requires development of a process to configure all new devices with the standard configuration. Many mobile devices cannot be centrally managed.
	Virtual Private Networking (VPN) and multifactor authentication	Requires multiple pieces of information to establish authenticated access. Makes attacker's job more difficult	Not all systems and devices support multifactor process.
	Network access control	Restricts network access to only authorized devices	Scanning and authorization of individual devices can be difficult. Does not work for all mobile devices; may need to implement device control service. Maintenance and management of service can be difficult in a large infrastructure.
	Disable "autorun" features	Reduces malware threat by eliminating automatic installation	May interfere with normal operation of some applications or media.
	Removing unnecessary data	Reduces amount of information lost if device is lost or stolen	Many users will find it difficult to reduce the amount of data they carry.

Table 8.1   Technology Controls Summary (Continued)

Technology	Control	Benefits	Challenges
	Physical protection	Provides the first layer of defense for a portable computer (e.g., locking cables, privacy screens, and storing out of sight)	Many users do not practice effective physical security of their devices.
Portable storage devices (PSD) and dual-use devices	Banning PSD use in the enterprise	Eliminates the risk of mobile data loss through PSDs	Users will find other means to mobilize data. Available technology may not support all PSD platforms in use.
	Encrypt data on PSDs	Provides effective protection for mobile data	Hardware-encrypted devices can be expensive. Software-based encryption may not be available for all PSD platforms. Requires user action and attention to encryption process.
	Data movement restrictions	Prevent sensitive data from moving to the PSD	Technology (e.g., DLP) may not support all PSDs. Blocking data movement to data portion of dual-use device may block access to whole device.
Smartphones and PDAs	Access controls	Passwords and PINs can restrict who has access to the device	Unless centrally managed and enforced, many users may not enable passwords. Many devices may not support access controls beyond passwords.

(Continued)

Table 8.1   Technology Controls Summary (Continued)

Technology	Control	Benefits	Challenges
	Feature restrictions	Can restrict or disable access to troublesome features (e.g., flash media storage or Bluetooth)	Difficult to enforce unless devices are centrally managed and administered.
Optical media	Encryption of data	Similar to encryption on other mobile devices	Similar to other encryption challenges. If encryption is not used, disk must be physically destroyed after use to ensure data is not leaked to unauthorized parties.
E-mail	Encryption	Can automatically encrypt all e-mail or certain classes of e-mail	Interoperability of e-mail with other organization (who may use different standards) may be difficult to achieve. Automated detection of e-mails requiring encryption is inexact. Reliance on end users to recognize the need for encryption of specific messages can be ineffective.
	Attachment blocking	Can reduce loss of sensitive information or intellectual property due to wayward attachments on unprotected systems	May prevent users from accessing important data. May not be available on all mobile device platforms.

Table 8.1   Technology Controls Summary (Continued)

Technology	Control	Benefits	Challenges
Instant messaging (IM)	Blocking access to public IM systems	Can reduce the potential for information leakage through IM chat with external parties	Most IM clients are port-agile and will find a way around any firewall restrictions.
Text messaging	User awareness of risks of text messaging for sensitive information	Can reduce potential for sensitive information leakage	Users can ignore the awareness information.

Note

1. Richard Kissel et al., *Guidelines for Media Sanitization*, Special Publication 800-88, National Institute for Standards and Technology, September 2006.

Chapter 9

Creating a Mobile Security Policy

We are all familiar with policies. In fact, many of us are inundated with policies: human resources policies, technology policies, accounting policies, travel policies, and (of course) security policies. Now you must face the task of defining your organization's policy for mobile data security, and all the discussions from previous chapters must come into play in order to create the best policy for your organization. When formulating that policy, you must start by clearly understanding what you are striving for with a mobile data security program. What are you trying to protect, and what general rules are you going to implement in order to protect it? You must understand whether technology is available that can support your goals, and if not, understand how to adjust those goals to fit within the capabilities of the available technology. Finally, you need to understand your own organization's culture, how establishing controls or restrictions on mobile technology will fit within that culture, and what resistance you may encounter from your organization's employees. In short, you need to start with a policy goal, work to understand the realism and limitations of that goal, then readjust the policy based on that understanding.

Once you have developed your objectives and target goals, you can start to develop the formal policy that will carry your mobile protection program forward. It's the policies that people will look to for guidance and reinforcement when trying to implement the organization's mobile security objectives. They will also look to the policy when trying to bypass, circumvent, or find loopholes in the organization's intent as a means of justifying their own particular actions or desires. The policy is where it all starts and where it all ends.

However, that doesn't mean that you need to develop your formalized policy as the very first task in your mobile data security program. While that may sound good in theory, it doesn't work well in practice, particularly for a subject as complex and fraught with obstacles as mobile security. Some types of policies can work well with this approach. For example, a policy requiring that all employees wear ID badges while on company premises is fairly straightforward. There is little need for advanced research on how people should wear their badges, or how wearing badges will affect their ability to perform their duties. In addition, there is surprisingly little variation in the way employees can apply badge-wearing technology, aside from the "clip vs. lanyard" discussion, the outcome of which has more implications as a fashion statement than as a security measure. Companies wishing to implement such a practice often begin with defining the policy itself—"Thou shalt wear badges"—and move quickly to the implementation and deployment phases, including any process or technology work that needs to be put into place.

Such an approach won't work well when it comes to implementing mobile data security policies. Because of the complexity of the issues discussed in previous chapters, implementing a mobile data security plan requires a great deal of thought, study, and planning. The organization may have a basic understanding of what it wants to do—usually a broad statement such as "secure all mobile data"—but the path to get there is full of compromises and trade-offs. You can encrypt hard disks, but encrypting flash drives is difficult. You can block certain devices, but that can affect the usefulness of those devices. You can filter content, but you run the risk of filtering too aggressively or missing some sensitive data that should have been blocked. There are many decision points and avenues to explore. At this point in your reading, you should be keenly aware of that fact.

This is why setting a mobile data security policy at the beginning of the process won't work well. It's certainly possible to set such a policy early in the planning, but the process of identifying approaches, researching available technology, determining what works and what doesn't, and factoring in the needs and pain points of the users affected by the policy may render such a preplanned policy useless before it even takes effect. Determining what you *want* to do before you even know if you are *able* to do it will inevitably lead to a policy that is ineffective, unenforceable, and ultimately useless. It's ineffective because the stated policy goals can't be achieved given the available (or practically deployable) technology. It's unenforceable because employees who can't conform to the policy may be forced to ignore it due to lack of technical support for the policy's objectives or practical alternatives to use as compensating controls. It's useless because any policy that is both ineffective and unenforceable is worse than having no policy at all.

As a result, this book intentionally didn't start out discussing mobile data security policy because it's important to have a clear understanding of all the areas that securing mobile data will impact before policy can even be addressed. This book has taken you through problem identification, risk management, threat modeling, and technology evaluation before addressing policy development because understanding these key areas is essential to setting an effective and enforceable policy. Only after going through that process, and understanding how all those subjects ultimately affect an organization's ability to deploy and sustain mobile data security, can you begin to formulate a policy (and associated standards and procedures) that will provide real security for your organization's mobile data.

Security is always about trade-offs. No organization ever has enough time, money, or people to implement all the security measures that it wants or needs, so it must make some trade-offs between the three in order to achieve an acceptable level of security. An organization must reconcile the trade-offs it is willing to make to enable mobile device use in the enterprise, and then translate those into a workable policy statement that is ultimately effective, enforceable, and useful. Even an outright ban on mobile devices is, itself, a trade-off, although one that heavily favors enterprise security over user productivity. That's why policy development was saved until after all the other aspects of mobile security have been discussed. It will bring together the disciplines, risk factors, and alternatives discussed so far.

Before going through the policy discussion, some terminology should be reviewed. Specifically, the terms *policy* and *standard* should be understood before getting too far into the discussion.

> **Policy**: A high-level statement of management intent and direction.
> **Standard**: A set of operational or technical requirements to be used to comply with, enact, and enforce the policy statements.

These distinctions are extremely important when you begin to take the ideas presented here (as well as those developed by your own security and business teams) and try to implement them in your organization. Different organizations treat each of these categories differently. Some make a clear distinction between policies and standards. Others lump both policies and standards into a single document and call them all the organization's "policy." The approach a particular organization takes is as much a matter of individual taste and organizational culture as anything else. It will be up to you to determine for your own organization how to categorize each of the discussion points presented in this chapter.

Setting the Goal Statement

Every policy published within an organization has a specific goal or purpose for its existence.* That goal should be clearly established at the beginning of the policy so that the reader (and those ultimately subject to the policy) will have a clear understanding of why the policy was put into place and what it hopes to achieve. Given that premise, let's start the discussion of mobile data policy formation where

---

* Of course, we've all seen way too many policies that seem vague or unclear. The intent here is to avoid that problem.

we started this book and where we've repeatedly referred when things begin to get confusing: by answering the question, "What are you trying to protect?" In order to create a clear and concise mobile data policy, you need to identify a clear and concise target risk or security gap that you are trying to mitigate with this policy. The typical goal statement is usually rather vague, such as in this example:

> The goal of this policy is to protect MoDevCo and its customers when data is transmitted or stored using mobile devices.

That certainly gets the point across, but it leaves too much to the reader's imagination to fill in the gaps of the statement. Initial questions that come to mind include:

- Why does the company or its customers need protection?
- What data does the policy refer to?
- What falls under the heading of "transmitted or stored"?
- What mobile devices are meant?

Pretty much every aspect of this goal statement is brought into question. Therefore, the goal statement should be clearer in its objective. Protecting mobile data on mobile devices is a lofty goal, but such security measures wouldn't be considered if they didn't serve some higher purpose. That higher purpose is what the objective is all about. For example:

> The goal of this policy is to protect MoDevCo intellectual property and sensitive customer data (including nonpublic consumer data) when that information is stored or transmitted on a mobile device.

That begins to get the goal across. The company is worried about the data it stores about (or for) its customers, consumers (including, presumably, such sensitive areas as personal, health, and financial information), and internal operations, including information that the company wants to protect, such as intellectual property. The only thing that remains to be clarified is the part about mobile devices. To fill in this gap, we could incorporate the definition of mobile device from Chapter 1:

> The goal of this policy is to protect MoDevCo intellectual property and sensitive customer data (including nonpublic consumer data) when that information is used or stored on easily transported electronic storage devices.

This provides us the clear purpose we are looking for. There is little room for vagueness in this statement, and a reader of this policy will understand at the outset what she is about to read. Keep in mind, however, that this goal—as it has throughout this book—must apply to *all* mobile devices, from computers to electronic storage devices to smartphones. This means that any policy statements you make must apply equally to all such devices. Alternatively, a distinction should be made when there are different policy approaches for different devices.

Mobile Device Policy Issues

Once the policy's goal is clearly defined, attention turns to the approach the policy (and, ultimately, the mobile security program) will take and how it will address the various risks and threats that have been discussed throughout this book. However, if there is one thing that should be clear by now, it's that no approach will be able to cover all the relevant risks and threats, and no technology will be able to protect against everything. Therefore, the organization will need to decide where it wants to place its emphasis.

The first approach, and the most basic, is to simply control the use of certain devices in the infrastructure. These may be the devices that the organization feels have the most risk associated with them (such as flash drives or optical media) or the devices for which it can create effective and manageable controls for optimal secure use (such as certain smartphones or PDAs [personal digital assistants]). This is not exactly the same as the device-centric approach discussed in Chapter 5, however. In that approach, the organization specifically targeted mobile devices as the sole method for managing the mobile security issue. As seen in that chapter, such an approach may not allow the organization to fully address the total spectrum of mobile security risks. As a response to that, the policy approach that addresses device restrictions does so as part of the overall policy and plan, not as an exclusive path to security. It still leaves the door open to using additional and complementary approaches as well.

As an opening example, such an approach might take the following form:

> The use of mobile storage drives, including external hard disks and flash-memory devices, is prohibited for storing or transporting MoDevCo data or the data of its customers.

This approach, while highly restrictive, clearly explains what is acceptable. If a device can be classified as a mobile storage drive, external hard disk, or flash-memory device, its use is forbidden, period. A different approach might represent a compromise wherein the organization has approved the use of certain devices:

> The use of mobile storage drives, including external hard disks and flash-memory devices, for storing or transporting MoDevCo data or the data of its customers must be approved by the Information Security Department. Only approved and supported devices may be used on MoDevCo's network or systems.

This approach tells the users that it's possible to use certain mobile devices, as long as those devices have been officially approved. Another example addresses the use of smartphones and PDAs, whose functionality is more complex than a standard flash drive.

The use of "smart" mobile phones and Personal Digital Assistants (PDAs) for synchronizing personal and corporate data with network-based services is limited to those devices that have been approved for use by the MoDevCo Information Technology organization.

The assumption here is that only smartphones that have strong security controls—either built-in or added on as a separate package—will be approved by IT for employee use. How those devices are selected will be based on their ability to support the security technology the company is able to build or acquire, and the extent to which it is willing to impose those restrictions on the various devices.

The final approach to mobile device security may work for organizations that do not want to place any restrictions on the specific devices it will allow employees to use. This may be the case if the company doesn't care at all about mobile security (an unlikely but possible scenario) or if it has chosen to apply its efforts on the data-management aspects of mobile security. This approach can take one of two general forms. The first is the wide-open approach:

MoDevCo employees may utilize mobile devices to enhance their business productivity or provide services to MoDevCo customers.

This seems a bit scary and potentially dangerous, but for the organization that sees the use of mobile technology as a low risk, this may be an acceptable approach. However, organizations that see a higher risk from mobile technology may want to implement some restrictions on particular devices without necessarily restricting what those devices are. For example:

MoDevCo employees may utilize mobile devices to enhance their business productivity or provide services to MoDevCo customers. However, sensitive internal or customer information may only be transferred to, or stored on, devices that have been approved by the Information Security Department.

Rather than restricting acceptable devices to a specific few (which will quickly become outdated as new models with newer features are introduced), this approach gives employees the "freedom of choice" they desire while still allowing the company to restrict the use of devices to store sensitive information only to those that meet certain security criteria. Such criteria might include the use of encryption, passwords and other access-control mechanisms, or antimalware capabilities. This will require the organization's employees to understand the security requirement before they purchase a new device to ensure their purchase will meet corporate standards, so clear education and guidance in this area is critical.

In the previous "only approved devices" approach, the organization must continuously keep up with new devices as they are introduced. In this "meets standards" approach, the organization need not keep up with each new device model on the market. Because fundamental security capabilities are introduced into the marketplace at a much slower rate than are new devices, the organization needs only to look at those devices that have those specific capabilities. While the two are related, a standards-based approach might relieve the organization of the pressure to continuously evaluate new devices and focus their efforts only on the subset of those devices that employees show interest in using and have support for the security criteria the organization requires, rather than every new device on the market. This will reduce the number of devices that require evaluation, but the number may still be large for an organization whose employees have diverse technology interests.

Device Ownership

The next basic policy decision the organization will face is whether or not it will own and operate the mobile devices in the enterprise or whether it will require its employees to purchase their own. There are several implications to this decision that affect the organization's finances as well as its security. The most authoritarian approach is for the organization to purchase all mobile devices for use within the enterprise. The company establishes official procurement procedures for the various permitted mobile devices, and any employee wishing to use one would need to obtain them through this official channel. This enables the organization to deploy only those devices that meet the organization's security requirements, and devices that don't meet those requirements will not enter the environment—at least not through official channels. If the organization has selected a device-management product or service that is only applicable to certain devices (for example, a single brand of mobile phone), this is a way to ensure that only those devices are available for employee use.

This is the most desirable route to take from a security perspective as it allows the organization to specify the devices it is willing or able to support. Ownership of the devices gives the organization the governance authority to dictate the specific security features and configuration options that will be established on those devices. In addition, when an employee leaves the organization or the device reaches the end of its useful life, the organization has the ability to reclaim the device to ensure that any confidential information or intellectual property on that device is properly erased. The device can then be redeployed or destroyed with the confidence that such confidential information will not be disclosed to an unauthorized person.

The following policy phrasing should cover this approach:

> All mobile devices to be used on MoDevCo's network or systems must
> be procured and provisioned by MoDevCo's Corporate Procurement

organization. No employee-purchased devices will be permitted to attach to MoDevCo's infrastructure.

While this approach makes the best security sense, the business impact of this approach should be immediately apparent. The organization's cost for purchasing, maintaining, and tracking all those devices can quickly mount. Even for a small organization taking advantage of volume discounts, the cost can be overwhelming to the organization's budget and may require one or more full-time employees just to manage the effort. These are resources that may be put to better use elsewhere, particularly if finances are tight and the company is looking to manage its expenses and save money wherever possible. This is a classic risk trade-off decision: maintaining ownership and total control over the devices vs. the financial and operational cost of such a process. This type of decision is not unique to mobile devices, but because of the large number of these devices entering the workplace and the rapid pace with which new devices are introduced, it is a problem that has become particularly acute in recent years.

Because of the potential cost of company device ownership, many organizations are taking the opposite approach by requiring their employees to purchase their own devices. This shifts a large part of the cost of allowing mobility over to the employee. Since they are now using their own funds to purchase the equipment, employees may also be more inclined to select more budget-priced or feature-limited devices. Subsequently, the organization is relieved of the cost of purchasing and maintaining the devices, as well as the staff overhead to manage and track them. However, along with the cost shifting comes a corresponding shift in security responsibilities. Because the employee (not the organization) owns the device, she may be freely able to configure, update, and customize that device to her own particular tastes, including the configuration of the device's security features. If the device is not placed under the control of a centralized management system, the responsibility for setting the proper security configuration on a particular device now rests with the end user, an unreliable source of security practices. Even if the device is under the control of a centralized system, such systems often do not cover all aspects of the device's configuration or operation. There may still be areas where the employee's ability to configure and operate the device will leave it open to security risks.

A more troublesome problem appears when the organization's data is intermingled on a device with the employee's personal data. Because the device is owned by the employee, they are more likely to populate it with personal information, such as friends' contact information, personal calendar appointments, music, videos, and personal photos. This is acceptable (and expected) behavior for a personal device, but when that personal information begins to mingle with the company's internal and confidential information, there's a potential for trouble. For instance, do the security controls the company establishes on the device restrict the user's ability to install new features or applications on the device? Do user-installed applications conflict with the organization's information security policies or pose a risk to the information leakage? Does the ability to randomly install new features or applications increase the risk of malware on the device? The employee may feel that he has the right to install whatever utilities or games he sees fit on his phone; however, the organization may have restricted that capability due to security concerns. This may be a culture shock to the user who feels that the device is his personal property and that the organization does not have the right to dictate what he can do with that property.

Another troublesome scenario occurs when the employee leaves the service of the organization, either voluntarily or involuntarily. In the case where the organization owns the device, it must be returned to the organization upon termination so it can be properly wiped of all sensitive information and potentially redeployed. However, when the device belongs to the employee, she will expect that the device is hers to take with her when she leaves. What happens to the company's information on that device? A former employee, particularly one who leaves the organization involuntarily, can't be trusted to properly remove sensitive company data from the device. If a central configuration service has the ability to remotely wipe the device, that process may also wipe out the employee's personal data along with the company data. Additionally, if the employee is no longer available, there is no way to ascertain whether the remote wiping commands were even successful. These issues are at the heart of the cost/security trade-off of device ownership. On the one hand, the company can increase security control by owning the devices but must incur higher costs in the process. On the other hand, the company can lower its costs by requiring employee ownership of the device, but the resulting security issues may pose an unacceptable risk.

Some organizations have addressed this problem by following a compromise path. They require employees to purchase their own mobile device technology to do with as they please. However, if an employee wishes to attach that device to the company's infrastructure to synchronize e-mail and calendars or move information to and from the device, the employee must agree to abide by any security restrictions imposed on that device (including configuration and application restrictions) and to submit that device for data erasure upon termination, even if that means they will lose some of their personal information. A policy statement enforcing this compromise might look like this:

> All mobile devices to be used on MoDevCo's network or systems must be procured by the employee, who is solely responsible for all charges and maintenance costs. If an employee requires device connectivity to MoDevCo's infrastructure, the employee must agree to abide by MoDevCo's policies and standards regarding mobile device use, including all security controls and processes required for that device. Upon termination of employment, the employee must submit the device to the Information Security group for proper erasure of *all* data on the device.

This policy statement may also be backed by a specific "Mobile Device Connectivity Agreement" that the employee is required to sign prior to receiving connectivity. This extra step may be necessary to emphasize the importance of central management of the device, even if it is personally owned. While adding some overhead to the device management process, this approach may be an effective way to allow the use of personal devices within the company's infrastructure while still maintaining security control over those devices.

As a last point, the policy may also wish to emphasize that all personally owned devices must be on the list of approved and supported devices mentioned earlier and support the required security controls established by the policy. This may be implied by the phrase "...*agree to abide by MoDevCo's policies and standards regarding mobile device use...*," but it might be worth mentioning separately in the policy to make clear that the owners must be mindful of the devices they use and not expect the organization to attach any random device to the network.

Device Management

No matter how ownership is ultimately defined, all mobile devices in the enterprise will need to be managed to a standard security configuration, as discussed in Chapter 8. Even if the devices are personally owned, they should still be required to conform to, and be controlled by, the centralized configuration and management service. Again, this may be considered part and parcel of the agreement to "...*abide by MoDevCo's policies and standards regarding mobile device use...*" mentioned previously, but it may be worth highlighting this point specifically in the mobile security policy to eliminate any confusion or resistance from end users about surrendering control of "their" devices to the central management service. A sample of this might include the statement:

> All mobile devices must integrate with, and be managed by, applicable MoDevCo management and configuration tools and services.

Device Personalization

Even in an employee-owned/company-managed mobile device environment, some concession must be made to allow for customization and personalization of the user's mobile device. This issue is most prevalent with mobile phones and PDAs, where a wide range of customization options are available, including background screens (also known as "wallpaper"), ring tones, music files, videos and movies, custom applications, and games. Some of these pose little risk to the organization's security, and most organizations allow their end users to customize their devices with such personalization. The organization may have some legitimate concern that the music and videos files on the device are legally obtained. This is more of a legal than a security issue, but many security-awareness programs emphasize the need for all employees to use only legally licensed copies of media on their systems. Where many organizations draw the line, however, is with the installation of customized applications or games, which have the potential to interfere with normal device operation and can compromise the security of the device or of the organization if written specifically with malicious intent. For this reason, your policy might want to specify the extent to which customization is permissible on mobile devices.

> Employees are permitted to customize or personalize the runtime environment of their mobile device with personal photos, wallpaper, or media files only if such images, music, or media have been legally obtained. Users may not install customized or third-party applications on mobile devices without written approval of the Information Technology organization.

Mobile Data Issues

Once you have decided how to address mobile devices in the enterprise, the next step is to address mobile data itself, and some decisions must be made here in order to strike a good balance between the efficient functioning of the business and the need for effective mobile data security. There are several paths to choose when it comes to mobile data:

1. Data can be moved to any mobile device.
2. Data cannot be moved to any mobile device.
3. Data is only allowed to be moved to approved devices.
4. Only certain types of data can be transferred to mobile devices.
5. All data transferred to a mobile device must have minimum security protections.

Option 1: Data Can Be Moved to Any Mobile Device

> The storage or transmission of MoDevCo internal information or customer information using a mobile device is permitted. Employees must take precautions to ensure that both the data and the mobile device have appropriate security in place to protect the information while it resides on the mobile device.

This first option, where any data can be moved to any mobile device, assumes that the organization has emphasized a device-centric approach to mobile security. This requires any potential mobile device to have adequate built-in or add-on security controls to ensure that any data moved to it will remain protected for as long as it is on that device. In this case, the organization may have required the use of encryption for all mobile devices, but this would be a difficult undertaking, given the wide variety of devices and the lack of standardization among encryption products on mobile platforms. Alternatively, it may have implemented multiple techniques (such as encryption, access control, and content filtering) to serve a similar purpose, but again this would require that a solution has been found for every type of device found in the organization: not an easy or inexpensive assumption to make.

If, however, the organization has been able to find suitable protections for the most common devices in the environment, and is able to ensure that only those devices are used for transporting the riskiest of mobile data, it may make the risk decision to forgo protection for other, less risky types of devices in the name of efficiency or resource conservation. For example, the organization may be most concerned with data leakage through smartphones and flash drives. If the organization is able to deploy technology to secure these two classes of devices to a satisfactory security level, it may be willing to accept the residual risk of potential leakage through other devices, such as music players and external hard disks, because these devices are not prevalent in the environment or the company does not feel that they pose enough of a data leakage threat. Given all this, the position that all data can be moved to any mobile device is within the realm of possibility. However, extreme caution is warranted when making such blanket statements, as users are very likely to take the policy at face value and begin using any and all mobile devices at their disposal to transport sensitive or confidential information. Many of these devices will be left unprotected and subject to loss or theft. In addition, if the process or technology used to protect the riskiest of those devices is overly cumbersome or interrupts the users' workflow too severely, they may decide to circumvent those protections by specifically employing devices that have not been targeted for special protection. By doing this, they are still acting within the policy yet leaving the data unprotected.

If this option is adopted into policy, it should also be accompanied by a warning to employees to ensure that sensitive data is protected on all mobile devices, even those for which specific security standards have not been established. Even if a device they are using has built-in protections, it is important that the policy place the burden of responsibility for the data's protection directly onto the user. After all, if the data is stolen or the device is lost, it is the user that should be held accountable, not the device. Informing employees of this accountability and reminding them of their role in protecting the information is essential when taking this policy approach.

Option 2: Data Is Not Allowed to Be Moved to Any Mobile Device

The storage or transmission of MoDevCo internal information or customer information using a mobile device is prohibited.

If the first option represents one extreme end of the mobile security spectrum, this option represents the other. In this approach, the organization specifically bans the movement of any data to any mobile device, regardless of the security controls available on that device. There is not much more to be said from a security perspective with this option. Prohibiting the use of any mobile device to store sensitive or confidential information means that all the organization's data is protected from mobile threats (at least from a policy perspective). If such a ban is reinforced with the implementation of appropriate device blocking on all computers within the organization, this may be possible. However, such a technology would need to be pervasive in order to be effective. Every PC, laptop, server, and network in the enterprise would need to have the blocking technology in place to ensure that mobile devices are not attached and used to transfer information.

An organization considering this approach must be clear on both its intent and the wording of the policy. Prohibiting all data movement to mobile devices would also prohibit e-mail and calendar synchronization with smartphones and PDAs. That may not be what the organization had in mind when formulating the policy. If taken to the extreme, adopting this option would also force the organization to consider banning the use of laptop and portable computers as well, since they fall within the definition of a "mobile device" and can be used to transport information outside of the corporate environment. Given the total blockade of all mobile technology that this option represents, it is easy to see why so few organizations have chosen this course of action. Doing so ignores the business benefit these devices can bring to an organization. While it is the most secure option, it does not strike that optimal balance between security needs and business needs that all good security solutions seek to achieve. Nevertheless, if the security needs of the organization are extreme and it is willing to restrict its employees' use of this technology, it is an option to explore.

Option 3: Data Is Allowed to Be Moved to Only Approved Devices

> The storage or transmission of MoDevCo internal information or customer information using a mobile device is permitted using only approved devices with the proper security controls. The use of unapproved mobile devices is prohibited.

Option three seeks to attain the effective balance between security and business needs that eluded the first two options. In this approach, the organization directly addresses the need for mobile data by permitting the use of that data only on devices that have been approved for use by the appropriate group in the company, most likely the IT or information security group. Adopting this approach leads the company down the path of actively engaging the mobile security issue and implementing the appropriate process and technology changes to enforce the policy across the enterprise. The list of "approved" devices will be based on the security features found on those devices and the ability for the organization to deploy technology to address specific devices or device types. For example, if the organization implements a central smartphone management service, only smartphones that are supported by that service will be on the approved list, and employees must use one of those phones if they wish to synchronize their data. Likewise, if the organization implements a device and port management technology that only supports a specific brand of encrypted flash drive, that brand will be the only one available for employees to use for their mobile data needs.

Ironically, this approach actually benefits both the organization and the employee by limiting the number of options available to both. The organization establishes its baseline security requirements for mobile data and devices and finds the appropriate security technology for both that it can support, manage, and afford. By restricting the acceptable ways that mobile data can be transported, it reduces its overall support costs while, at the same time, reducing its risk from data transported on unmanaged (or unmanageable) devices.

From the employees' perspective, this approach gives them specific guidance as to which devices they can use to transport their data or manage their business affairs. If they stay within the guidelines of the supported device list they can be assured that the technology they employ will work within the organization's infrastructure and that it will be supported by the appropriate technical and security groups. In addition, they will have the assurance that the device has the appropriate security controls to enable it to carry sensitive or confidential information. Of course, that doesn't mean that all employees will be happy with this approach. There will always be devices that employees want to use that do not make it onto the approved list because the device does not support the minimum security control standards set by the organization.

In this "only approved devices" approach, the goal is to keep the list of approved devices to a minimum. This enforces standardization of security features and allows for ease of device management. The organization will need to determine the criteria for adding new devices or technology onto the approved list. It should add only those devices that fulfill the baseline mobile security requirements, but should not feel pressured to include every single device that users decide they "absolutely must have." Some decisions and limitations will have to be made, and this is bound to annoy some users whose favorite "must-have" device is not included on the approved list.

Option 4: Only Certain Types of Data Can Be Transferred to Mobile Devices

Data classified as "Public," "Internal," or "Confidential" may be stored or transported via a mobile device only if the device supports the baseline security controls established by the Information Security group. Data classified as "Secret" may not be stored or transported on any mobile device.

Like option 3 before it, option 4 addresses the need for mobility in the environment but approaches the issue from a data-oriented perspective rather than a technology or device-oriented one. In this option, the content and the sensitivity of the data is what permits potential mobility, not the transport mechanism. If the data has a lower sensitivity level, it is permitted to move onto a secured mobile device for storage or transport. The assumption here is that the security controls the organization is able to deploy in its mobile environment are sufficient to protect information with that level of sensitivity. If, however, the sensitivity of the information is high enough, the available mobile protection mechanisms may not be able to provide sufficient security to ensure its safe transport. The organization can selectively identify certain types of data that can be moved to mobile devices and certain types that can't.

There are many factors that can be used as criteria for inclusion or exclusion. In the example policy statement, inclusion is based on the classification level of the data itself. Classification levels are, of course, highly dependent on the organization's definition of sensitivity and the type of information it needs to classify. Nevertheless, classification is a good place for the organization to begin defining what information is acceptable for movement to a mobile device.

When considering how to categorize the data that can be allowed mobility, the decision may also be based on restrictions placed on the organization by outside parties. There may be regulatory requirements, industry standards, or contractual obligations that restrict or prohibit the ability to move certain types of data to mobile devices. In addition, the use of strong security controls—encryption, most notably—when transporting information on mobile devices is quickly becoming a standard part of privacy legislation. If the information contains financial data, health care information, or personal information, it is a safe bet that the owner of that data, the data subject, or a government agency will require the data to be protected on the mobile device. The example shown below gives you a sample policy statement based on the need to satisfy such external requirements.

> All financial data, health care records, or other Personally Identifiable Information pertaining to MoDevCo customers must be encrypted when moved to a mobile device.

Option 5. All Data Transferred to a Mobile Device Must Have Minimum Security Protections

> Appropriate security protections must be in place before any MoDevCo internal or customer data is stored or transported on any mobile device.

This last policy approach emphasizes specific security requirements for the mobilization of data. In this option, data can only be moved to a mobile device if the appropriate security protections are in place, regardless of its sensitivity, legal requirements, or potential impact to the organization. This approach does not specify if the security controls must be implemented on the data or on the device itself, only that proper controls must be in place. To properly address this approach, the organization must establish clear standards and guidelines as to what data and device security controls are required for data transport. The user, or sufficiently advanced data-monitoring technology, must ensure that those controls are in place before allowing the data to migrate to a mobile device.

For example, the organization may specify that all data must be encrypted before it can move to a mobile device. As we have seen, there are two ways to approach this requirement. The document itself can be encrypted, in which case it can be moved to any mobile device and still meet the requirements of the policy. Alternatively, the user can use an encrypted flash drive or encrypted external hard disk to store the data, filling the requirement without needing to alter the source data. Both solutions comply with the policy and are acceptable means of securely transporting information.

However, some decisions have fewer options from which to choose. For example, suppose the data has to be sent to another organization, but the receiving organization does not use the same encryption program as the sender. Encrypting the file itself is of no use, because the receiving company will not be able to decrypt the data. In this case, using a device with built-in hardware encryption may be the only option. The sender moves the data to the encrypted device and sends the device to the receiver. The receiver extracts the data from the encrypted device and the transmission is complete. This requires the sender to give the appropriate decryption keys to the receiver, but the assumption is made that the secure exchange of keys is possible. In this scenario, device protections are the only option because data-centric protections were not viable.

As an alternative example, suppose that data must be exchanged between two companies, and the specification for the data exchange requires that compact disks be used to store and transport the data. Because the standard specification for a data CD has no provision for encryption or access control, the data itself needs to be encrypted before it is placed on the CD and sent to the receiver. This ensures that the data will be protected even if the underlying transport mechanism (i.e., the CD) has no native security support.

Defining Technology Standards

The policy items discussed thus far only give the general rules for management of mobile data and devices, and give broad and general guidance as to what is expected of employees for protecting mobile assets. Very few employees can be expected to do the right thing based solely on such high-level policy statements. To be fair, most policies are so broad as to be open to interpretation in a variety of ways, leading to a situation where employees may be left on their own to determine the best approach to securing their mobile data. In addition, many policies (including the examples in this chapter) use terms such as "appropriate protection," "proper controls," and "authorized devices." It is only fair to employees that these terms be clearly defined to enable them to follow the rules correctly. A policy without supporting clarification is ultimately an ineffective policy.

That's where standards come in. The standards supporting the policy provide the clarification employees need in order to understand what they can (and can't) do with their mobile devices and their mobile data. Standards also inform the appropriate technology and business teams in the organization what features and controls must be established within the infrastructure to support the security of mobile data. As we have seen numerous times, the protection of mobile data often involves more than just restrictions on the mobile devices themselves. It also may involve similar restrictions on servers, network devices, and end-user workstations that carry that information before and after it is mobilized. Therefore, the mobile data standards must also address the general infrastructure and process changes that need to be made in order to properly protect mobile data and devices.

End-User Standards

First and foremost, end users will need to know what to expect when utilizing mobile devices. To begin with, changes to their workstations may be required in order to conform to the new mobile security policies and standards. These changes may include restrictions on the types of devices that may be attached to their workstations and the permitted functionality of those devices. For example, the standards may specify that "all USB-based devices are prohibited on end-user workstations." This, of course, will rule out the use of newer keyboards and mice, as they all now connect to the computer via USB. Therefore, the standards need to be very specific as to what technology restrictions are being established. The specification that "all USB-based *storage devices* are prohibited on end-user workstations" would be a better choice of wording. Likewise, other technology restrictions or device controls to be established on end-user systems should be documented in the standards as well. Specific ports to be restricted or specifically permitted should also be defined. Finally, if certain applications are restricted, such as peer-to-peer applications or desktop-based PDA synchronization software, users need to know so they have a chance to understand and properly comply with the new standards.

If content monitoring or filtering services will be used to detect mobile data and block or alter it before it reaches a mobile device, the standards should describe the type of service to be used and the filtering criteria to be established. If it is looking for all data marked "Confidential" or any file containing a list of credit card numbers, users should know that files with these characteristics will be blocked. The purpose is not to give them insight into how to circumvent the system (for example, by changing all instances of "Confidential" to "Public" in the document to evade the blocking mechanism), but rather to give them a way of understanding what is happening when they find that they can't move a certain document to a flash drive or their e-mail attachment is repeatedly blocked. The use of content filtering and blocking services will have a disruptive effect on the way people work. Letting them know what to expect will minimize the time spent determining the cause of their troubles and also reduce help desk or technical support costs from uninformed users trying to understand what is happening to their data.

Finally, if encryption or access-control services are added to the user's workstation they need to understand what those services are, how they work, and when they are required to be used. Encryption can be difficult enough to understand and use when the user is familiar with the software and how to manage keys and encrypt/decrypt files. It is nearly impossible for the uneducated user to understand without some instruction and guidance. The use of encryption can be a powerful tool, but unless the encryption is applied automatically, the user will need to intervene in order to employ the encryption properly to its greatest effect.

Device Standards

If the organization determines that it will restrict the use of mobile devices to only a few standard models or types, it must identify those specific technologies and models. There may be many categories of devices in use within the organization and varying degrees of specificity for each type of permitted device, depending on how the organization has developed and deployed its mobile security program. For example, the organization may have standardized on a single brand of smartphone (with, perhaps, several available models within that brand) because of the security features that brand supports. However, to address security on flash drives and optical media, it may deploy an automated encryption program that encrypts all data sent to a flash drive or disk. As a result, any brand of drive or optical media can be used, as the encryption service will work with any model of CD or DVD burner and any disk brand. The potential combinations of devices, models, and modes of operation (reading, writing, and synchronization for example) can be bewildering to a user trying to do the right thing.

To ensure that users are able to comply with the policy and provide the best protection for the organization's mobile data, the standards should describe, in as much detail as necessary, the specific mobile devices that employees are permitted to use and any restrictions that they must comply with when trying to move data to and from those devices. Table 9.1 shows an example of such a listing.

The list can be as simple or as complicated as it needs to be for employees to clearly understand what devices are available to them and how they can be used. The most important thing is that the list be as complete as possible and include all the devices that users will expect to attach (or are permitted to attach) to their systems. A matrix like this can go a long way toward employees' understanding of both the policy and the resulting changes in their computing and communications environment.

Table 9.1   Example Device Standards Matrix

Category	Brand	Model(s)	Operating Modes (Read, Write, Synchronize)
Flash drive (nonencrypted)	Any	Any	Read-only for flash drives without built-in hardware encryption; restriction enforced by desktop device-management service.
Flash drive (encrypted)	Kingston	Data Vault	Read and write data.
	IronKey	All models	Read and write data.
Smartphone	Blackberry	All models	All modes; must be connected to corporate BES service; stand-alone synchronization not permitted.
	Apple iPhone	All models	All modes; must be connected to IMO service; stand-alone synchronization not permitted.
CD/DVD drives	Any	Any	Read-only for locally attached optical drives; creation of optical media must be managed through copy services.
External hard disk (nonencrypted)	Any	Any	Drive must be encrypted with PGP whole-disk encryption; restriction enforced by desktop device-management service.
External hard disk (encrypted)	BusLink	BUSL0JR	Drive must be provisioned through Purchasing Dept.; keys must be provisioned and managed by Information Security Dept.
Media devices (music players, video players, digital cameras)	Any	Any	Not permitted to attach to end-user systems; restriction enforced by desktop device-management service.

Data Protection Standards

Finally, the standards must enable users to understand how they are to treat specific types of information and what controls are required to protect those different information classes. If the organization has already established an information classification program, this direction might come from that program and employ many of the same controls. The difference is that the controls developed for the information-classification program must now be applied to mobile data and devices, which may have a different risk profile than the storage and transport media that was anticipated when the classification program was first established. If the required protections for mobile data are radically different from what was originally established for information classification, that program's documentation and standards should be updated to reflect the inclusion of this newer technology.

The data protection standards should first specify what types of data actually need protection while stored or transported on a mobile device. The classification levels from the classification program can create a natural categorization for defining what types of information need protection and the forms that protection will take. As the classification level rises (meaning higher and higher levels of sensitivity or criticality), the greater and more restrictive the mobile data controls must be to adequately protect the data. Table 9.2 shows an example of how those protection levels might be defined.

If the organization does not have an information classification program, it needs to define what types of data it is most concerned about and how that data must be protected when it is mobile. Table 9.3 gives an example of how that might be defined.

It would be impossible to categorize every type of data element or business document that may end up on a mobile device, but it is important to identify the most common data and document types used within the organization and specify how that data is to be protected. Given enough examples, employees will be able to apply those examples to the data they manage on a daily basis, even if it isn't specified in the policy. This allows them to gain a much better understanding of how to best protect the information they manage.

Table 9.2   Example Classification Levels Protection Matrix

Classification Level	Minimum Required Mobile Protection
Public	No protection required
Internal	Password protection or other access controls
Sensitive	Encryption
Secret	Not permitted on mobile devices

Table 9.3 Example Data-Type Protection Matrix

Data Type	Minimum Required Mobile Protection
Public or commonly available information	No protection required
Internal memos, documents, project plans, etc.	Password protection
Source code or technical specifications	Encryption
Internal financial or business forecast data	Encryption
Consumer financial or health care data	Not allowed on mobile devices

When Are Protections Required?

There may be situations where mobile data controls are relaxed because the information is protected by other environmental elements. As a result, the policy may wish to specify whether mobile data protections are mandatory in some circumstances but optional in others. For example, if an external hard drive is used only within the confines of a single building, the requirement for encryption may not be necessary if the building's physical security and access-control mechanisms provide enough protection against unauthorized personnel infiltrating the building. The requirement for passwords and screen locks on a smartphone may be relaxed if that phone is only used by on-site personnel for emergency communications within a building or small geographic location. There may be circumstances where the mobile security policy may have varying levels of protection based not on the type of data or device, but the circumstances of the data or device's use.

Be very careful when considering this type of approach, however. Because of the highly portable nature of mobile devices, they can quickly go from stationary to mobile in an instant or leave the confines of the protected area either through theft or unintentional occupation in an employee's pocket when they leave the premises. If the organization is absolutely certain that a particular mobile device will remain within the confines of an already-secured location and the possibility of it leaving that location is extremely small, the policy might make provisions for lesser data protection controls in light of the more stringent physical security controls.

Conclusion

As discussed in Chapter 7, security policies are considered directive controls. They specify what the organization expects from its employees and give guidance and requirements for how they are expected to comply. However, policies by themselves rarely provide much protection. They must be coupled with strong standards and an effective enforcement mechanism if there is any hope that they will result in good mobile security for the organization and its information. Policies are also highly dependent on the people within the organization to follow them and make the effort to apply them to their work environments.

Getting policy right is a tricky matter. If you make the policy too lax, it won't provide effective control against the problem the policy was designed to address. Make it too stringent or restrictive, and you run the risk of preventing employees from getting their work done or driving them to ignore or bypass the policy. That delicate balance—between the needs of the business to continuously move forward and the need to secure the business against known or anticipated mobile hazards—is difficult to achieve and even more difficult to maintain. The mobile security policy, however, is the place where that balance starts.

The organization needs to start with a clear understanding of where it wants to go and the general approach it wants to take. From there, it may conduct the program research, technology development, and implementation plans to see if that approach is attainable and practical. Once those steps are complete, the organization must then revisit the initial policy direction and create a formal, detailed policy and associated standards to establish a company-wide direction.

The ideas in this chapter are meant to provide examples of policy directions and statements to consider, and these can serve as a starting point for your own efforts. They should provide the springboard for a thoughtful and thorough discussion of your own organization's mobile security needs and how those needs should translate into policy. Every policy is as different and individual as the organization that establishes it, so no single format or statement can thoroughly capture all of the options, considerations, and nuances that creating a good mobile security policy must account for. However, this springboard should launch you, and your organization, well into the process of developing your own mobile security policy.

Action Plan

Although it is not the first step in the process, creating a mobile security policy is an important milestone in securing the organization's mobile data and ensuring that the mobile devices in use have the appropriate security in place to protect that data. To guide you in the formulation of that policy, use the following steps to help align the work you have done to this point with the organization's goals and objectives for its mobile security program.

1. Determine the position the organization wishes to establish with respect to the issues discussed, including:
   - The extent to which mobile devices will be permitted
   - Device ownership

- The organization's ability to control and manage the device
- The extent to which users will be able to personalize their devices
- The extent to which corporate information will be permitted on mobile devices

2. Review the policy options presented in this chapter. Use the sample statements as the starting point for developing your own policy.

3. Establish the supporting standards that will guide the implementation of the policy. Consider all of the following:
   - Technology standards
   - Device standards
   - Data-protection standards
   - End-user standards

4. Review the proposed policies and standards with the appropriate constituent groups within the organization to solicit their feedback and gain their concurrence.

Chapter 10

Building the Business Case for Mobile Security

Nobody secures mobile information because it is easy. And nobody implements mobile security because it is cheap.

If mobile security were either easy or cheap, there would be more of it in place today, and more products and services would have security built in to their feature set and functionality. It's true that there has been some movement in this area; Microsoft includes its Encrypting File System (EFS) and BitLocker in some versions of its Windows software; Apple has FileVault in its OS X operating system; BlackBerry devices have security built into their base architecture; and flash drives and hard disks are now available with built-in hardware encryption. These, however, are the exceptions. For the rest of the mobile technology world, security must be enabled through add-on software and hardware upgrades. Neither of these is easy or cheap to implement.

The same is true when you try to introduce mobile security into an organization. The modern corporate enterprise (even on the smallest of scales) is a melting pot of locations, networks, servers, storage, services, service providers, and—you guessed it—mobile devices. We have seen throughout this book that implementing security for mobile data and devices is difficult even in the best of circumstances, and most enterprises rarely exhibit the best of circumstances. As a result, the lucky individual that gets tapped on the shoulder to develop and implement security for mobile data and devices in the enterprise has a lot of work to do, both to convince the "powers that be" that the effort and expense are worth it and to actually make mobile security work effectively. Because you are reading this book, it's safe to assume you are that lucky individual. Congratulations. It's not going to be easy, or cheap.

That's why this chapter will discuss developing the business case for mobile security. Implementing a security plan that can have such a wide-ranging impact on the way employees work and move information will be a difficult task. Because many organizations are currently experiencing financial and industry difficulties, any plans to enable additional security functionality or to restrict data movement will inevitably meet with a great deal of resistance. Ironically, that resistance won't be for ideological reasons. There are few in the enterprise who will argue against the need for mobile security. They may point to capabilities already available and wonder why additional measures are needed, but in this age of public breach disclosures and heavy privacy regulation, almost no one will argue against the need for better security controls. Rather, the resistance will come from the impact such security will have on the organization's operations and, more importantly, the expense of the effort. In order to counter those arguments and present the best possible case for moving forward with security plans for mobile data and devices in your organization, this chapter will present the basis for a justifiable business case that can be presented to management* to help gain their approval. Some of the material will draw on information and methods already discussed in previous chapters, but they will be revisited here specifically with an eye toward convincing those who will approve such a plan to invest the time, resources, and financial backing necessary to make the mobile security program work.

Keep in mind that every organization has its own culture and approach for developing, submitting, and obtaining approval of a business plan for any endeavor. Some organizations have a very formal process, with documentation, approval chains, extensive financial analysis, and case presentations required at each step of the process. Others are more informal, where documentation may be required, but where the socialization and approval process is more informational, conversational, and consensus-driven. As a result, there is no way that one approach or format will be able to cover all the possible scenarios and methodologies every organization may require. Rather, this chapter will focus on the different areas that must be addressed when building a business case for mobile security, give examples of different approaches to consider, explore methods for driving home the impact that mobile security (or the lack of it) may have on an organization, and give some advice for the best ways to state and reinforce the case for bringing security of mobile data and devices to the enterprise. It will be up to the reader to take the methods and approaches presented here and apply them to the needs (and format) of a particular organization.

---

* Throughout this chapter, the term "management" will be used as a catch-all to indicate the people within the organization who have the authority to approve your business case.

Identifying the Catalyst

This book started out with a simple question, "What are you trying to protect?" Likewise, the business case should start out addressing that question as well. A business case (and the subsequent program implementation that the case describes) seeks to persuade management to invest the company's resources in an area that has not been given the proper attention or whose existing processes and technology are not adequately addressing current threats. As a result, your business case must start by focusing on the actual problem. Here's an example of a problem statement that is well meaning but too broad to capture management's attention:

> MoDevCo must enact a program to protect mobile data and mobile devices.

While this may be true, it doesn't give any sense as to why this is a problem and why the company must act on this problem now. The business case should not only present the problem, it must also give the proper context for both the problem and the company's need for prompt action. There must be some catalyst that has prompted the organization to even consider the issue of mobile security and forced someone to research potential solutions. For many organizations, this catalyst can be one of several primary factors:

- Forward-thinking leadership
- Recent incidents or losses
- Fear of publicity and reputational damage
- Audit findings
- Legislative or regulatory changes
- Contractual or business obligations
- Alignment with company objectives

Forward-Thinking Leadership

Some organizations are blessed with leadership that has the foresight to understand the current business and security landscape and understand the security threats that are poised to strike at the company's revenue-generating capabilities. These are the leaders who understand that security is more than just "gates, guns, and guards" or "firewalls and antivirus." For these leaders, security enables an organization to move ahead with its business and establish appropriate preventive and detective controls to address the specific threats that are a part of its industry or business. These leaders do not wait for incidents, headlines, or trade magazines to tell them what to do or simply react to today's incidents; they use the resources and expertise at their disposal to look ahead to tomorrow's problems. If your organization has this style of leadership, the decision to investigate and plan a mobile data security program will come from the top. A directive from forward-thinking leadership to establish such a program is often all the endorsement that the program will need to get started.

Sadly, however, those leaders are few and far between. While there are many, many business leaders that take security seriously (most, in fact, do these days), many of them will hesitate before committing to security programs that have as broad an impact as the security of mobile data and devices will have. More often, they will react to some change in the environment or some external force that has caused them to consider such a program. For these managers, the knowledge that mobile security is the "right thing" to do is not enough. They will need to be convinced of the need for such a program and led down the path of acceptance. Even forward-thinking leaders will not hand over a blank check. They need to be convinced that the concern or threat they believe needs to be addressed is, in fact, being addressed by the proposed program.

The business case can address the needs and directives of forward-thinking leadership through some of the following examples:

> MoDevCo's leadership has identified a strategic initiative to protect company and customer information in any form, including information that travels on mobile devices. As a result, the company is launching a mobile security program to address the future protection needs of MoDevCo and its customers.

> Although MoDevCo has not yet experienced a large-scale loss of company or customer information, senior management is concerned that our current prevention and detection capabilities in the area of mobile data security do not adequately protect the company. Therefore, additional controls over mobile data protection need to be established to prevent such an attack in the future.

> MoDevCo has traditionally met or exceeded industry and regulatory guidelines in the areas of information security and privacy. MoDevCo's leadership has identified a growing trend toward establishing advanced protection of mobile data and the use of mobile devices to manage company information. In order to maintain our industry leadership position and maintain the trust and confidence of our customers, the MoDevCo leadership has requested the creation of a comprehensive mobile data security program.

Recent Incidents or Losses

Recall the Chapter 4 discussion of Newton's laws of motion, specifically the notion that an object at rest will tend to stay at rest until acted upon by an external force. In the case of many organizations, the "object" at rest is the current state of the security program, which may be steadily addressing most of the security problems the organization may face on a regular basis. One of the most powerful "external forces" an organization may experience is a security breach of its systems or unauthorized access or theft of its information. Nothing can shake an organization out of complacency more quickly than a security incident targeted at them or a competitor in the same industry. For example, the security breaches at TJX Company sent shockwaves that were felt by any company that processes large volumes of credit card data, not just those in the retail clothing industry. Likewise, the many media reports of government agencies disclosing taxpayer and employee information from stolen laptops and flash drives have an impact even on organizations that are not part of the government or that perform services for those particular agencies. Any such incident, if its circumstances and consequences can be applied to a particular organization, can be the Newtonian force for change in the company's approach to mobile security. If recent incidents or losses are such a catalyst, the business plan should highlight these incidents as a driving force and establish the proposed course of action as the way to avoid such an incident from occurring (or, perhaps, recurring) in the enterprise.

> As a result of the recent loss of secret product development plans through the theft of a company laptop computer, MoDevCo must institute a comprehensive program to maintain the security of data that is stored or transported on mobile devices.

> Recent security incidents regarding the theft of consumer data at one of MoDevCo's competitors have forced the company to reevaluate its controls surrounding the use of mobile data and mobile devices. Those incidents have forced our competitors into multimillion-dollar legal settlements and subjected them to increased scrutiny by our industry's regulators. In order to prevent such an occurrence from affecting MoDevCo or its customers, and to avoid the losses and additional regulation such a loss would incur, MoDevCo must enact a comprehensive mobile data security program.

Fear of Publicity and Reputational Damage

As bad as incidents and data losses may be, some organizations are able to absorb them both financially and operationally. The organization may have enough financial backing or insurance to cover any damages that may result from a data loss, and may even be willing to weather the resulting pressure from regulators or public lawsuits that might result from the breach. However, most organizations are unwilling to expose themselves to the negative public exposure and publicity that a large-scale breach or loss can bring, nor are they willing to suffer any damage to their reputation. This is especially true of public companies, whose stock price and market valuation often rise and fall based on the positive and negative publicity they receive as a result of their activities. A company that finds itself in the middle of a negative publicity storm can quickly see the public's opinion of the company turn against them, and the resulting impact on the company from nervous customers and business partners can have financial repercussions that last far beyond the effect of the original incident. As a result, the business case should highlight what the effect of such negative publicity might be and highlight ways in which the proposed plan can avoid it.

> After the state's largest insurance carrier reported the loss of a CD containing 100,000 personal health records, its stock price plummeted 35%, and it is reportedly losing several of its largest customers. Should a similar incident happen to MoDevCo, the resulting negative publicity would pose a considerable threat to our market position, particularly as we struggle to maintain market share in this troubling economic climate. MoDevCo must implement a program to secure mobile data and mobile devices in order to properly defend against this threat and prevent such a publicly damaging event.

> MoDevCo's recent marketing campaign—"We Care About You"—has successfully increased the company's brand recognition and customer loyalty ratings well beyond expectations. An incident involving the loss of customer or consumer data through the theft or mishandling of mobile data could result in a wave of negative publicity and negate many of the gains the company has experienced. A program to secure mobile data and mobile devices will help prevent such an event from negatively affecting the company's position or reputation.

Audit Findings

A review of an organization's security controls (performed either internally or by an independent party) is a common method for forcing an organization to address mobile security issues. In most organizations, audit results are reported to the board of directors (or a similar authoritative body), which is responsible and accountable for ensuring that audit items having material impact on the organization are properly addressed. An audit report indicating that the organization is lacking effective security controls for mobile data and devices can be an effective way to jump start a mobile security program. The audit in question may have been specifically directed at reviewing the organization's mobile security program, or it may have been part of a larger audit of information-protection controls. No matter what path the audit took to get to the conclusion, once a finding concerning mobile data is documented, it must be addressed to the satisfaction of the auditors and business leadership. "Addressed" can mean many different things, and the business may (after careful review) decide to "address" the finding by accepting the risk of inaction.

When building the mobile security business case, the audit findings should be acknowledged and addressed explicitly, pointing out how the proposed plan addresses the findings, better secures the organization, and is a much better alternative than the acceptance of the risk.

> A recent audit by MoDevCo's Internal Audit Department resulted in a finding that the company does not have adequate controls around the protection of mobile data or the configuration and use of mobile devices. The company must establish a program to address this finding and better secure its mobile data.

Legislative or Regulatory Changes

The regulatory landscape surrounding the protection of mobile data and devices has been evolving for the past several years. In the past, laws regarding the protection of consumer financial and health information have been general in nature and have not singled out any particular technology as a specific threat or point of concern. Recently, however, several laws have specifically identified mobile data and mobile devices as an area of concern, either as part of a more general security requirement or as a specific point to address. In addition, specific industries or industry segments may have their own requirements, such as the Payment Card Industry (PCI) standards for protection of card data, which crosses all industries. An organization has a responsibility to comply with applicable laws and regulations in the jurisdictions and industries within which it operates. This obligation gets much more complex as the organization grows to service multiple states, regions, countries, or industries, each with its own laws and regulations. The business case must show how the establishment of the proposed plan will help the organization remain in compliance with such regulations and keep the organization from facing penalties or legal proceedings as a result of noncompliance.

> Compliance with numerous regulatory mandates and industry guidelines (including the Sarbanes-Oxley Act, the Massachusetts Data Protection Law, and the Payment Card Industry (PCI) Data Security Standard) is essential for MoDevCo to continue to serve its customers. Without clear and audited compliance with these laws, MoDevCo may face penalties from various states if a data breach should occur or face the loss of its ability to process credit card and payment transactions. To prevent these potential restrictions on MoDevCo's business, a program to secure mobile data and mobile devices must be enacted.

Contractual or Business Obligations

Finally, establishing a mobile device security program may simply be a requirement that the company has agreed to as part of a contract with one of its customers, or a basic functionality that customers expect. Many organizations are willing to make concessions to their largest customers (or a desirable potential customer) that require changes to their security program. Because mobile data security is currently such a hot topic, companies that outsource part of their business to service providers or who share confidential information with business partners are paying more attention to the security controls those partners have in place, including controls around mobile data and devices. If such a contractual obligation exists, the business case should highlight that fact, as a breach of the contract might be equally as damaging to the organization (both to its finances and its reputation) as a security breach from a hostile attacker.

> MoDevCo's recent agreement with Flotsam Industries requires us to establish controls to secure all Flotsam Confidential Information on mobile devices and over publicly accessible networks. The Flotsam contract makes it one of MoDevCo's largest customers. In order to comply with the terms of the agreement, and to continue to enhance the relationship between MoDevCo and Flotsam, a program to secure mobile data must be established.

> Several recent bids with major new customers have been lost because MoDevCo does not have a program to protect confidential information on mobile devices. Customer interest in such a program will continue to increase, and the lack of these controls is affecting MoDevCo's ability to compete against its industry competitors, all of whom have established mobile device protections. In order to position MoDevCo as having the proper controls in place to protect its customers' confidential information, MoDevCo must establish a program to protect mobile data and mobile devices.

Alignment with Company Objectives

A positive method of highlighting the benefits of your proposal is to describe how your plan aligns with the organization's market, financial, or growth objectives. This is a more positive approach that demonstrates to management that the program is being implemented to benefit the needs of the business, not just to meet regulatory concerns or align with general security practices. For example, the following statement demonstrates such an objective:

> Establishing the proposed mobile security program will allow the company to meets its stated objective to equip its sales force with the tools they need to better reach customers. The proposed security controls will enable more secure movement and storage of data on the mobile devices that the sales force relies on, thus providing them with better and timelier information with which to service their customers and prospects.

There may be many similar business plans or goals in your organization that can be used to bolster the positive benefits of the proposed program. Aligning your proposal with one or more of these shows that you understand the needs of the business and that your proposed action will support and enhance those needs while, at the same time, providing the organization with the protection and control it requires.

The organization may be concerned with more than one of these issues. This is a good thing for the business case, as it shows that the implementation of a mobile device security program can address multiple business concerns. However, be sure to maintain focus when developing the business case. If there are too many forces in play, the case might get bogged down trying to address too many problems at once. If you find that is the case, select one or two of the most important considerations to address with the plan and make those the highlight of the business case. The other considerations can be mentioned, but not overly emphasized.

Determining the Impact of the Problem

Once you have effectively stated the problem, the next step is to describe the impact the problem is having on the organization. Too many security efforts are implemented simply because the organization's security team identifies a security need of which the rest of the organization is not cognizant. This stems from the inability of the security team to properly communicate to management the impact that the perceived security weakness can have on the organization. This lack of communication can lead management to consider the actual threat minimal, leading to a false sense of security that the current controls are adequate to address this new threat. If someone in the organization has determined that mobile data and mobile devices present a real and potentially damaging threat to the organization, he must do an effective job of communicating that to management. A good approach is to address the potential impact in terms that the business can understand:

- Financial losses
- Reputational damage
- Cost of remediation and cleanup
- Operational impact

These may appear to mirror some of the categories presented in the Catalyst section of the business case, and they are related in many ways. However, the Catalyst section served to introduce management to the weakness or gap in the organization's security program. The Impact section, on the other hand, informs management about what *could* happen if that gap is exploited and information is lost. In this section, it is important to use as many facts and figures as possible, as these are the things that will sway opinion in favor of approving the business case; however, avoid creating unnecessary fear within management through the inflation of negative impact or overestimating potential losses.* Doing so may have a greater emotional impact on management and create a favorable response to your business case; however, anyone digging deeper into the facts and statements made in the business case will quickly uncover the exaggerated facts. This will not only hurt your chances of gaining approval for your proposal, it may also impact your credibility, which will have longer business and career implications.

Financial Losses

All organizations run on money, and companies are adverse to losing money in any form, much less from a security breach or data loss. That's why the Impact section can carry such weight in the business case. It can speak directly to the organization's primary interest (money) and show how the gap in the organization's mobile security program can directly affect the organization's ability to acquire or maintain cash. To assist this effort, the business case might draw on direct experience the organization has had from previous mobile data incidents. It is important that the financial impact be as specific as possible. For example, the following loss statement might not be the most effective:

> If a laptop containing sensitive information was lost or stolen, MoDevCo could end up paying millions in fines or regulatory penalties.

While this statement gives a sense of the potential impact a loss could have, it is too vague to apply to the company's particular situation. Is there a quantitative value for how many "millions" would be lost? What regulations would MoDevCo be violating? More details specifying the potential issue the program is designed to address will help the business case.

When contemplating a potential security problem, especially one that might have an impact on the organization's operations, a natural tendency is for the organization to collectively believe that "it can't happen here," or "it hasn't happened yet, so we must be doing something right." Even if the organization has been the victim of a loss or theft, many in the organization will believe that lightning won't strike the same place twice. It is important for the business case to dispel this myth by highlighting issues the organization has had in the past that the program could have prevented.

> In 2006, the theft of a MoDevCo laptop resulted in the loss of technical specifications for an upcoming product. Shortly thereafter, Flotsam Industries introduced a similar product months ahead of its previously announced schedule. Although no direct evidence of Flotsam's

---

* This is often referred to as "F.U.D.," which stands for "Fear, Uncertainty, and Doubt."

involvement in the theft has ever been produced, its unexpected early entry in the market cost MoDevCo an estimated $16 million in potential revenue as the sole source for this product.

Last month, a flash drive containing 300,000 credit card records was lost by an employee whose car was burglarized. Because the data was not encrypted, the company was forced to notify over 250,000 card holders and offer one year of credit-monitoring services for affected customers. In addition, notification to several state attorneys general and federal agencies were required. The total cost of the loss has been estimated to be over $15 million.

If the company has not had a direct incident that it can draw from, there are many publicly available incidents to choose from for support. Chapter 2 gave some examples, and the Privacy Rights Clearinghouse study mentioned in that chapter is an excellent place to begin researching cases from companies or industries similar to your own. The point to make when utilizing others' experiences is that, although the particular incident happened to someone else, the situation and circumstances surrounding the loss were very similar to the circumstances within your own organization. For example:

In February 2009, CVS Pharmacies was found to be disposing of sensitive patient information in unsecured receptacles. A settlement with the U.S. Department of Health for HIPAA violations cost CVS $2.25 million. A recent audit of MoDevCo's information-disposal practices showed that the company does not adequately dispose of our backup DVDs containing customers' health care records. As a result, if such information was ever stolen or leaked to unauthorized parties, MoDevCo could face a fine similar to, or exceeding, that which CVS had to pay.

Real numbers speak very loudly. Use the Impact section as the place to speak directly to the organization's self-interest.

Reputational Damage

Nobody likes to look bad; that's human nature. Organizations are composed of humans who collectively do not want to make themselves or the organization look bad. Therefore, an impact on the company's reputation can be an important consideration in the business case. Although not a direct financial loss, a loss of reputation can have both short- and long-term ramifications on the company's bottom line. For example:

When Choicepoint announced in 2005 that data thieves had stolen over 163,000 consumer records, its stock dropped nearly 10% in the days following the announcement. If MoDevCo were to experience a similar loss of information through the loss or theft of a mobile device, it would have a similar impact on the company's stock and negatively affect the company's reputation with investors and market analysts. Although Choicepoint's stock price eventually regained its value, there is no guarantee that MoDevCo's stock would rebound as well.

Cost of Remediation and Cleanup

The aftermath of a data-loss incident will involve an investigation to find the root cause of the incident and the development of remediation efforts to prevent a recurrence. If the incident involves a lost or stolen mobile device, there may be no physical evidence to examine, and thus the organization may not be able to determine if the confidential information on the device has been compromised or copied from that device. If the device was encrypted, the organization might be able to determine that the information remained secure, but there is always room for doubt. Was the password protecting the decryption keys strong enough? Was the device taken by someone who might have knowledge of the password (such as a friend or coworker)? If the device had a remote-deletion capability and the organization sent it the "kill" signal, did the device receive that signal? There will be a cost for the investigation, and that cost must be factored into the business case.

> If MoDevCo were to suffer a mobile data loss incident, it is estimated that the investigative efforts would require the services of three internal investigators for at least 2 weeks, resulting in a cost of approximately $18,000, exclusive of any travel expenses that may be required.

If third-party investigators are involved, the cost can be considerably higher. An external investigator charging $250 per hour can cost close to $20,000 (plus expenses) for the same 2-week investigation. If the investigation lasts longer (and many do), the costs can add up quickly.

Finally, the remediation efforts—the process for cleaning up the damage (possibly including reloading and installing new systems and reloading application and system data onto those rebuilt systems) and implementing new controls to prevent a recurrence of the incident in the future—will have a cost. Unfortunately, unless one can know the specifics of the incident, it is difficult to predict the cost to prevent a future incident. However, there is ample case evidence of past incidents that one can draw on, which have been highlighted both in this chapter and in Chapter 2.

Operational Impact

So far, the impact of a mobile data loss has been limited solely to financial considerations. However, the organization may also experience an impact on its operation as a result of the loss. A mobile data incident will, by definition, indicate a lapse in the way the organization manages and transports its information. That lapse may be a one-time event or a systemic problem, but the organization must quickly act to make changes in those areas or be at risk for further incidents. The most immediate problem is that the organization may be without the lost data for some time. If the mobile data was the sole copy in existence—or if the backup of that data will take some time to recover—the organization may have to work around the data's absence. If the data was critical to the organization's operation, it may be unable to operate effectively until the data can be restored. This lost time will need to be accounted for in the business case, as this will have important repercussions on the organization's ability to deliver goods and services to its customers.

> If critical mobile data is lost or stolen and the backup for that data cannot be located or its restoration delayed, MoDevCo could be unable to produce new Gadgetrons for its customers, resulting in a production loss of $375,000 for every day of data unavailability.

As an alternative, the organization may have to re-create the data, which can be a time-consuming task. For example, if the data is the result of a nightly batch run of several programs that gather input from multiple sources, the source data may have to be regathered from those sources, and the programs may have to be reexecuted in an "out of cycle" process, one for which the organization is not prepared or which may involve participation of external data suppliers.*

> If critical mobile data is lost from the Milwaukee division—a division that makes heavy use of mobile devices to move and manage data—it will take up to 3 days to re-create the data from its component feeder systems, resulting in missed service levels to our customers and contractual penalties of $90,000.

Finally, if the loss is serious enough, the organization may suspend the use of mobile devices for a period of time until it can make a determination of how to proceed with their use more securely. If the organization (or the specific affected area) is a heavy user of mobile devices, that will most certainly have an impact on the organization's workflow and productivity. Definitive statistics on how the impact will affect the organization or its business may be difficult to quantify, but a statement addressing the severity of this impact is certainly in order.

> The Milwaukee plant's order-processing system relies heavily on the ability to manage order information through an application on employees'

---

* While some may point to such a case as a failure in the organization's disaster-recovery planning, it is nevertheless something that must be taken into account in the business case.

mobile phones. If one of those devices is lost or stolen, the mobile component of the system will need to be shut down to prevent further compromise of the system through unauthorized access. This will force the Milwaukee plant to switch to a manual order-processing system, resulting in delays fulfilling orders for MoDevCo's customers.

By now the point should be clear. A loss or compromise of mobile data will have a clear impact on the organization and its ability to continue business as usual. That impact may be financial, reputational, or operational, but there will be an impact. The business case must be clear about what those potential impacts may be and how they will affect the organization. The objective, of course, is to try to show that the impact can be mitigated or prevented by the implementation of the proposed plan. Failure to make the impact apparent to management (or to understate the extent of the impact) will cause management to undervalue the risk of the problem and, perhaps, not approve the business case.

Describe the Current State of Controls

Once the problem statements have been addressed and the impact is clearly understood, the next step is to inform management of the current state of mobile controls in the enterprise. This step is critical to ensure that all who must review and approve the business case have a uniform understanding of where the organization is and where it needs to go. It is likely that different people in the organization, especially at the higher levels, will not have a clear understanding of the role mobile devices play in the organization, nor will they have a good sense of what protections are in place and what risks exist.

Some in the organization will believe that the current security program-controls (such as firewalls, antimalware, and intrusion-detection systems) are already covering the potential threat from mobile devices. For this group, the Current State section provides an understanding of which existing controls are able to address various mobile data issues. A select few in the organization will truly understand the mobility issue and already have a good sense of what additional protections might be needed. For these people, the Current State section serves to confirm their knowledge and reinforce or refine their opinions on what needs to be done. Finally, the majority of the people reading the business case will likely not be knowledgeable about either the issue or the current state. They have probably taken advantage of mobile technology in their work but are unaware of the risks these items bring to the organization or of the need to apply any additional security controls. For this group, the Current State section serves as a wake-up call. These are the people who need to be most convinced of a need for change in the organization, and are the most likely to offer resistance to your efforts. This group believes firmly in the adage, "If it ain't broke, don't fix it." The task of the Current State section of the business case is to explain why it's "broke" as a lead-in to how this proposal will "fix it."

Start by explaining what mobile security protections are in place now. This part may be short if the organization hasn't yet done anything in particular to secure its mobile data. Even so, you may be able to identify some security controls that are already in place that will have an impact on mobile data and devices. For example:

> MoDevCo uses BlackBerry devices for all corporate smartphone users. BlackBerry has a rich set of security features that are centrally managed from the BlackBerry Enterprise Server.

> MoDevCo's e-mail service automatically detects e-mail messages that contain customer account numbers or credit card numbers and sends those messages to an automated encryption service.

> MoDevCo computers do not have built-in CD or DVD writers installed as standard equipment. All requests for such devices must be approved by the Information Security Department.

> The use of flash-memory sticks on end-user systems is prohibited by corporate policy.

If the organization has already taken steps to specifically protect mobile data or establish security settings on mobile devices, this is also the place to enumerate and highlight those efforts. This will establish that the organization is addressing the issue of mobile security and that some incremental activity has already taken place. While this may lead some to believe that these steps are sufficient to protect the company's mobile data, highlighting what's already been done will lay the groundwork for describing the gaps that still remain in the mobile security program. Those gaps, of course, will be filled (at least in part) by the actions described in the business case.

> MoDevCo has blocked the use of all USB devices through the activation of Active Directory controls for all Windows systems. This prevents users from attaching USB flash drives or external hard disks to their computers. However, technical controls for USB devices on Macintosh and Unix/Linux systems are not in place.

> MoDevCo has installed full-disk encryption on all end-user workstations. Encryption has not been implemented on internal servers or network storage devices.

> MoDevCo sends all outbound e-mail through its encryption service. However, the company does not block employee access to external e-mail systems such as Gmail or Yahoo! Mail. Employees are permitted to access these services from their work computers for limited personal use.

> MoDevCo's information-classification program has a special category for mobile data. All mobile data is automatically classified at the

highest level, regardless of the classification of that data while at rest on MoDevCo's systems. The protection requirements for mobile data are described in the corporate policy guide. However, technical controls to enforce those requirements are not yet in place.

The use of flash-memory sticks on end-user systems is prohibited by corporate policy. However, technical controls are not in place to restrict such use on end-user systems.

Encrypted flash-memory devices for protecting confidential MoDevCo data are available from the Purchasing Department. However, due to their high cost, employees are still purchasing lower-cost, nonencrypted devices from local retailers using either their corporate charge cards or paying for them out of their own pockets.

The point here is to give credit for mobile data protection efforts that are already in place. Those efforts will establish the fact that mobile security is already seen as a risk point by the organization and that some work in this area has been started to combat the threats. However, it is important to describe the limitations of those efforts, as the above examples illustrate. The goal of the business case is to establish the need for additional controls to protect mobile data. Simply listing the controls already in place will give the false impression that enough has already been done and that any additional controls are unnecessary. Likewise, simply listing the gaps in current controls without mentioning the work that has already been done does not establish that previous efforts have been insufficient.

As with much of the business case, the organization's corporate culture will determine some of this section's content and approach. Some organizations just want to know what's been done, while others are only concerned with what's left to do. However, providing as much information as possible in the Current State section establishes a clear path for what is to come next: the Proposed Solution. The information in this section shows the path that the organization has already been down, including what has transpired along that path. As a result, what gaps remain should be apparent to the readers, and should lead them quite naturally to the proposed solution.

The Proposed Solution

If the sections that have come before are the appetizer of the business plan, the Proposed Solution section is the main course, serving up a proposal to close the gap between where the organization currently stands on mobile security and where it needs to be in the future. This section should explain specifically what needs to be done along with the policy, process, and technology changes that need to be made. Because the primary purpose of a business case is to solicit financial backing for a project or program, the emphasis will most likely be on the financial and personnel resources required to complete the proposed plan. However, any changes in the organization's policies or processes that are critical to the success of the plan must be explained as well.

The best place to start this effort is with a simple declaration of the proposed solution. Example summary descriptions of proposed solutions might include some of these elements:

> To address the remaining risks associated with the movement of confidential data to mobile storage devices (such as flash drives and optical media), MoDevCo must purchase and implement BrandX's Mobile Control product. This product will block access to USB-based devices as well as restrict the ability to save media to CDs and DVDs.

> To provide better security for mobile data shared with smartphones and PDAs, MoDevCo must standardize by using BrandY smartphones and PDA products. This will allow the use of BrandY's MobileManager system for maintaining proper security controls and access restrictions on smartphones and PDAs used within the organization.

> To ensure that mobile data is protected throughout the enterprise, MoDevCo must invest in the BrandZ Universal Device Encryption software. BrandZ enables all devices in the organization to support full-disk and file-based encryption for all data on the device, and integrates with MoDevCo's e-mail, desktop, and mobile device platforms currently in use.

From those opening introductions, the business case would proceed to detail specifically why the proposed product or service fits the organization's mobile security needs. For example, the proposal should address the following issues:

- What specific features or functions does the proposed solution have?
- How do those features or functions fit the gaps identified in the business case's previous sections?
- How does the proposed solution integrate with (or replace) existing technology currently in use?
- How does the proposed solution increase the overall security of the organization's mobile data and its mobile devices?

After the specific details of the proposed activity have been laid out, attention should move to required changes to the technical and operational environment as a result of the proposal. Unless you can manage to implement security technology that is totally transparent to the end user, there will need to be some adjustment to the way employees work and the way they move information around the environment. In addition, if there are processes or operational changes required, these will most definitely have an impact on the way people work. As a result, these should be clearly noted and described in the business case. After all, when users start complaining because your new mobile security program has implemented restrictions that they don't approve of, it helps to be able to tell them that management knew of the changes and approved of them. It will not help your case or your credibility with management if the proposal involves sweeping operational or end-user impacts that they were not informed of. Therefore, it is best to specify what these changes will be up front to minimize confusion and renegotiation.

> As a result of the proposed program, end users will no longer be able to synchronize e-mail, calendar, and contact information with the corporate e-mail system unless they are using one of the approved and supported mobile devices.

> All flash drives used to store company information will have built-in hardware encryption and be procured through the corporate purchasing department. The new proposed desktop configuration manager will block all attempts to write data to a nonencrypted drive.

> Optical media creation facilities will be established in all Copy Service locations. End users will no longer be permitted to create CDs or DVDs from their desktop computers, and must send their data to Copy Services to burn onto optical media. All information must be reviewed and approved by an Information Security representative before Copy Services will be allowed to create the requested media.

> The new system will automatically identify data classified as "Confidential" or "Restricted" and prevent it from being moved to a mobile device or transported over mobile media.

These examples are but a few possibilities; the specifics of how the proposal will affect the organization's operation and users' workflow is impossible to comprehensively catalog here. Nevertheless, there are several important types of changes that should be identified.

■ *Changes to internal processes*: Any change that requires employees to change the way they move and manage information, or that changes the way they can access that information, must be described. Explaining those changes to management and describing both why the changes are necessary and (potentially) how to minimize the impact on employees will go a long way toward gaining acceptance of the proposal.

■ *Changes to technology standards*: If the proposal requires the organization to change the technology used for a particular area, those changes must be noted and addressed. For example, if the end users must move to a more secure desktop operating system, that will have a significant impact on the way end users work and are supported. If a particular device is required to engage in some mobile activity, it will have a financial and operational impact on the organization as well. Changes in technology do not only impact the end user, they also affect the support and maintenance services of the IT organization. If new backup systems that encrypt all backup tapes in the data center are required, that will require support and process changes from the data-center IT staff. Their support and endorsement of the proposal will be critical to its successful approval and eventual implementation.

■ *Changes to procurement processes*: The business case needs to explain how users will purchase goods and services in order to comply with the new mobile security plan. Will the old products or service still be available for use? Who will pay for the changes or upgrades? Does the Purchasing Department have the information it needs to make the transition smoothly? Employees rely on their ability to have their work materials readily available when they need them. If that availability is delayed because the newly required materials, technology, or services are not available, the program will fail.

■ *Changes in information flow and availability*: Finally, it ultimately comes down to the data itself. Users have become accustomed to having their data available to them in whatever mobile platform they desire, so changes or new restrictions to that approach must be documented as part of the plan. The description of those changes must be coupled with the reason why those changes are necessary to protect mobile data, the employee, and the organization.

The imposition of new mobile security practices and technology will undoubtedly have an impact on the organization, and that impact will be met with resistance (in some cases, a great deal of resistance) by both end users and management (who must ultimately respond to angry end users). The business case must be very clear about what those changes are, how they will impact the users' or the organization's work processes, and what has been done to minimize that impact. However, the emphasis must remain at all times on the need to secure mobile data and, ultimately, protect the organization. That's why the business case is being developed in the first place. While efforts can (and should) be made to minimize the impact of those changes, it should be clear that the changes set forth in the business case are required if the organization truly wants to address its mobile security issues.

Program Time Line

Once the details of the plan have been established, management will want to know how long the plan will take to implement. This will have an impact on its approval of the plan, as shorter and smaller projects tend to be seen more favorably than longer, drawn-out programs. Explicitly detailing the project's time line will set the proper expectations for results. A program that will take 9 months to implement should not give the impression that visible results will be apparent in the first month. Likewise, a technology that is easily implemented should be able to show results after the first several weeks of operation, not after 18 months of use.

If the proposed program is large enough, it might be advantageous to split its implementation into several phases. This will allow for a quicker, more visible implementation of the program's phases and a shorter turnaround time for positive results. A program that is too large, too expensive, and takes too long to implement risks being rejected at the outset, as management is often reluctant to take on such large undertakings, especially if the company's finances or business outlook are tenuous. Even if the large, grandiose plan were to be approved in full, it runs the risk of collapsing under its own weight by trying to change too much at once. Steady, incremental change is often easier to implement and more successful than rapid, massive change.

If the plan is to be split into phases, this will change the scope and approach of the business case. In such a situation, the initial case might be an umbrella proposal for the entire program. This umbrella proposal would include all the information we've discussed thus far for the entire project, but the Time Line section will explain that the project will be split into phases, with a brief description of what each phase will entail. This is crucial, as you want management to see the implementation of mobile security as a continuous program, not a series of independent projects. After the initial case gets approved, subsequent business case documents might need to be submitted for the individual phases. Although these will have to stand on their own merits, the initial approval of the overall plan will go a long way toward gaining approval of the subsequent incremental cases.

In any event, whether the program is established as one large implementation or a series of smaller projects, the Time Line section should give an estimate of when the project will commence, how long it will take to implement, and the expected completion date. Although the implementation of mobile security is not a "project"—in fact, once it's enabled it will be in effect in perpetuity—the initial implementation will take a finite amount of time to complete, and the proposal should explain what that time will be. Specific milestones to ensure that the program is meeting its target goals must also be included, so management can get a good sense of how the program's progress and success will be measured. Although such information is usually reserved for a separate project plan and not a business case, inclusion in the business case will show management that the plan is well thought out and that the team has thoroughly researched its implementation and impact.

A more complex proposal, or one that will take several phases to fully implement, may raise questions as to whether or not the proposal will have an impact on other programs or projects already underway within the organization. Therefore, the business case should discuss why that particular time line was selected and how other company priorities affected the program's planning. Any effort to secure mobile data must align with other ongoing business programs and priorities and should not disrupt those initiatives. It's critical to demonstrate to management that the proposal has been designed to coexist and complement other activities in progress within the enterprise.

> The program will be implemented in several phases to coincide with the deployment of the new network device upgrade project. As each network segment is upgraded, the new device-monitoring system will be implemented in that segment. This will maximize the use of the network engineering team's time and minimize disruption to end users.

Financial Analysis

So far, the business case has been used to explain the purpose and goals of the project, describe the benefits and impact to the organization, and outline the timing and integration considerations. Management may embrace the proposal, marvel at the innovative use of leading-edge technology, and praise you on the creativity and business-focused methodology of protecting the organization without any undue burden on the users. They may even be ready to sign off on your proposal—almost. One last thing stands in the way of gaining that final approval, and eventually the discussion must turn to money. No great effort ever succeeds solely on the merits of its objectives, and in the current economic environment no project—much less a security project—will be given unlimited funds to pursue its goals. Therefore, it's critical that the business case provides a thorough analysis of the true cost and resource requirements of the mobile security program.

Every organization has its own methodology for developing a financial analysis, but there are some basic categories of financial information that must be included. At a minimum, the case must present the capital expenditures (or CapEx) associated with the project. Capital expenses are defined as those that are used to purchase fixed assets, such as computers, furniture, or buildings. Capital expenses are also often defined as funds that are allocated to purchase goods that will be used for more than one year. The counterpart to capital expenses is operating expenses (or OpEx). Operating expenses are those that go to the day-to-day and ongoing operation of the business, and are usually separated from capital expenses in a financial analysis. There are strict accounting rules for classifying expenses as CapEx or OpEx, so it's essential to consult with the finance experts in the organization when building the business case to ensure that all expenses are thoroughly and properly accounted for.

Most mobile data protection programs are multiyear efforts. Even if the initial deployment will occur within a single year, the ongoing support and maintenance will be a continuing expense to the organization. Therefore, the business case should give detailed information on any ongoing or recurring expenses for the program. It is important to show management that an ongoing commitment will

Table 10.1 Basic Multiyear Financial Analysis

Item	Initial Cost	Year 2	Year 3	3-Year Total	Ongoing Costs
Encryption software licensing	$30,000	$4,500	$4,500	$39,000	$4,500
DLP[a] software blocking	$50,000	$9,000	$9,000	$68,000	$9,000
Key management servers	$60,000	$0	$0	$60,000	$0
Software deployment servers	$13,000	$0	$0	$13,000	$0
Additional hardware (flash drives)	$10,000	$1,000	$1,000	$12,000	$1,000
Staff (head count)	4	2	2		2
Staff cost ($150K per full-time employee)	$600,000	$300,000	$300,000	$1,200,000	$300,000
Totals	$763,000	$314,500	$314,500	$1,392,000	$314,500

[a] Data loss prevention.

be needed to maintain the program and to give them an indication of the required level of that commitment. For example, Table 10.1 shows a basic multiyear analysis for a typical business case.*

Although overly simplistic, Table 10.1 gives you a good sense for how to break out the major items required in the financial analysis. This is why it's so critical to involve experts from your financial or business analysis team. They will know how the organization breaks out different categories of expenses, and will be able to provide guidance on how to minimize those expenses, thus helping your overall case.

Calculating the Return on Investment

For any mobile security program, management will want to know what the organization is gaining from the effort as a result of the expense it is allocating. This

---

* "Basic" here is a gross understatement. Most business cases will have a much more detailed financial analysis. The point here is to illustrate the type of information that might go into such a case, not to define a formal format for the information.

is commonly known as the return-on-investment (ROI) calculation. The expectation of ROI is that, for any program investment in the business, the organization should be able to recoup that investment within a particular amount of time to the point where the investment should pay for itself. The typical time frame for an ROI calculation is 1 to 3 years, meaning that by the end of the third year the financial benefits to the company should have met or exceeded the cost to implement the program. There has been a great deal of discussion over the years relating to the ROI of security investments. Books and papers have been written, models have been developed, and nearly the entire industry has been seeking a definitive and convincing ROI case for information security. Although this effort has produced some very interesting methodologies and literature, by and large the effort has been a complete failure.

Do not expect that the ROI for your business case will magically break that mold. Here's why. ROI assumes that, for any given investment, that investment will eventually bring money back into the organization. This is typically demonstrated by showing that the project will either directly enable revenue or prevent financial loss in a systematic and repeatable way. Most security efforts fall into the latter category; they are enabled to prevent financial or intellectual-property loss to the organization. Determining a specific future loss potential implies that you can make predictions based on historical experience. Unfortunately, security incidents do not follow predictable trends. For example, given a random sample of 1,000 humans of a known age, race, or geographic location, it would be possible to tell with a high degree of accuracy how many of them are left-handed, how many will die of cancer, how many will be hit by lightning, or how many will win the lottery. This will be based on an analysis of historical data for those statistics and the mathematical probability of their recurrence in the given population. Unfortunately, the actuarial calculations for security don't follow standard patterns. While there are certainly historical trends and incident data to select from, the field is still too young to have a solid statistical history.

Because security incidents are random, unpredictable acts, and because the losses to an organization are based on the individual circumstances of the incident itself, there is no repeatable or predictable pattern or model on which to base an ROI calculation. For example, if the effort to protect mobile data costs $750,000, and it prevents a single $1-million data loss in the first year, the ROI for the project is $250,000 in that first year. If the same $750,000 project prevents a series of $10,000 data losses, it will take 75 such incidents before the company can see a positive return on its investment. However, those 75 incidents may occur in the first year or the fifth or the tenth—there is no way to predict.

This is not to say that the business case should ignore the concept of ROI altogether; it just means that the return will need to be based on more qualitative information rather than straight mathematical calculations. The point is to show that enacting the proposed mobile security protections will prevent the organization from experiencing losses through information theft or the resulting legal, regulatory, reputational, and (of course) financial losses that often accompany such incidents. The following business-case language samples are based on earlier examples:

> The theft of an employee's flash drive cost MoDevCo an estimated $10 million in direct and incidental losses. The implementation of the proposed mobile security program could prevent a similar incident from occurring in the future. The prevention of a single similar incident can quickly recoup the cost of the program's implementation.

> The lack of mobile data protection controls has cost other organizations in MoDevCo's industry millions of dollars in regulatory fines for mishandling of consumer data. Implementation of the proposed program will prevent MoDevCo from incurring similar fines.

> MoDevCo's contract with Flotsam requires that it implement protection for all mobile data and mobile devices that may contain Flotsam's confidential information. Contractual penalties for noncompliance include a refund of one month's licensing fees for each occurrence of noncompliance. As a result, three instances of noncompliance will cost MoDevCo in excess of the cost of implementing the proposed mobile data protection program.

You can see that none of these examples demonstrated a definitive financial return on investment. Nevertheless, using examples of previous losses (by the company or other organizations) can serve a similar purpose: demonstrating that the investment in the mobile data program is a wise one to protect the organization from future financial losses or legal troubles.

Alternatives Considered

Management likes to have alternatives and options. It likes to know that any request for the organization's investment has been through careful consideration and that viable, less expensive alternatives have been evaluated. To address that need, the business case must present the alternatives that were included, considered, and ultimately rejected during the program development process. There are no ideal or perfect solutions to security problems, and almost all security decisions represent trade-offs between cost, ease of use, and control effectiveness. Balancing these three aspects of any security solution is critical, and evaluating alternatives for mobile data protection will require trade-off decisions that create an optimal combination for your particular enterprise.

Some of these alternatives may have had a lower cost, some may have had easier implementations, and others may have had better controls (or at least a different approach to control implementation). However, none of these alternatives was selected for the final recommendation for one reason or another. The case should make mention of the alternatives that were considered and why they were deemed inappropriate to protect the organization as well as the proposed solution.

> The use of UberWare's MobileProtect product was considered for device blocking on end-user systems. However, MobileProtect does not recognize certain types of encrypted flash devices, a capability that was deemed critical by the project team.

> Alpha Systems's MobileSafe was evaluated due to its lower licensing cost. However, MobileSafe requires the use of dedicated command servers on each network segment, increasing the overall implementation cost to $75,000 higher than required by the proposed solution.

> DeviceGuard was considered due to its similar feature set and current market dominance. However, its licensing costs were nearly double that of the proposed solution. The feature comparison between the two products was nearly identical, making the proposed solution a more cost-effective alternative.

One alternative that should be part of every business case is the "do nothing" alternative. This alternative examines what would happen to the organization if no changes are made and no additional processes or technologies are implemented. The point of the "do nothing" option is to give management a point of comparison for determining whether the proposed solution is sufficient to cover the present gaps in the mobile security program. For any business proposal, whether for security programs or any other business activity, there is always an option to do nothing—to keep the organization as it is and let the status quo prevail. Clearly, that is not a desirable option, and the content of the business case should make it clear that other more desirable options are available, but it is one that management can consider once presented with the alternatives. Some or all of the information contained in the description of the "do nothing" option will have already been covered in other sections of the proposal, but placing this information as a specific option in the Alternatives Considered section of the business plan gives management the ability to formally say it will not address the mobile security issue with any of the options presented in the plan.

Conclusion

This chapter has been a bit of a departure from the other chapters in this book. Although it discusses the presentation and proposal for a mobile protection program, it also discusses the general development of a business case, one that just happens to concern the implementation of security for mobile data and devices. The presentation of security issues to management has not, historically, been a strong point for security professionals. As a result, security-oriented business cases tend to be very heavy in technical detail and security jargon and light on business benefit and impact.

Through the examples in this chapter, and the suggestion for the topics that a security-oriented business case needs to cover, you should begin to get a good sense of how to present the risk, threat, and technology information to management. These are the areas that are the most difficult to translate from "security speak" to "business speak." Security professionals are very comfortable in the world of threats, attacks, hackers, data leakage, and incident management. Unfortunately, they often have a difficult time relating those areas of expertise into terms that owners of the business can relate to. How do data-loss threats relate to business threats? How does mobile device risk relate to general business risk? How does an insecure flash drive pose a million-dollar threat to the business? How does the synchronization of e-mail to a smartphone pose an intellectual-property or social-engineering risk to the company? In the best of all worlds, these are issues that the leadership of the organization's information-security function has routinely communicated to the company's senior leadership, who should thus have a good grasp of the issues. As a result, the business case is an opportunity to reinforce those ideas and capitalize on the previous discussions to lead management to a swift approval.

Unfortunately, the business case may be the first opportunity many in management have to understand the extent of these problems. If this is the case, the business case must be clear, precise, and descriptive enough to present a thorough and accurate description of the problems, impacting considerations, and proposed solution. Without management's prior knowledge of these issues, the business case will have a difficult time gaining approval, and a great deal more socialization will be required to gain its passage.

As stated at the outset of this chapter, the ideas and guidelines presented here are representative of a "typical" business case for presenting mobile security solutions to management. There is no doubt that you will need to take these ideas and fit them to your own organization's process and format standards. Certainly, the inclusion of any incident information that the organization has experienced should be included, as this is the best source of validation that the proposal is necessary to properly protect the organization (assuming that such an incident is not already the catalyst).

In the end, the approval or rejection of a business case for mobile security will come down to the completeness of the risk analysis and the ability to adequately and accurately portray the risk of inaction to the organization. That analysis should be performed and completed long before the business case is ever written; the business case is merely the vehicle for conveying the results to management. Recall from the beginning of this chapter that implementing effective mobile security is not easy and it's not cheap. If you have performed the analysis properly, you can convince management to provide adequate time, resources, and financial backing to overcome these obstacles. If you are able to state your case using business language that management can understand, and if you can include the proper facts and circumstances to establish a compelling case, your proposal should have a better chance of gaining approval.

Action Plan

This chapter has been about relating security to the business and ensuring that your plan to secure the organization's mobile data has the best possible chance to gain approval from those in the organization's leadership who have the power to move your program forward. After all the analysis, technical research, implementation planning, and policy making, it all comes down to convincing management that changes in the way the organization manages and secures its mobile data require a commitment and an investment in the policy, process, and technology changes represented in the business case.

To ensure that the business case covers all the required discussion points, use the following checklist as a guide during its development:

1. *Identifying the catalyst*: What has changed that has forced the organization to require better mobile security?
   - Forward-thinking leadership?
   - Recent incidents or losses?
   - Fear of publicity and damaged reputation?
   - Audit findings?
   - Legislative or regulatory changes?
   - Contractual or business obligations?
2. *Impact determination*: What is the effect of the problem on the organization?
   - Financial losses?
   - Reputational damage?
   - Cost of remediation and cleanup?
   - Operational impact?
3. *Current state analysis*: What mobile security currently exists in the enterprise?
   - Policies?
   - Processes?
   - Technologies?
4. *Proposed solution*: What is your proposal to change the mobile security program and close the identified gap(s)?
   - Changes to internal processes?
   - Changes to technology standards?
   - Changes to procurement processes?
   - Changes in information flow and availability?

5. *Schedules and timing*: When will the program begin, and how long will it take?
   - Single implementation?
   - Phased implementation?
6. *Financial analysis*: How much will it cost?
   - Capital expenses?
   - Operating expenses?
   - Multiyear expenses?
   - Return on investment?
7. *Alternatives considered*: Why was this path selected?
   - Lower-cost alternatives?
   - Feature set comparisons?
   - "Do nothing" scenario?

Index